Distinctive Home Designs - *Home Plans Encyclopedia* is a collection of best ...... the nation's leading designers and architects. Only quality plans with sound design ...... ncy and affordability have been selected.

This plan book covers a wide range of architectural styles in a popular range of sizes. A broad assortment is presented to match a wide variety of lifestyles and budgets. Each design page features floor plans, a front view of the house, and a list of special features. All floor plans show room dimensions, exterior dimensions and the interior square footage of the home.

Technical Specifications - Every effort has been made to ensure that these plans and specifications meet most nationally recognized building codes (BOCA, Southern Building Code Congress and others). Drawing modifications and/or the assistance of a local architect or professional designer are sometimes necessary to comply with local codes or to accommodate specific building site conditions.

Detailed Material Lists - An accurate material list showing the quantity, dimensions, and description of the major building materials necessary to construct your new home can save you a considerable amount of time and money.

Blueprint Ordering - Fast and Easy - Your ordering is made simple by following the instructions on page 322. See page 321 for more information on what type of blueprint packages are available and how many plan sets to order.

Your Home, Your Way - The blueprints you receive are a master plan for building your new home. They start you on your way to what may well be the most rewarding experience of your life.

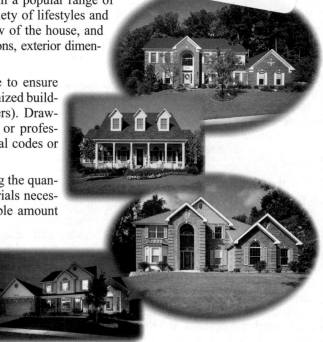

Home Plans Encyclopedia is published by Home Design Alternatives, Inc. (HDA, Inc.) 4390 Green Ash Drive, St. Louis, MO 63045. All rights reserved. Reproduction in whole or in part without written permission of the publisher is prohibited. Printed in U.S.A © 1999. Artist drawings shown in this publication may vary slightly from the actual working blueprints.

How *You* Can Customize Our Plans Into *Your* Dream Home

Custom homes once were the product of a lengthy and often expensive design process requiring numerous meetings between owner, builder and architect.

Now there's an alternative, a faster and less expensive means of acquiring a custom home. Instead of starting from scratch, you can select any design from this book and with the Customizer Kit™, change it to suit your particular needs and preferences.

With the Customizer Kit you have unlimited design possibilities available to you when building a new home. It allows you to alter virtually any architectural element you wish, both on the exterior and interior of the home. The Kit comes complete with simplified drawings of your selected home plan so that you can sketch out any and all of your changes. To help you through this process, the Kit also includes a workbook called "The Customizer," a special correction pen, a red marking pencil, an architect's scale and furniture layout guides. These tools, along with customizer drawings, allow you to experiment with various design changes prior to having a design professional modify the actual working drawings.

Before placing your order for blueprints consider the type and number of changes you plan to make to your selected design. If you wish to make only minor design changes such as moving interior walls, changing window styles, or altering foundation types, we strongly recommend that you purchase reproducible

masters along with the Customizer Kit. These master drawings, which contain the same information as the blueprints, are easy to modify because they are printed on erasable, reproducible paper. Also, by starting with complete detailed drawings, and planning out your changes with the Customizer Kit, the cost of having a design professional or your builder make the required drawing changes will be considerably less. After the master drawings are altered, multiple blueprint copies can be made from them.

If you anticipate making a lot of changes, such as moving exterior walls and changing the overall appearance of the house, we suggest you purchase only one set of blueprints as a reference set and the Customizer Kit to document your desired changes. When making major design changes, it is always

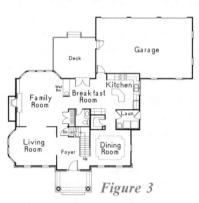

Figure 3

advisable to seek out the assistance of an architect or design professional to review and redraw that portion of the blueprints affected by your changes.

Typically, having a set of reproducible masters altered by a local designer can cost as little as a couple hundred dollars, whereas redrawing a portion or all of the blueprints can cost considerably more depending on the extent of the changes. Like most projects, the more planning and preparation you can do on your own, the greater the savings to you.

Finally, you'll have the satisfaction of knowing that your custom home is uniquely and exclusively yours.

Figure 2

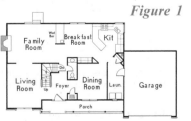

Figure 1

Examples of Customizing

Thousands of builders and home buyers have used the Customizer Kit to help them modify their home plans, some involving minor changes, many with dramatic alterations. Examples of actual projects are shown here.

Figure 1 shows the front elevation and first floor plan for one of our best-selling designs.

Figure 2 shows how one plan customer made few but important design changes such as completely reversing the plan to better accommodate his building site; adding a second entrance for ease of access to the front yard from the kitchen; making provisions for a future room over the garage by allowing for a stairway and specifying windows in place of louvers, plus other modifications.

Figure 3 shows another example of an actual project where the design shown in Figure 1 was dramatically changed to achieve all of the desired features requested by the customer. This customized design proved to be so successful that we obtained permission to offer it as a standard plan.

GLENWOOD

Apartment Garage With Surprising Interior

632 total square feet of living area

Special features

- Porch leads to vaulted entry and stair with feature window, coat closet and access to garage/ laundry
- Cozy living room offers vaulted ceiling, fireplace, large palladian window and pass-through to kitchen
- A garden tub with arched window is part of a very roomy bath
- 1 bedroom, 1 bath
- Slab foundation
- 122 square feet on the first floor and 510 square feet on the second floor

Price Code AA

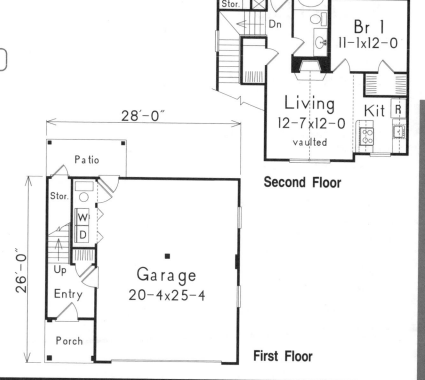

Second Floor

First Floor

MULTI-STORY
under 2,000 square feet

Plan #X20-0655

To order blueprints use the form on page 322 or call toll-free 1-800-DREAM HOME (373-2646)

Open Layout Ensures Easy Living

976 total square feet of living area

Special features

- Cozy front porch opens into large living room
- Convenient half bath is located on first floor
- All bedrooms are located upstairs for privacy
- Dining room has access to the outdoors
- 3 bedrooms, 1 1/2 bath
- Basement foundation
- 488 square feet on the first floor and 488 square feet on the second floor

Price Code A

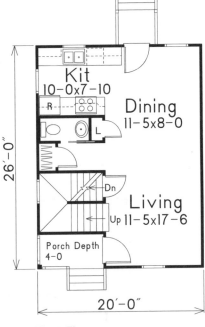

First Floor

Kit
10-0x7-10

Dining
11-5x8-0

Living
Up 11-5x17-6

Dn

Porch Depth
4-0

26'-0"

20'-0"

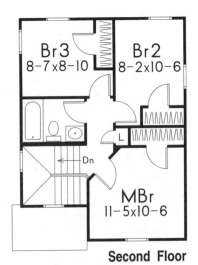

Second Floor

Br3
8-7x8-10

Br2
8-2x10-6

Dn

MBr
11-5x10-6

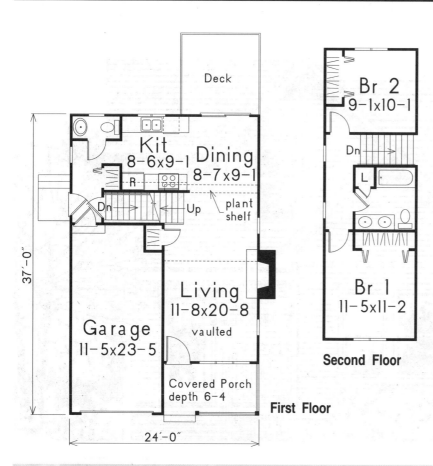

Kit
8-6x9-1

Dining
8-7x9-1

Deck

plant shelf

Dn   Up

R

37'-0"

Living
11-8x20-8
vaulted

Garage
11-5x23-5

Covered Porch
depth 6-4

24'-0"

First Floor

Br 2
9-1x10-1

Dn

L

Br 1
11-5x11-2

Second Floor

Special Planning In This Compact Home

977 total square feet of living area

Special features

- Comfortable living room features a vaulted ceiling, fireplace, plant shelf and coat closet
- Both bedrooms are located upstairs and share a bath with double-bowl vanity and linen closet
- Sliding glass doors in dining room provide access to the deck
- 2 bedrooms, 1 1/2 baths, 1-car garage
- Basement foundation
- 545 square feet on the first floor and 432 square feet on the second floor

Price Code A

MULTI-STORY
under 2,000 square feet

Plan #X20-0496

To order blueprints use the form on page 322 or call toll-free 1-800-DREAM HOME (373-2646)

Compact Home, Perfect Fit For Narrow Lot

| 1,085 total square feet of living area |

Special features

- Rear porch has a handy access through the kitchen
- Convenient hall linen closet located on the second floor
- Breakfast bar in kitchen offers additional counter space
- Living and dining rooms combine for open living atmosphere
- 3 bedrooms, 2 baths
- Basement foundation
- 685 square feet on the first floor and 400 square feet on the second floor

Price Code A

MULTI-STORY under 2,000 square feet

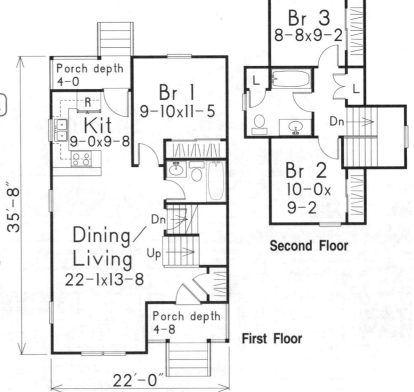

Porch depth 4-0

Kit
9-0x9-8

Br 1
9-10x11-5

35'-8"

Dn

Dining/
Living
22-1x13-8

Up

Porch depth
4-8

First Floor

22'-0"

Br 3
8-8x9-2

L   L

Dn

Br 2
10-0x
9-2

Second Floor

Plan #X20-0494

Spacious Vaulted Great Room

1,189 total square feet of living area

Special features

- All bedrooms are located on the second floor
- Dining room and kitchen both have views of the patio
- Convenient half bath located near the kitchen
- Master bedroom has private bath
- 3 bedrooms, 2 1/2 baths, 2-car garage
- Basement foundation
- 615 square feet on the first floor and 574 square feet on the second floor

Price Code A

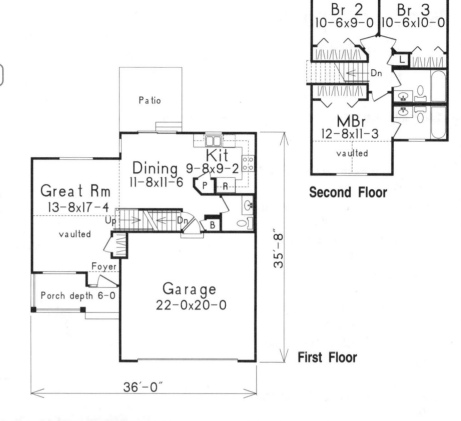

Br 2
10-6x9-0

Br 3
10-6x10-0

MBr
12-8x11-3
vaulted

Second Floor

Patio

Kit 9-8x9-2

Dining
11-8x11-6

Great Rm
13-8x17-4
vaulted

Up

Dn

Foyer

Porch depth 6-0

Garage
22-0x20-0

35'-8"

36'-0"

First Floor

Plan #X20-0487

Floor-To-Ceiling Window Expands Compact Two-Story

1,246 total square feet of living area

Special features

- Corner living room window adds openness and light
- Out-of-the way kitchen with dining area; back garden close by
- Private first floor master bedroom with corner window
- Large walk-in closets are located on both floors
- Easily built perimeter allows economical construction
- 3 bedrooms, 2 baths, 2-car garage
- Basement foundation
- 846 square feet on the first floor and 400 square feet on the second floor

Price Code A

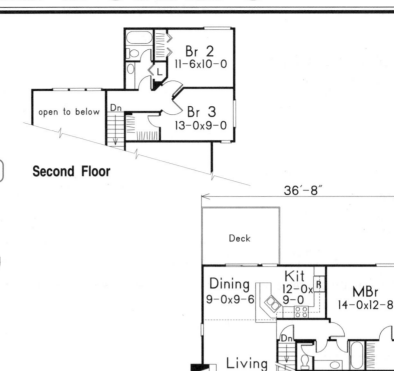

Second Floor

Br 2 11-6x10-0
Br 3 13-0x9-0
open to below
Dn

First Floor

36'-8"
38'-8"
Deck
Dining 9-0x9-6
Kit 12-0x9-0
MBr 14-0x12-8
Living 12-4x17-0
vaulted
Garage 20-0x20-0
plant shelf
Dn
Up

Plan #X20-0102

To order blueprints use the form on page 322 or call toll-free 1-800-DREAM HOME (373-2646)

PENFIELD

Unique Step Up From Entry To Living Space

1,261 total square feet of living area

Special features

- Great room, brightened by windows and doors, features vaulted ceiling, fireplace and access to sun deck

- Vaulted master bedroom with private bath

- Split level foyer leads to living space or basement

- Centrally located laundry area near bedrooms

- 3 bedrooms, 2 baths, 2-car drive under garage

- Basement foundation

Price Code A

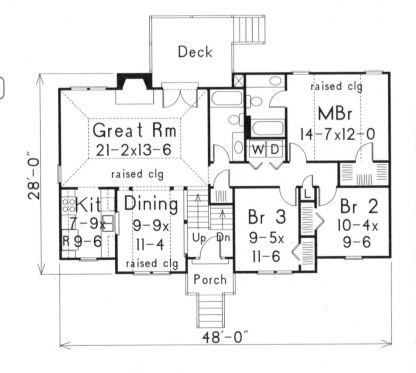

MULTI-STORY under 2,000 square feet

Openness Reflects Relaxed Lifestyle

1,330 total square feet of living area

Special features

- Vaulted living room is open to bayed dining room and kitchen creating ideal spaces for entertaining

- Two bedrooms, a bath and linen closet complete the first floor and are easily accessible

- The second floor offers both bedrooms with walk-in closets, a very large storage room and an opening with louvered doors which overlooks the living room

- 4 bedrooms, 2 baths, 1-car garage

- Basement foundation

    Price Code A

MULTI-STORY under 2,000 square feet

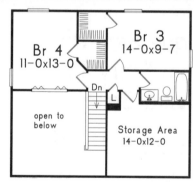

Second Floor

Br 4
11-0x13-0

Br 3
14-0x9-7

Dn   L

open to below

Storage Area
14-0x12-0

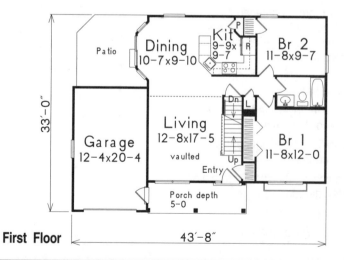

First Floor

Patio

Dining
10-7x9-10

Kit
9-9x9-7

P

R

Br 2
11-8x9-7

33'-0"

Dn   L

Garage
12-4x20-4

Living
12-8x17-5
vaulted

Up

Br 1
11-8x12-0

Entry

Porch depth
5-0

43'-8"

Plan #X20-0483

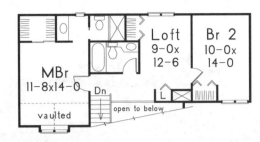

Second Floor

Loft
9-0x
12-6

Br 2
10-0x
14-0

MBr
11-8x14-0

Dn

vaulted

open to below

L

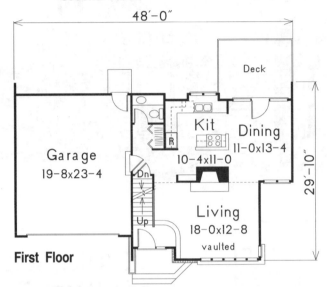

48'-0"

Deck

Kit
10-4x11-0

Dining
11-0x13-4

Garage
19-8x23-4

R

Dn

Up

Living
18-0x12-8
vaulted

29'-10"

First Floor

Tall Windows, Sweeping Roof Lines Make A Sizable Impression

1,351 total square feet of living area

Special features

■ Roof lines and vaulted ceilings make this home look larger than its true size

■ Central fireplace provides a focal point for dining and living areas

■ Master bedroom suite is high-lighted by a roomy window seat and a walk-in closet

■ 3 bedrooms, 2 1/2 baths, 2-car garage

■ Basement foundation

■ 674 square feet on the first floor and 677 square feet on the second floor

Price Code A

MULTI-STORY
under 2,000 square feet

Plan #X20-0103

To order blueprints use the form on page 322 or call toll-free 1-800-DREAM HOME (373-2646)

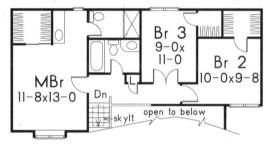

Second Floor

First Floor

Exterior Accents Add Charm To This Compact Cottage

1,359 total square feet of living area

Special features

- Lattice-trimmed porch, stone chimney and abundant windows lend outside appeal
- Spacious, bright breakfast area with pass-through to formal dining room
- Large walk-in closets in all bedrooms
- Extensive deck expands dining and entertaining area
- 3 bedrooms, 2 1/2 baths, 2-car garage
- Basement foundation
- 668 square feet on the first floor and 691 square feet on the second floor

Price Code A

MULTI-STORY under 2,000 square feet

DEXTER

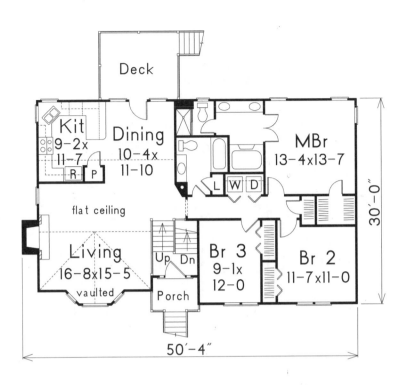

Deck

Kit
9-2x
11-7

R   P

flat ceiling

Dining
10-4x
11-10

MBr
13-4x13-7

L W D

Living
16-8x15-5

vaulted

Up   Dn

Br 3
9-1x
12-0

Br 2
11-7x11-0

Porch

30'-0"

50'-4"

Compact Home
Yet Charming
And Functional

1,404 total square feet of living area

Special features

- Split foyer entrance
- Bayed living area features unique vaulted ceiling and fireplace
- Wrap-around kitchen has corner windows for added sunlight and a bar that overlooks dining area
- Master suite features a garden tub with separate shower
- Back deck provides handy access to dining room and kitchen
- 3 bedrooms, 2 baths, 2-car drive under garage
- Basement foundation, drawings also include partial crawl space foundation

Price Code A

MULTI-STORY under 2,000 square feet

Plan #X20-0176

To order blueprints use the form on page 322 or call toll-free 1-800-DREAM HOME (373-2646)

15

BALDWIN

Exciting Split-Foyer Entrance

1,407 total square feet of living area

Special features

- Large living room with fireplace and access to the rear deck
- Kitchen and dining areas combine to create open gathering area
- Convenient laundry room and broom closet
- Master bedroom includes private bath with large vanity and separate tub and shower
- 3 bedrooms, 2 baths, 2-car drive under garage
- Basement foundation

Price Code A

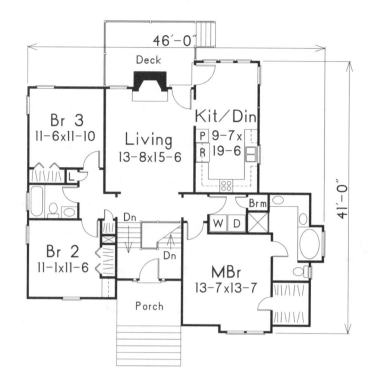

46'-0"

Deck

Br 3
11-6x11-10

Living
13-8x15-6

Kit/Din
P 9-7x
R 19-6

41'-0"

Br 2
11-1x11-6

Dn

Dn

Brm

W D

MBr
13-7x13-7

Porch

Plan #X20-0251

To order blueprints use the form on page 322 or call toll-free 1-800-DREAM HOME (373-2646)

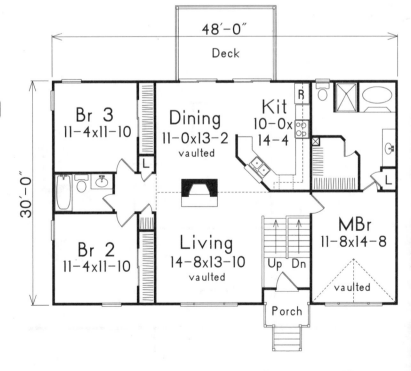

Large Windows Grace This Split Level Home

1,427 total square feet of living area

Special features

- Practical storage space situated in the garage
- Convenient laundry closet located on lower level
- Kitchen and dining both have sliding doors that access the deck
- Large expansive space created by vaulted living and dining rooms
- 3 bedrooms, 2 baths, 2-car garage
- Basement foundation

  Price Code A

48'-0"

Deck

Br 3
11-4x11-10

Dining
11-0x13-2
vaulted

Kit
10-0x
14-4

30'-0"

L

Br 2
11-4x11-10

Living
14-8x13-10
vaulted

Up Dn

MBr
11-8x14-8

vaulted

Porch

MULTI-STORY under 2,000 square feet

Plan #X20-0671

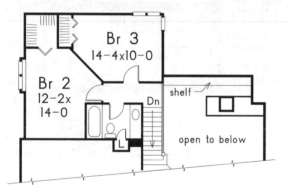

Second Floor

Br 3
14-4x10-0

Br 2
12-2x
14-0

shelf

Dn

open to below

Gabled Front Porch Adds Charm And Value

1,443 total square feet of living area

Special features

- Raised foyer and cathedral ceiling in living room
- Impressive full-wall fireplace between living and dining rooms
- Open U-shaped kitchen with breakfast bay
- Angular side deck accentuates patio and garden
- First floor master bedroom suite has a walk-in closet and a corner window
- 3 bedrooms, 2 baths, 2-car garage
- Basement foundation
- 1,006 square feet on the first floor and 437 square feet on the second floor

Price Code A

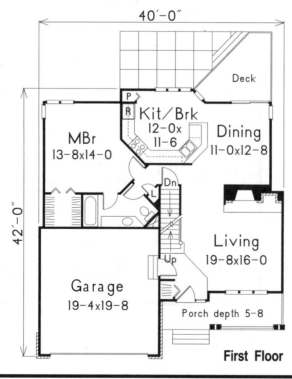

40'-0"

Deck

Kit/Brk
12-0x
11-6

MBr
13-8x14-0

Dining
11-0x12-8

Dn

42'-0"

Living
19-8x16-0

Up

Garage
19-4x19-8

Porch depth 5-8

First Floor

MULTI-STORY under 2,000 square feet

18

FERNWOOD

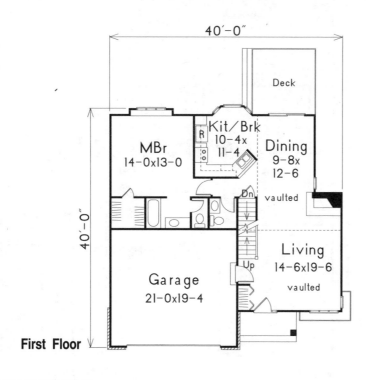

40'-0"

40'-0"

Deck

MBr
14-0x13-0

Kit/Brk
10-4x
11-4

Dining
9-8x
12-6
vaulted

Dn

Living
14-6x19-6
vaulted

Up

Garage
21-0x19-4

First Floor

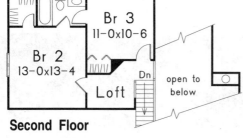

Br 3
11-0x10-6

Br 2
13-0x13-4

Loft

Dn

open to
below

Second Floor

Vaulted Living Area With Corner Fireplace

1,448 total square feet of living area

Special features

- Dining room conveniently adjoins kitchen and accesses rear deck
- Private first floor master bedroom
- Secondary bedrooms share a bath and cozy loft area
- 3 bedrooms, 2 1/2 baths, 2-car garage
- Basement foundation
- 972 square feet on the first floor and 476 square feet on the second floor

Price Code A

MULTI-STORY
under 2,000 square feet

Plan #X20-0270

To order blueprints use the form on page 322 or call toll-free 1-800-DREAM HOME (373-2646)

Home For Narrow Lot Offers Wide Open Spaces

1,492 total square feet of living area

Special features

- Cleverly angled entry spills into living and dining rooms which share warmth of fireplace flanked by arched windows
- Master suite includes double-door entry, huge walk-in closet, shower and bath with picture window
- Stucco and dutch hipped roofs add warmth and charm to facade
- 3 bedrooms, 2 1/2 baths, 2-car garage
- 760 square feet on the first floor and 732 square feet on the second floor
- Basement foundation

Price Code A

First Floor

Second Floor

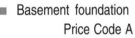

MULTI-STORY under 2,000 square feet

J.N. HANSEN S.DG.

Plan #X20-0415

To order blueprints use the form on page 322 or call toll-free 1-800-DREAM HOME (373-2646)

WOODFIELD

Dining With A View

1,524 total square feet of living area

Special features

- Delightful balcony overlooks two-story entry illuminated by oval window
- Roomy first floor master suite offers quiet privacy
- All bedrooms feature one or more walk-in closets
- 3 bedrooms, 2 1/2 baths, 2-car garage
- Basement foundation
- 951 square feet on the first floor and 573 square feet on the second floor

Price Code B

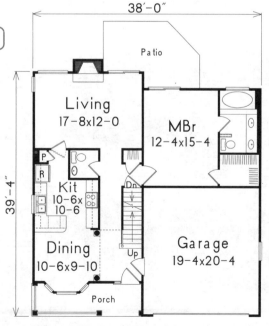

38'-0"

Patio

Living
17-8x12-0

MBr
12-4x15-4

Kit
10-6x
10-6

Dn

39'-4"

Dining
10-6x9-10

Up

Garage
19-4x20-4

Porch

First Floor

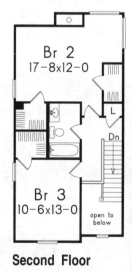

Br 2
17-8x12-0

Dn

Br 3
10-6x13-0

open to
below

Second Floor

MULTI-STORY
under 2,000 square feet

Plan #X20-0652

To order blueprints use the form on page 322 or call toll-free 1-800-DREAM HOME (373-2646)

21

Relax On The Covered Front Porch

1,543 total square feet of living area

Special features

- Fireplace serves as the focal point in the large family room

- Efficient floor plan keeps hallways at a minimum

- Laundry room connects the kitchen to the garage

- Private first floor master bedroom has walk-in closet and bath

- 3 bedrooms, 2 1/2 baths, 2-car detached side-entry garage

- Slab foundation, drawings also include crawl space foundation

- 1,040 square feet on the first floor and 503 square feet on the second floor

Price Code B

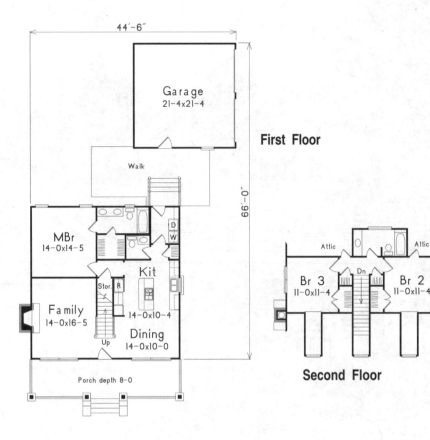

44'-6"

Garage
21-4x21-4

First Floor

Walk

66'-0"

MBr
14-0x14-5

D
W

Kit
14-0x10-4

Stor. R

Family
14-0x16-5

Dining
14-0x10-0

Up

Porch depth 8-0

Attic | Attic

Dn

Br 3
11-0x11-4

Br 2
11-0x11-4

Second Floor

MULTI-STORY
under 2,000 square feet

Plan #X20-0489

Ornate Corner Porch Catches The Eye

1,550 total square feet of living area

Special features

- Impressive front entrance with a wrap-around covered porch and raised foyer
- Corner fireplace provides a focal point in the vaulted great room
- Loft is easily converted to a third bedroom or activity center
- Large family/kitchen area includes greenhouse windows and access to the deck and utility area
- Secondary bedroom has a large dormer and window seat
- 2 bedrooms, 2 1/2 baths, 2-car garage
- Basement foundation
- 818 square feet on the first floor and 732 square feet on the second floor

Price Code B

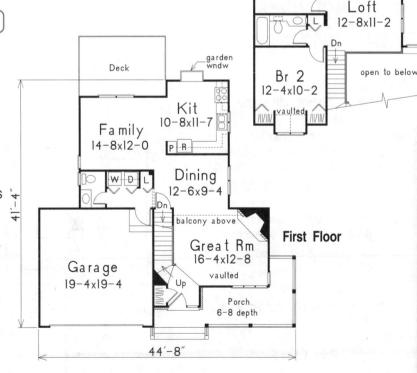

Second Floor

MBr 12-4x14-0

Loft 12-8x11-2

L

Dn

Br 2 12-4x10-2

open to below

vaulted

Deck

garden wndw

Kit 10-8x11-7

Family 14-8x12-0

P R

Dining 12-6x9-4

W D L

Dn

balcony above

First Floor

Great Rm 16-4x12-8

vaulted

Garage 19-4x19-4

Up

Porch 6-8 depth

41'-4"

44'-8"

MULTI-STORY under 2,000 square feet

Country Kitchen Center Of Living Activities

| 1,556 total square feet of living area |

Special features

- A compact home with all the amenities
- Country kitchen combines practicality with access to other areas for eating and entertaining
- Two-way fireplace joins the dining and living areas
- Plant shelf and vaulted ceiling highlight the master bedroom
- 3 bedrooms, 2 1/2 baths, 2-car garage
- Basement foundation
- 834 square feet on the first floor and 722 square feet on the second floor

Price Code B

MULTI-STORY under 2,000 square feet

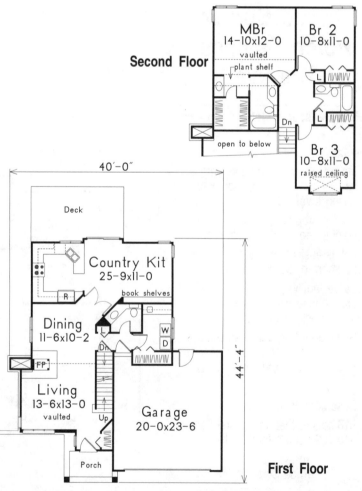

Second Floor

MBr
14-10x12-0
vaulted
plant shelf

Br 2
10-8x11-0

open to below

Dn

Br 3
10-8x11-0
raised ceiling

40'-0"

Deck

Country Kit
25-9x11-0
book shelves

R

Dining
11-6x10-2

W
D

FP

Dn

Living
13-6x13-0
vaulted

Up

Garage
20-0x23-6

44'-4"

Porch

First Floor

Plan #X20-0209

Country-Style With Wrap-Around Porch

1,597 total square feet of living area

Special features

- Spacious family room includes fireplace and coat closet

- Open kitchen/dining room provides breakfast bar and access to outdoors

- Convenient laundry area located near kitchen

- Secluded master suite with walk-in closet and private bath

- 4 bedrooms, 2 1/2 baths, 2-car garage

- Basement foundation

- 982 square feet on the first floor and 615 square feet on the second floor

Price Code C

First Floor

Porch Depth 7-0

MBr 12-0x14-0

Dining 11-0x10-0

Kit 10-0x10-0

Garage 21-4x25-4

Family 14-0x16-10

Second Floor

Br 4 12-0x12-4

Br 3 14-0x10-0

Br 2 14-0x10-10

MULTI-STORY under 2,000 square feet

Plan #X20-0448

To order blueprints use the form on page 322 or call toll-free 1-800-DREAM HOME (373-2646)

Stylish Living For Narrow Lot

1,575 total square feet of living area

Special features

- Inviting porch leads to spacious living and dining room with attractive bay
- Kitchen with corner windows features an island snack bar, breakfast room bay, convenient laundry and built-in pantry
- A luxury bath and walk-in closet adorn master bedroom suite and is convenient to both secondary bedrooms
- 3 bedrooms, 2 1/2 baths, 2-car garage
- Basement foundation
- 802 square feet on the first floor and 773 square feet on the second floor

Price Code B

36'-0"

46'-8"

First Floor

Kit 9-0x11-7
Brkfst 10-0x11-0
Dining 12-0x11-0
Living 15-7x14-4
Dn
Up
R
D W
P

Garage 19-4x20-4

Second Floor

MBr 12-0x14-8
vaulted clg
Br 2 12-0x11-0
Dn
L
Br 3 12-0x11-3
vaulted clg
plant shelf

J.N. HANSEN S.D.6.

Plan #X20-0711

To order blueprints use the form on page 322 or call toll-free 1-800-DREAM HOME (373-2646)

COUNTRY CHARM I

Old-Fashioned Porch Gives Welcoming Appeal

1,664 total square feet of living area

Special features

- L-shaped country kitchen includes pantry and cozy breakfast area

- Bedrooms located on second floor for privacy

- Master bedroom includes walk-in closet, dressing area and bath

- 3 bedrooms, 2 1/2 baths, 2-car garage

- Crawl space foundation, drawings also include basement and slab foundations

- 1,664 square feet of living space, with 832 square feet on the first floor and 832 square feet on the second floor

Price Code B

Second Floor

MBr 12-11x12-11

Br 2 11-8x12-2

Br 3 11-3x12-2

Dn

56'-0"

26'-0"

Dining 10-5x11-6

Kitchen 14-11x11-6

P

W D

R

Furn

Living 18-9x13-7

Foyer

Up

Garage 23-8x23-5

Porch depth 6-0

First Floor

MULTI-STORY
under 2,000 square feet

Plan #X20-0536

To order blueprints use the form on page 322 or call toll-free 1-800-DREAM HOME (373-2646)

27

Two-Story Home With Uncommon Charm

1,695 total square feet of living area

Special features

- Facade features cozy wrap-around porch, projected living room window and repeating front gables

- Balcony overlooks to entry below

- Kitchen has full view corner window with adjacent eating space that opens to screened porch

- Vaulted master bedroom with his and her closets and private bath

- 3 bedrooms, 2 1/2 baths, 2-car garage

- Basement foundation

- 870 square feet on the first floor and 825 square feet on the second floor

Price Code B

Second Floor

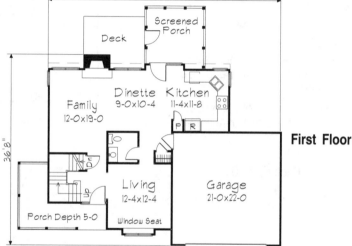

First Floor

MULTI-STORY under 2,000 square feet

Plan #X20-0388

To order blueprints use the form on page 322 or call toll-free 1-800-DREAM HOME (373-2646)

WEDGEWOOD

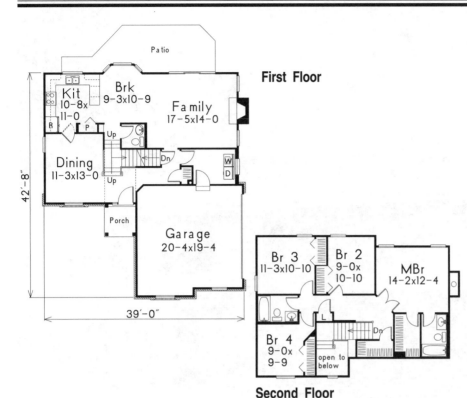

First Floor

Patio

Kit
10-8x
11-0

Brk
9-3x10-9

Family
17-5x14-0

Dining
11-3x13-0

Up
Dn
Up

W
D

42'-8"

Porch

Garage
20-4x19-4

39'-0"

Second Floor

Br 3
11-3x10-10

Br 2
9-0x
10-10

MBr
14-2x12-4

Br 4
9-0x
9-9

open to
below

Smaller Home Offers Stylish Exterior

1,700 total square feet of living area

Special features

- Two-story entry with T-stair is illuminated with decorative oval window
- Skillfully designed U-shaped kitchen with built-in pantry
- All bedrooms have generous closet storage and common to spacious hall with walk-in cedar closet
- 4 bedrooms, 2 1/2 baths, 2-car garage
- Basement foundation
- 896 square feet on the first floor and 804 square feet on the second floor

Price Code B

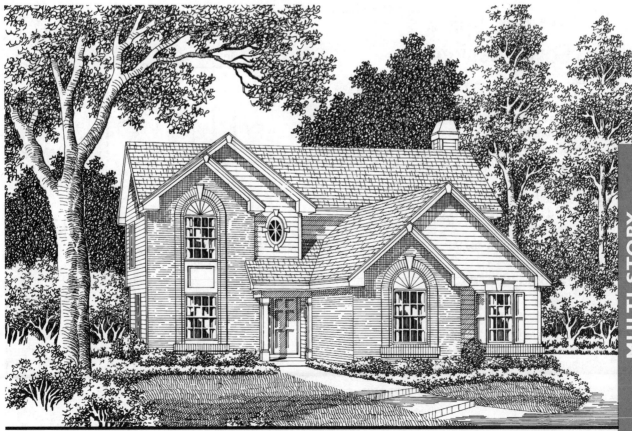

MULTI-STORY under 2,000 square feet

Plan #X20-0656

To order blueprints use the form on page 322 or call toll-free 1-800-DREAM HOME (373-2646)

WOODLAND II

Unique Split Foyer Design

1,720 total square feet of living area

Special features

- Lower level includes large family room with laundry area and half bath

- L-shaped kitchen with convenient serving bar and pass-through to dining area

- Private half bath in master bedroom

- 3 bedrooms, 1 full bath, 2 half baths

- Basement foundation

- 502 square feet on the lower level and 1,218 square feet on the upper level

    Price Code B

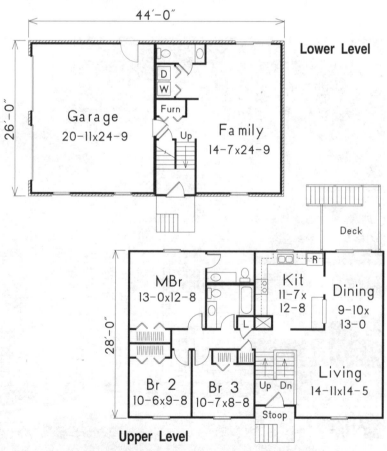

44'-0"

26'-0"

Lower Level

Garage
20-11x24-9

Family
14-7x24-9

D
W

Furn

Up

Deck

28'-0"

MBr
13-0x12-8

Kit
11-7x
12-8

Dining
9-10x
13-0

L

R

Br 2
10-6x9-8

Br 3
10-7x8-8

Up Dn

Living
14-11x14-5

Stoop

Upper Level

Plan #X20-0520

To order blueprints use the form on page 322 or call toll-free 1-800-DREAM HOME (373-2646)

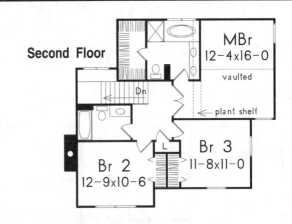

Second Floor

MBr
12-4x16-0
vaulted

← plant shelf

Dn

Br 3
11-8x11-0

Br 2
12-9x10-6

Cozy Columned Archway Defines Foyer

1,777 total square feet of living area

Special features

- Large master bedroom and bath with whirlpool tub, separate shower and spacious walk-in closet

- Large island kitchen with breakfast bay and access to the three-seasons porch

- Convenient laundry room with half bath

- 3 bedrooms, 2 1/2 baths, 2-car garage

- Basement foundation

- 887 square feet on the first floor and 890 square feet on the second floor

Price Code B

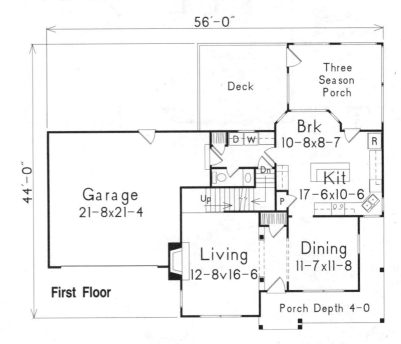

56'-0"

44'-0"

Deck

Three Season Porch

Brk
10-8x8-7

Garage
21-8x21-4

Kit
17-6x10-6

Up

Dn

P

Living
12-8x16-6

Dining
11-7x11-8

First Floor

Porch Depth 4-0

Plan #X20-0389

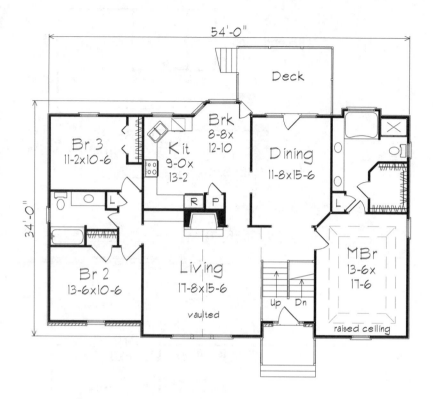

Dimensions: 54'-0" × 34'-0"

Rooms: Deck, Br 3 (11-2×10-6), Kit (9-0×13-2), Brk (8-8×12-10), Dining (11-8×15-6), Br 2 (13-6×10-6), Living (17-8×15-6) vaulted, MBr (13-6×17-6) raised ceiling, Up / Dn

Split Entry With Lots Of Room For Future Growth

1,803 total square feet of living area

Special features

- Master bedroom features raised ceiling and private bath with walk-in closet, large double-bowl vanity and separate tub and shower
- U-shaped kitchen includes corner sink and convenient pantry
- Vaulted living room complete with fireplace and built in cabinet
- 3 bedrooms, 2 baths, 3-car drive under garage
- Basement foundation

    Price Code C

MULTI-STORY under 2,000 square feet

Plan #X20-0395

To order blueprints use the form on page 322 or call toll-free 1-800-DREAM HOME (373-2646)

Second Floor

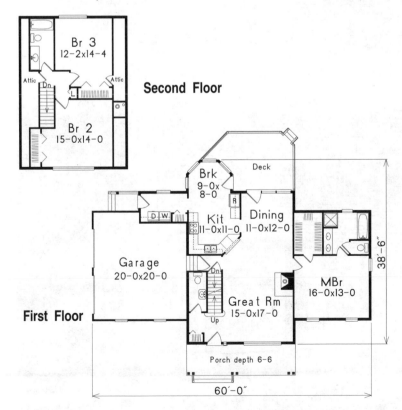

First Floor

Farmhouse Style Offers Great Privacy

1,805 total square feet of living area

Special features

- Energy efficient home with 2" x 6" exterior walls
- Master suite forms its own wing
- Bedrooms upstairs share a hall bath
- Large great room with fireplace spacially blends into a formal dining room
- 3 bedrooms, 2 1/2 baths, 2-car garage
- Basement foundation
- 1,245 square feet on the first floor and 560 square feet on the second floor

Price Code C

MULTI-STORY under 2,000 square feet

Plan #X20-0673

To order blueprints use the form on page 322 or call toll-free 1-800-DREAM HOME (373-2646)

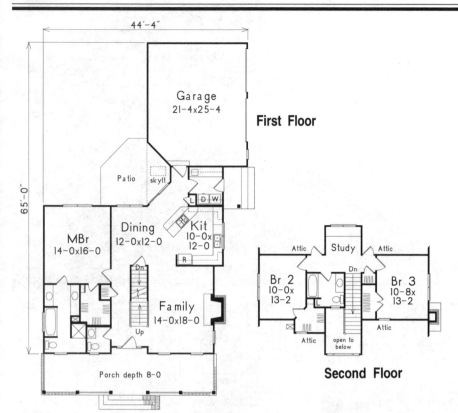

First Floor

44'-4"

Garage
21-4x25-4

Patio

skylt

L D W

65'-0"

MBr
14-0x16-0

Dining
12-0x12-0

Kit
10-0x
12-0

R

Dn

Family
14-0x18-0

Up

Porch depth 8-0

Second Floor

Attic   Study   Attic

Br 2
10-0x
13-2

Dn

Br 3
10-8x
13-2

Attic   open to   Attic
below

Covered Porch Highlights This Home

> 1,808 total square feet of living area

Special features

- Master bedroom has a walk-in closet, double vanities and separate tub and shower

- Two bedrooms upstairs share a study area and full bath

- Partially covered patio is complete with a skylight

- Side entrance opens to utility room with convenient counter space and laundry sink

- 3 bedrooms, 2 1/2 baths, 2-car garage

- Basement foundation

- 1,271 square feet on the first floor and 537 square feet on the second floor

Price Code C

MULTI-STORY
under 2,000 square feet

Plan #X20-0491

To order blueprints use the form on page 322 or call toll-free 1-800-DREAM HOME (373-2646)

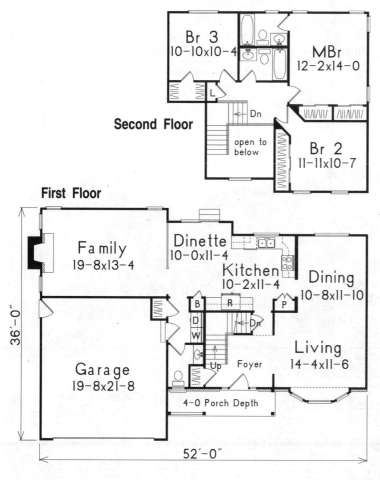

Second Floor

Br 3
10-10x10-4

MBr
12-2x14-0

Dn

open to
below

Br 2
11-11x10-7

First Floor

Family
19-8x13-4

Dinette
10-0x11-4

Kitchen
10-2x11-4

Dining
10-8x11-10

B
R
D
W
P

Dn

Up   Foyer

Living
14-4x11-6

Garage
19-8x21-8

36'-0"

4-0 Porch Depth

52'-0"

Great Plan For Formal And Informal Entertaining

1,813 total square feet of living area

Special features

- Bedrooms located upstairs for privacy
- Living room with large bay window joins dining room for expansive formal entertaining
- Great family area created by family, dinette and kitchen
- Two-story foyer and L-shaped stairs create an impressive entry
- Inviting covered porch
- 3 bedrooms, 2 1/2 baths, 2-car garage
- Basement foundation
- 1,094 square feet on the first floor and 719 square feet on the second floor

Price Code C

MULTI-STORY under 2,000 square feet

Plan #X20-0383

To order blueprints use the form on page 322 or call toll-free 1-800-DREAM HOME (373-2646)

Wrap-Around Porch Adds Outside Living

1,814 total square feet of living area

Special features

- Vaulted master bedroom features walk-in closet and private bath
- Exciting two-story entry with views through the dining room
- Family room, dining room, and kitchen combine to make great entertaining space with lots of windows
- 3 bedrooms, 2 1/2 baths, 2-car garage
- Basement foundation
- 924 square feet on the first floor and 890 square feet on the second floor

Price Code C

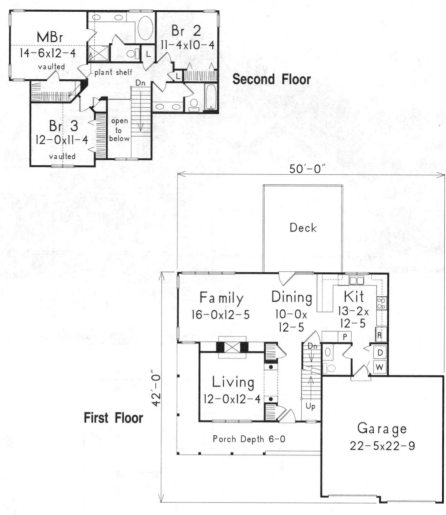

Second Floor

MBr 14-6x12-4 vaulted

Br 2 11-4x10-4

plant shelf

Dn

Br 3 12-0x11-4 vaulted

open to below

50'-0"

Deck

First Floor

42'-0"

Family 16-0x12-5

Dining 10-0x 12-5

Kit 13-2x 12-5

Living 12-0x12-4

Dn

Up

Porch Depth 6-0

Garage 22-5x22-9

MULTI-STORY under 2,000 square feet

Plan #X20-0385

To order blueprints use the form on page 322 or call toll-free 1-800-DREAM HOME (373-2646)

Country Home With Plenty Of Style

1,829 total square feet of living area

Special features

- Entry foyer with coat closet opens to large family room with fireplace
- Two bedrooms upstairs share a full bath
- Optional second floor bedroom can be finished as your family grows
- Cozy porch provides convenient side entrance into home
- 3 bedrooms, 2 1/2 baths, 2-car side entry garage
- Slab foundation
- 1,339 square feet on the first floor and 490 square feet on the second floor

Price Code C

MULTI-STORY under 2,000 square feet

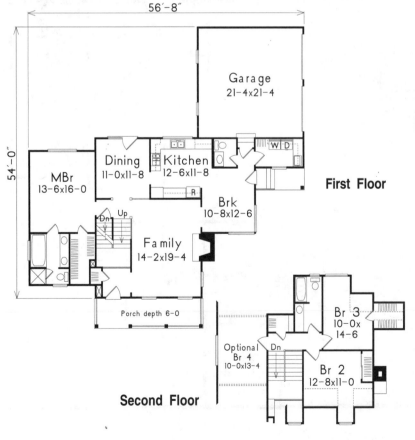

56'-8"

54'-0"

Garage
21-4x21-4

W D

Dining
11-0x11-8

Kitchen
12-6x11-8

MBr
13-6x16-0

R

Brk
10-8x12-6

First Floor

Dn   Up

Family
14-2x19-4

Porch depth 6-0

Br 3
10-0x
14-6

Optional
Br 4
10-0x13-4

Dn

Br 2
12-8x11-0

Second Floor

Open Living Area, Plan Designed For Sloping Lot

1,835 total square feet of living area

Special features

- Family room opens onto balcony through double doors
- Living room offers expansive living space with windows and cathedral ceiling
- Kitchen features angled breakfast bar and corner sink
- Master bedroom boasts vaulted ceiling, walk-in closet, and deluxe bath
- 3 bedrooms, 2 1/2 baths, 2-car garage
- Basement foundation
- 1,022 square feet on the first floor and 813 square feet on the second floor

Price Code D

MULTI-STORY under 2,000 square feet

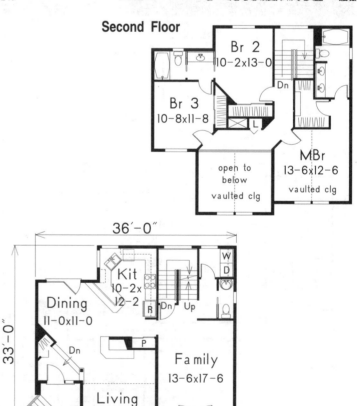

Second Floor

Br 2
10-2x13-0

Br 3
10-8x11-8

Dn

MBr
13-6x12-6
vaulted clg

open to below
vaulted clg

First Floor

36'-0"

33'-0"

Kit
10-2x
12-2

W D

Dining
11-0x11-0

Dn   Up

R

Dn

Family
13-6x17-6

P

Living
13-0x14-4

Porch

Plan #X20-0328

To order blueprints use the form on page 322 or call toll-free 1-800-DREAM HOME (373-2646)

Vaulted Great Room Home With Open Entrance

(1,851 total square feet of living area)

Special features

- High-impact entrance to great room also leads directly to the upper floor

- First-floor master bedroom suite with corner window and walk-in closet

- Kitchen/breakfast room with center work island and pass-through to the dining room

- Upper floor bedrooms overlook the great room

- 4 bedrooms, 2 1/2 baths, 2-car garage

- Basement foundation

- 1,199 square feet on the first floor and 652 square feet on the second floor

Price Code D

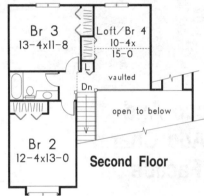

Br 3
13-4x11-8

Loft/Br 4
10-4x
15-0
vaulted

open to below

Dn

Br 2
12-4x13-0

Second Floor

52'-0"

Deck

41'-4"

P

Kit/Brk
14-8x15-0

R

Dining
11-0x15-0

MBr
13-0x15-0
vaulted

Dn

W
D

Great Rm
21-4x14-0
vaulted

Up

Garage
21-4x19-4

Porch

First Floor

MULTI-STORY under 2,000 square feet

Stucco And Stone Add Charm To Facade

1,854 total square feet of living area

Special features

- Front entrance enhanced by arched transom windows and rustic stone
- Isolated master bedroom with dressing area and walk-in closet
- Family room features sloped high ceilings and large fireplace
- Breakfast area accesses covered rear porch
- 3 bedrooms, 2 1/2 baths, 2-car side entry garage
- Basement foundation
- 1,317 square feet on the first floor and 537 square feet on the second floor

Price Code D

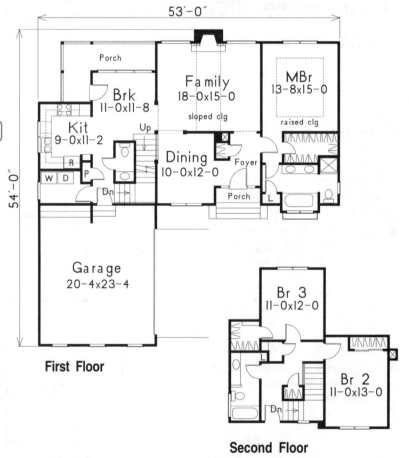

53'-0"

54'-0"

Porch

Brk
11-0x11-8

Kit
9-0x11-2

R

W D P

Dn

Up

Family
18-0x15-0
sloped clg

Dining
10-0x12-0

Foyer

Porch

MBr
13-8x15-0
raised clg

Garage
20-4x23-4

First Floor

Br 3
11-0x12-0

Br 2
11-0x13-0

Dn

Second Floor

Plan #X20-0302

To order blueprints use the form on page 322 or call toll-free 1-800-DREAM HOME (373-2646)

Striking, Covered Arched Entry

1,859 total square feet of living area

Special features

- Fireplace highlights vaulted great room
- Master suite includes large closet and private bath
- Kitchen adjoins breakfast room providing easy access to outside
- 3 bedrooms, 2 1/2 baths, 2-car garage
- Basement foundation
- 1,070 square feet on the first floor and 789 square feet on the second floor

Price Code C

Second Floor

First Floor

MULTI-STORY under 2,000 square feet

Plan #X20-0372

To order blueprints use the form on page 322 or call toll-free 1-800-DREAM HOME (373-2646)

41

Wrap-Around Country Porch

1,875 total square feet of living area

Special features

- Country-style exterior with wrap-around porch and dormers
- Large second floor bedrooms share a dressing area and bath
- Master bedroom suite includes bay window, walk-in closet, dressing area and bath
- 3 bedrooms, 2 baths, 2-car side entry garage
- Crawl space foundation, drawings also include basement and slab foundations
- 1,055 square feet on the first floor and 820 square feet on the second floor

Price Code C

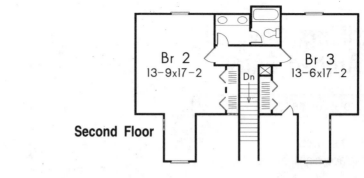

Second Floor

Br 2
13-9x17-2

Br 3
13-6x17-2

Dn

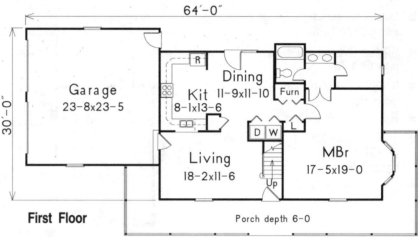

First Floor

64'-0"

30'-0"

Garage
23-8x23-5

Kit
8-1x13-6

R

Dining
11-9x11-10

Furn

D W

Living
18-2x11-6

Up

MBr
17-5x19-0

Porch depth 6-0

MULTI-STORY under 2,000 square feet

Plan #X20-0523

To order blueprints use the form on page 322 or call toll-free 1-800-DREAM HOME (373-2646)

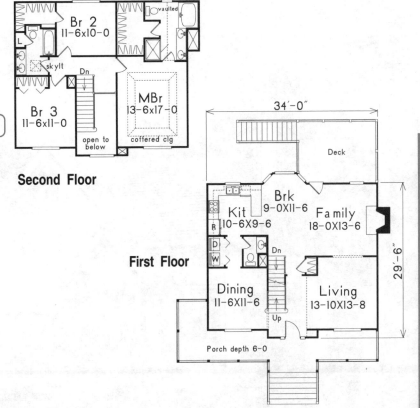

Charming Extras Add Character To This Home

1,880 total square feet of living area

Special features

- Master suite enhanced with coffered ceiling
- Generous family and breakfast areas are modern and functional
- Front porch compliments front facade
- 3 bedrooms, 2 1/2 baths, 2-car drive under garage
- Basement foundation
- 981 square feet on the first floor and 899 square feet on the second floor

Price Code C

Second Floor

Br 2
11-6x10-0

vaulted

Br 3
11-6x11-0

Dn

open to below

MBr
13-6x17-0

coffered clg

skylt

First Floor

34'-0"

Deck

Brk
9-0X11-6

Kit
10-6X9-6

Family
18-0X13-6

29'-6"

Dining
11-6X11-6

Living
13-10X13-8

Dn

Up

Porch depth 6-0

MULTI-STORY under 2,000 square feet

FERGUSON

Well Sculptured Design, Inside And Out

1,889 total square feet of living area

Special features

- The striking entry is created by a unique stair layout, an open high ceiling and a fireplace
- Garage bonus area converts to a fourth bedroom or activity center
- Second floor bedrooms share a private dressing area and bath
- 3 bedrooms, 2 1/2 baths, 2-car garage
- Basement foundation
- 1,128 square feet on the first floor and 761 square feet on the second floor, including the bonus room above the garage

Price Code C

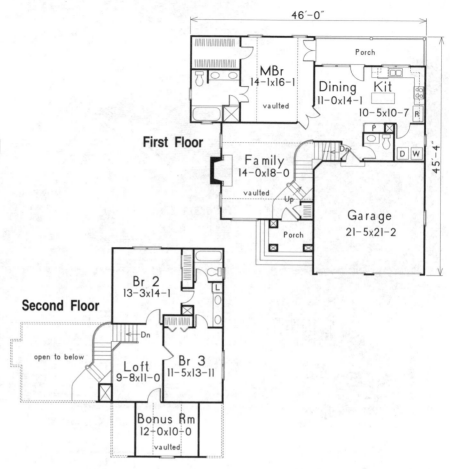

First Floor

46'-0"

45'-4"

MBr 14-1x16-1 vaulted

Porch

Dining 11-0x14-1

Kit 10-5x10-7

Family 14-0x18-0 vaulted

Garage 21-5x21-2

Porch

Second Floor

Br 2 13-3x14-1

open to below

Loft 9-8x11-0

Br 3 11-5x13-11

Bonus Rm 12-0x10-0 vaulted

MULTI-STORY under 2,000 square feet

Plan #X20-0206

To order blueprints use the form on page 322 or call toll-free 1-800-DREAM HOME (373-2646)

44

Country Classic With Modern Floor Plan

> 1,921 total square feet of living area

Special features

- Sunken family room with built-in entertainment center and coffered ceiling
- Sunken formal living room with coffered ceiling
- Dressing area with double sinks, spa tub, shower and french door to private deck
- Large front porch adds to home's appeal
- Energy efficient home with 2" x 6" exterior walls
- 3 bedrooms, 2 1/2 baths, 2-car garage
- Basement foundation
- 1,058 square feet on the first floor and 863 square feet on the second floor

Price Code D

Second Floor

Deck

Br 2
12-2x 11-6

MBr
13-2x14-2

Dn

open to below

Br 3
10-8x11-6

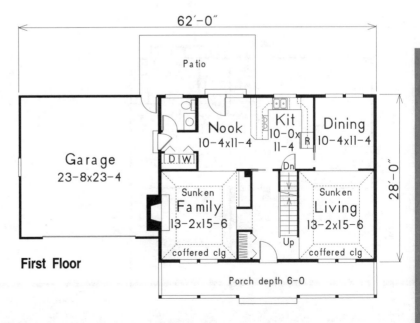

62'-0"

Patio

First Floor

Garage
23-8x23-4

Nook
10-4x11-4

Kit
10-0x 11-4

Dining
10-4x11-4

D W

R

Dn

Sunken Family
13-2x15-6

coffered clg

Up

Sunken Living
13-2x15-6

coffered clg

28'-0"

Porch depth 6-0

MULTI-STORY under 2,000 square feet

Lower Level

46'-0"

24'-4"

Br 3
9-9x10-4

Atrium
9-6x7-7

Br 2
12-3x11-6

Up

Family
16-0x15-5

Bar

Br 4
9-9x10-1

Storage
18-0x9-3

D
W

Deck

Dining
10-8x12-0
vaulted

Skylts

Dn

plant shelf   vaulted

plant shelf

Kit
10-4x11-4
vaulted

Great Room
16-0x15-9
vaulted

MBr
12-5x15-0

P

R

Porch

Garage
18-4x20-4

46'-8"

46'-0"

First Floor

Big Features In A Small Package

1,941 total square feet of living area

Special features

- Dramatic, exciting and spacious interior
- Vaulted great room brightened by sunken atrium window wall and skylights
- Vaulted U-shaped gourmet kitchen with plant shelf opens to dining room
- First floor half bath features space for stackable washer and dryer
- 4 bedrooms, 2 1/2 baths, 2-car garage
- Walk-out basement foundation
- 996 square feet on the first floor and 945 square feet on the lower level

Price Code C

MULTI-STORY
under 2,000 square feet

Plan #X20-0420

To order blueprints use the form on page 322 or call toll-free 1-800-DREAM HOME (373-2646)

DORCHESTER

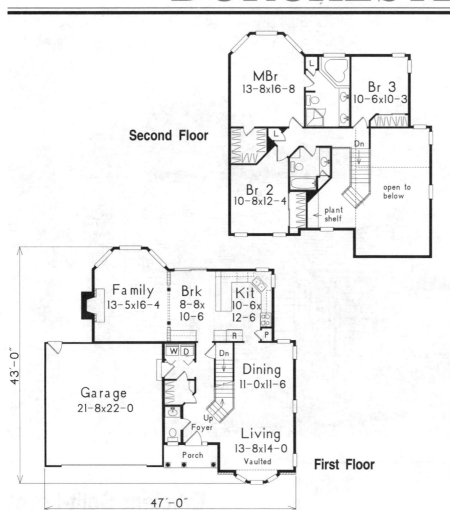

Second Floor

MBr
13-8x16-8

Br 3
10-6x10-3

L

Dn

open to
below

Br 2
10-8x12-4

plant
shelf

First Floor

43'-0"

Family
13-5x16-4

Brk
8-8x
10-6

Kit
10-6x
12-6

R

P

W D

Dn

Dining
11-0x11-6

Garage
21-8x22-0

Up
Foyer

Living
13-8x14-0
Vaulted

Porch

47'-0"

Columned Breakfast Room Adds Appeal

1,954 total square feet of living area

Special features

- Living and dining areas include vaulted ceilings and combine for added openness
- Convenient access to laundry room from garage
- Appealing bay window in family room attracts light
- Raised jacuzzi tub featured in master bath
- 3 bedrooms, 2 1/2 baths, 2-car garage
- Basement foundation
- 1,052 square feet on the first floor and 902 square feet on the second floor

Price Code C

C. Kolupski

MULTI-STORY
under 2,000 square feet

Plan #X20-0375

To order blueprints use the form on page 322 or call toll-free 1-800-DREAM HOME (373-2646)

Br 2
10-4x
10-0

Kit
9-10x
10-0
R
plant shelf

Dining
9-8x
10-0

MBr
11-6x14-4
L

Up   vaulted clg

Dn

Br 3
11-0x11-0

Living
19-6x13-0

First Floor

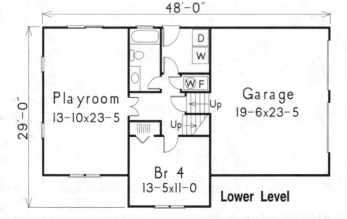

48'-0"

29'-0"

Playroom
13-10x23-5

D
W

W F

Up

Garage
19-6x23-5

Up

Br 4
13-5x11-0

Lower Level

Efficient Split-Level Design

[1,978 total square feet of living area]

Special features

- Master bedroom includes walk-in closet and private full bath
- Entry opens into large living area with bay window, fireplace and plant shelf
- Open kitchen/dining area includes bar and access to deck
- 3 bedrooms, 2 baths, 2-car drive under garage
- Partial basement/slab foundation
- 742 square feet on the lower level and 1,236 square feet on the upper level

Price Code C

Plan #X20-0248
To order blueprints use the form on page 322 or call toll-free 1-800-DREAM HOME (373-2646)

HOLLYHILL

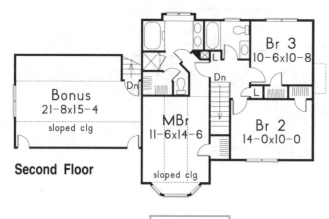

Second Floor

- Bonus 21-8x15-4 sloped clg
- Dn
- Br 3 10-6x10-8
- L
- MBr 11-6x14-6 sloped clg
- Dn
- L
- Br 2 14-0x10-0

- Patio
- Up
- Up
- Brk 9-4x9-6
- Up
- DW
- Kit 11-6x 8-6
- R
- Living 14-0x23-4
- Garage 21-8x27-4
- 30'-0"
- Dining 11-6x9-0
- Porch depth 5-0
- 52'-0"
- Up

First Floor

Double Bay Enhances Front Entry

1,992 total square feet of living area

Special features

- Distinct living, dining and break-fast areas
- Master bedroom boasts full end bay window and a cathedral ceiling
- Storage and laundry area located adjacent to the garage
- Bonus room over the garage for future office or playroom
- 3 bedrooms, 2 1/2 baths, 2-car garage
- Crawl space foundation, drawings also include basement foundation
- 868 square feet on the first floor and 1,124 square feet on the second floor, including the bonus room above the garage

Price Code C

MULTI-STORY
under 2,000 square feet

Plan #X20-0113

To order blueprints use the form on page 322 or call toll-free 1-800-DREAM HOME (373-2646)

Blends Open And Private Living Areas

1,996 total square feet of living area

Special features

- Dining area features octagonal coffered ceiling and built-in china cabinet

- Bedrooms are arranged with a view to the foyer, a coffered ceiling in the master bedroom and a bright skylight for each bath

- Family room includes wet bar and fireplace flanked by attractive quarter round windows

- 9' ceilings throughout first floor with plant shelving in foyer and dining area

- 3 bedrooms, 2 1/2 baths, 2-car side entry garage

- Basement foundation, drawings also include crawl space and slab foundations

- 1,137 square feet on the first floor and 859 square feet on the second floor

Price Code C

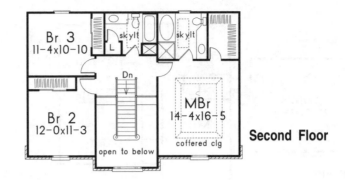

Second Floor

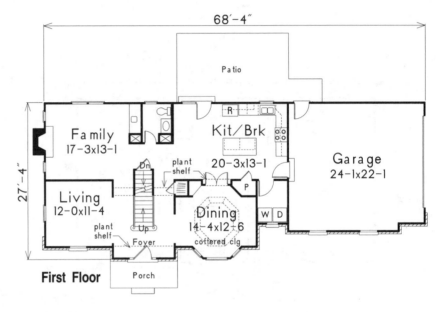

First Floor

MULTI-STORY under 2,000 square feet

Plan #X20-0228

To order blueprints use the form on page 322 or call toll-free 1-800-DREAM HOME (373-2646)

50

Distinctive Front Facade With Generous Porch

2,024 total square feet of living area

Special features

- King-sized master suite with sitting area

- Living room features include corner fireplace, access to covered rear porch, 18' ceilings and a balcony

- Closet for handling of recyclables

- 3 bedrooms, 2 1/2 baths, 2-car side entry garage

- Crawl space foundation, drawings also include slab and basement foundations

- 1,460 square feet on the first floor and 564 square feet on the second floor

Price Code C

First Floor

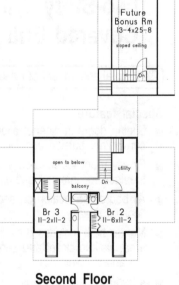

Second Floor

MULTI-STORY over 2,000 square feet

Charming Two-Story With Covered Entry

2,013 total square feet of living area

Special features

- Sliding doors in dinette, allow convenient outside access
- Family room includes cozy fireplace for informal gathering
- All bedrooms located on second floor for privacy
- Master bath includes dressing area, walk-in closet and separate tub and shower
- 4 bedrooms, 2 1/2 baths, 2-car garage
- Basement foundation
- 1,025 square feet on the first floor and 988 square feet on the second floor

Price Code C

MULTI-STORY
over 2,000 square feet

Second Floor

Br 3
11-0x11-4

Br 4
8-6x11-0

Br 2
10-10x11-2

open to below

MBr
13-0x16-10

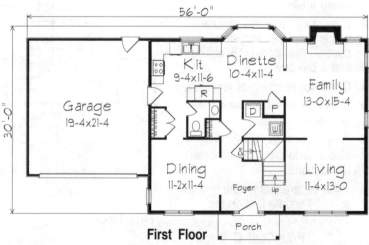

First Floor

56'-0"

30'-0"

Garage
19-4x21-4

Kit
9-4x11-6

Dinette
10-4x11-4

Family
13-0x15-4

Dining
11-2x11-4

Foyer

up

Living
11-4x13-0

Porch

Plan #X20-0384

SUMMIT

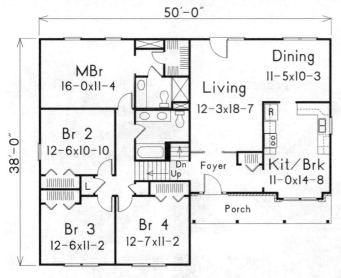

First Floor

- MBr 16-0x11-4
- Br 2 12-6x10-10
- Br 3 12-6x11-2
- Br 4 12-7x11-2
- Living 12-3x18-7
- Dining 11-5x10-3
- Kit/Brk 11-0x14-8
- Foyer
- Porch
- Dn / Up

50'-0"
38'-0"

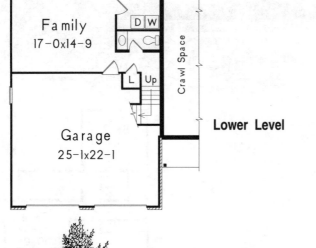

Lower Level

- Family 17-0x14-9
- Garage 25-1x22-1
- Crawl Space
- L / Up

Plan Is Ideal For Growing Family

2,015 total square feet of living area

Special features

- Master bedroom features walk-in closet and private bath
- Secondary bedrooms include ample closet space
- Lower level complete with large family room, half bath and laundry area
- Breakfast area window seat and pass-through country kitchen
- 4 bedrooms, 2 1/2 baths, 2-car garage
- Partial basement/crawl space foundation
- 403 on the lower level and 1,612 on the first floor

Price Code C

MULTI-STORY over 2,000 square feet

Plan #X20-0516

Rustic Stone Enhances Front Entrance

| 2,024 total square feet of living area |

Special features

- Impressive fireplace and sloped ceiling in the family room
- Master bedroom features vaulted ceiling, separate dressing room and a walk-in closet
- Breakfast area includes work desk and accesses deck
- 4 bedrooms, 2 1/2 baths, 2-car side entry garage
- Basement foundation
- 1,395 square feet on the first floor and 629 square feet on the second floor

Price Code C

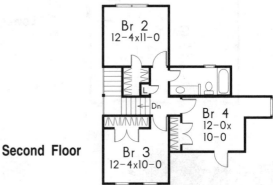

Second Floor

Br 2
12-4x11-0

Br 4
12-0x 10-0

Br 3
12-4x10-0

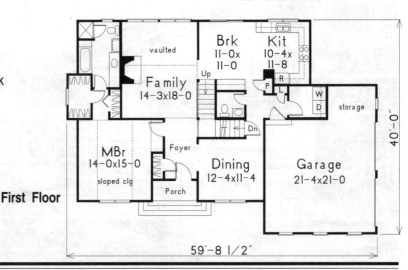

First Floor

vaulted

Brk
11-0x 11-0

Kit
10-4x 11-8

Family
14-3x18-0

Up

storage

W
D

MBr
14-0x15-0

sloped clg

Foyer

Dining
12-4x11-4

Garage
21-4x21-0

Porch

Dn

40'-0"

59'-8 1/2"

MULTI-STORY over 2,000 square feet

Handsome Facade, Compact Design

2,041 total square feet of living area

Special features

- Wonderful sunken family room features fireplace and accesses patio

- The kitchen with island cooktop and nook combines with family room creating open area

- Dining room accessible from kitchen and vaulted living room

- Bedroom 4 - possible study or den

- 4 bedrooms, 3 baths, 2-car side entry garage

- Partial basement/slab foundation

- 1,385 square feet on the first floor and 656 square feet on the second floor

Price Code C

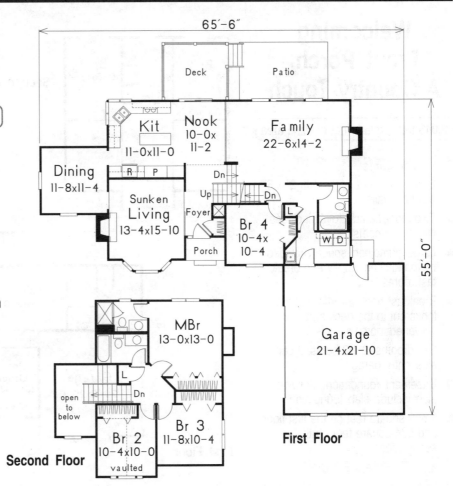

65'-6"

Deck   Patio

Kit
11-0x11-0

Nook
10-0x
11-2

Family
22-6x14-2

Dining
11-8x11-4

R P

Dn

Up   Dn

Sunken
Living
13-4x15-10

Foyer

Br 4
10-4x
10-4

Porch

L

W D

Garage
21-4x21-10

55'-0"

First Floor

MBr
13-0x13-0

L
Dn

open
to
below

Br 2
10-4x10-0
vaulted

Br 3
11-8x10-4

Second Floor

Plan #X20-0311

To order blueprints use the form on page 322 or call toll-free 1-800-DREAM HOME (373-2646)

Welcoming Front Porch, A Country Touch

2,043 total square feet of living area

Special features

- Energy efficient home with 2" x 6" exterior walls

- Two-story central foyer includes two coat closets

- Large combined space provided by the kitchen, family and breakfast rooms

- Breakfast nook for informal dining looks out to the deck and screened porch

- 3 bedrooms, 2 1/2 baths, 2-car side entry garage

- Basement foundation, drawings also include slab foundation

- 1,509 square feet on the first floor and 534 square feet on the second foor

Price Code C

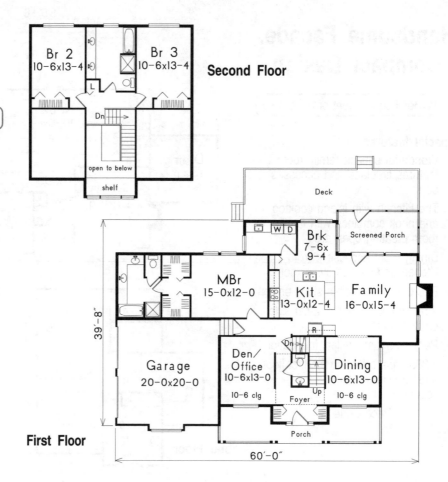

Second Floor

Br 2 10-6x13-4
Br 3 10-6x13-4
L
Dn
open to below
shelf

First Floor

39'-8"
60'-0"

Deck
W D
Brk 7-6x 9-4
Screened Porch
MBr 15-0x12-0
Kit 13-0x12-4
Family 16-0x15-4
Garage 20-0x20-0
Den/Office 10-6x13-0
10-6 clg
R
Dn
Up
Foyer
Dining 10-6x13-0
10-6 clg
Porch

MULTI-STORY over 2,000 square feet

Plan #X20-0672

Breakfast Nook
Fits In Cozy Bay

2,045 total square feet of living area

Special features

- Master bedroom includes walk-in closet and private bath with corner tub and separate shower
- Both family and breakfast rooms access outside doors
- Two-story foyer with attractive transom windows opens into formal living room
- 3 bedrooms, 2 1/2 baths, 2-car garage
- Basement foundation
- 1,136 square feet on the first floor and 909 square feet on the second floor

Price Code C

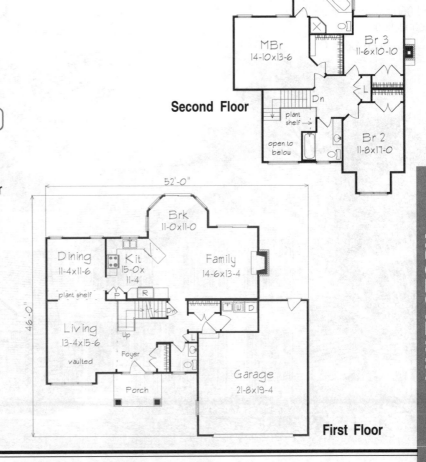

Second Floor

MBr
14-10x13-6

Br 3
11-6x10-10

Dn

plant shelf →

open to below

Br 2
11-8x17-0

52'-0"

46'-0"

Brk
11-0x11-0

Dining
11-4x11-6

Kit
15-0x11-4

Family
14-6x13-4

plant shelf

P R

Living
13-4x15-6

Up

W D

Foyer

vaulted

Garage
21-8x19-4

Porch

First Floor

MULTI-STORY over 2,000 square feet

Plan #X20-0381

To order blueprints use the form on page 322 or call toll-free 1-800-DREAM HOME (373-2646)

57

Practical Two-Story, Full Of Features

2,058 total square feet of living area

Special features

- Handsome two-story foyer with balcony creates a spacious entrance area
- Vaulted ceiling in the master bedroom with private dressing area and large walk-in closet
- Skylights furnish natural lighting in the hall and master bathroom
- Conveniently located second floor laundry near bedrooms
- 3 bedrooms, 2 1/2 baths, 2-car garage
- Basement foundation, drawings also include slab and crawl space foundations
- 1,098 square feet on the first floor and 960 square feet on the second floor

Price Code C

Second Floor

Br 3
11-0x13-5

MBr
16-5x13-5
vaulted

W D

Br 2
13-0x11-0

open to below

Dn

skylt

skylt

First Floor

Deck

Dining
11-7x13-5

Kit
11-6x
10-3

Brk
9-6x12-3

Family
16-5x13-5

R

Living
13-5x13-4

Up

Foyer

Dn

Garage
20-5x21-4

Porch

36'-0"

50'-0"

MULTI-STORY over 2,000 square feet

Plan #X20-0171

To order blueprints use the form on page 322 or call toll-free 1-800-DREAM HOME (373-2646)

WEDGEGROVE

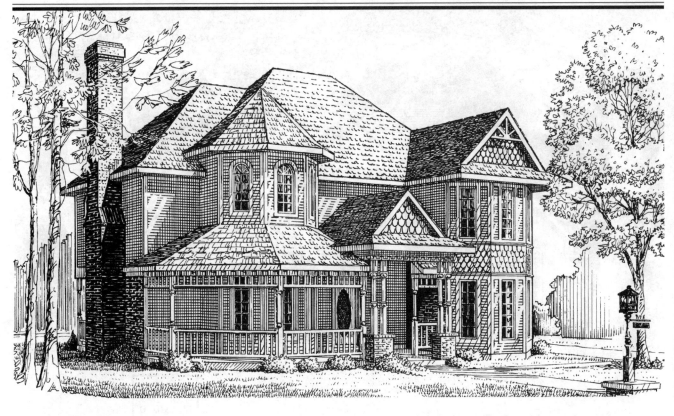

Victorian-Style Home Features Double Bays

2,066 total square feet of living area

Special features

- Large master bedroom includes sitting area and private bath
- Open living room features a fireplace with built-in book shelves
- Spacious kitchen accesses formal dining area and breakfast room
- 3 bedrooms, 2 1/2 baths
- Slab foundation
- 997 square feet on the first floor and 1,069 square feet on the second floor

Price Code C

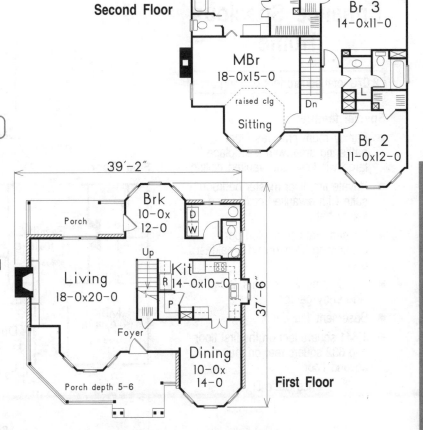

Second Floor

Br 3
14-0x11-0

MBr
18-0x15-0

raised clg

Sitting

Dn

Br 2
11-0x12-0

39'-2"

Brk
10-0x
12-0

Porch

D
W

Up

Living
18-0x20-0

Kit
14-0x10-0

37'-6"

R

P

Foyer

Dining
10-0x
14-0

Porch depth 5-6

First Floor

Plan #X20-0234

To order blueprints use the form on page 322 or call toll-free 1-800-DREAM HOME (373-2646)

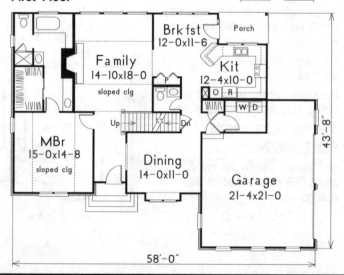

Br 3
12-0x10-0

L

Br 4
12-0x10-0

Dn

Br 2
14-0x11-0

optional
bonus room

Second Floor

Vaulted Ceilings Enhance Spacious Home

2,073 total square feet of living area

First Floor

Brkfst
12-0x11-6

Porch

Family
14-10x18-0

sloped clg

Kit
12-4x10-0

O R

W D

Up

Dn

Special features

- Family room provides ideal gathering area, with a fireplace, large windows and vaulted ceiling

- Private first floor master bedroom suite with a vaulted ceiling and luxury bath

- Kitchen features angled bar connecting kitchen and breakfast area

- 4 bedrooms, 2 1/2 baths, 2-car side entry garage

- Basement foundation

- 1,441 square feet on the first floor and 632 square feet on the second floor

Price Code D

MBr
15-0x14-8

sloped clg

Dining
14-0x11-0

Garage
21-4x21-0

43'-8"

58'-0"

Plan #X20-0230

MOUNTFAIR

Palladian-Style Window Highlights Front Entrance

2,081 total square feet of living area

Special features

- 11'-2" ceilings in living room, dining room and den
- Living and dining rooms divided by columns and plant shelf
- Impressive fireplace with tile hearth in family room which accesses kitchen
- Master bedroom features double-door entrance to master bath and walk-in closet
- 3 bedrooms, 2 1/2 baths, 3-car garage
- Crawl space foundation
- 1,186 square feet on the first floor and 895 square feet on the second floor

Price Code C

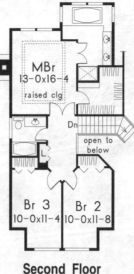

Second Floor

MBr
13-0x16-4
raised clg

Dn

open to below

Br 3
10-0x11-4

Br 2
10-0x11-8

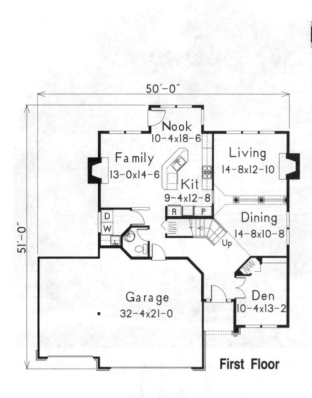

50'-0"

51'-0"

Nook
10-4x18-6

Family
13-0x14-6

Living
14-8x12-10

Kit
9-4x12-8

Dining
14-8x10-8

Up

Garage
32-4x21-0

Den
10-4x13-2

First Floor

Plan #X20-0327

Distinctive Country Look And Feel

2,127 total square feet of living area

Special features

- Energy efficient home with 2" x 6" exterior walls
- Kitchen includes island cooktop, built-in desk, and a cozy nook with outside access
- Double-door entrance to master suite and deluxe bath
- Large covered wrap-around porch
- Bedroom 4 accesses attic storage above garage
- 4 bedrooms, 2 1/2 baths, 2-car garage
- Crawl space foundation
- 1,037 square feet on the first floor and 1,090 square feet on the second floor including the bonus room

Price Code C

MULTI-STORY
over 2,000 square feet

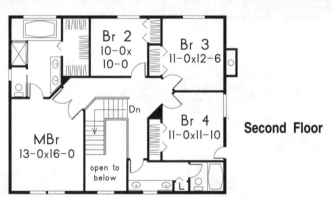

Second Floor

Br 2
10-0x 10-0

Br 3
11-0x12-6

Br 4
11-0x11-10

MBr
13-0x16-0

Dn

open to below

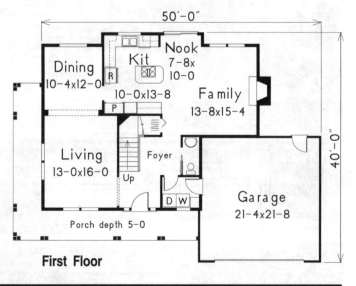

First Floor

50'-0"

40'-0"

Nook
7-8x 10-0

Kit
10-0x13-8

Dining
10-4x12-0

Family
13-8x15-4

Living
13-0x16-0

Foyer

Up

Garage
21-4x21-8

Porch depth 5-0

D W

R

P

Plan #X20-0325

ROBERTSON

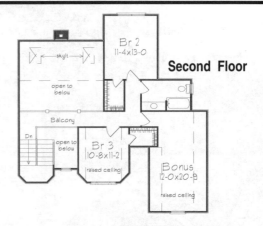

Second Floor

Balcony Overlooks Skylighted Family Room

2,128 total square feet of living area

Special features

■ Large bonus room offers many possibilities

■ Convenient laundry room located near kitchen

■ Private master bath features raised ceiling, large walk-in closet and deluxe bath

■ 3 bedrooms, 2 1/2 baths, 2-car garage

■ Basement foundation

■ 1,299 square feet on the first floor and 829 square feet on the second floor, including the bonus room above the garage

Price Code C

First Floor

Plan #X20-0363

To order blueprints use the form on page 322 or call toll-free 1-800-DREAM HOME (373-2646)

MULTI-STORY over 2,000 square feet

Second Floor

First Floor

Excellent Design For Comfortable Living

2,180 total square feet of living area

Special features

- Informal dinette and formal dining area flank kitchen
- Fireplace is focal point in vaulted family room
- Master bedroom includes bath with walk-in closet, shower and corner garden tub
- 3 bedrooms, 2 1/2 baths, 2-car garage
- Basement foundation
- 1,228 square feet on the first floor and 952 square feet on the second floor

Price Code C

Plan #X20-0378

HUNTINGTON

MBr
19-4x13-0
Vaulted

Br 2
14-0x11-0

Br 3
12-9x12-0
Vaulted

Second Floor

Great Rm
19-4x15-0

Breakfast
11-8x13-0

Kit
12-0x14-6

Entry

Porch Depth 7-8

Dining
15-0x12-0

Garage
21-4x21-10

48'-8"

57'-0"

First Floor

Distinctive Country Porch

2,182 total square feet of living area

Special features

- Meandering porch creates inviting look
- Generous great room with four double-hung windows and gliding doors to exterior
- Highly functional kitchen features island/breakfast bar, menu-desk and convenient pantry
- Each secondary bedroom includes generous closet and private bath
- 3 bedrooms, 3 1/2 baths, 2-car side entry garage
- Basement foundation
- 1,112 square feet on the first floor and 1,070 square feet on the second floor

Price Code C

MULTI-STORY over 2,000 square feet

Plan #X20-0413
To order blueprints use the form on page 322 or call toll-free 1-800-DREAM HOME (373-2646)

65

Centralized Living Area Is Functional And Appealing

2,186 total square feet of living area

Special features

- See-through fireplace a focal point in family and living areas
- Built-in bookshelves grace living area
- Large laundry room with adjoining half bath
- Ideal second floor bath includes separate vanity with double sinks
- 3 bedrooms, 2 1/2 baths, 2-car garage
- Basement foundation
- 1,166 square feet on the first floor and 1,020 square feet on the second floor

Price Code C

MULTI-STORY over 2,000 square feet

Br 2
11-0x10-9

plant shelf

MBr
16-8x14-0
vaulted

Dn

open to below

Br 3
12-0x13-0

vaulted

Second Floor

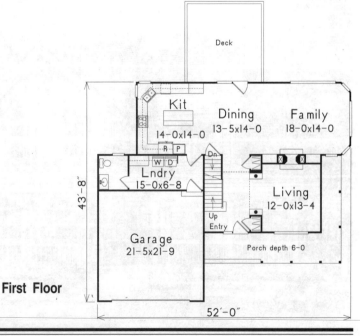

Deck

Kit
14-0x14-0

Dining
13-5x14-0

Family
18-0x14-0

Lndry
15-0x6-8

Dn

Living
12-0x13-4

43'-8"

W D

Up
Entry

Garage
21-5x21-9

Porch depth 6-0

52'-0"

First Floor

Stylish Corner Entry Porch

2,195 total square feet of living area

Special features

- Elegant parlor features attractive bay window
- Open floor plan in the family room, nook and kitchen
- Master bedroom with walk-in closet and private bath
- Energy efficient home with 2" x 6" exterior walls
- 4 bedrooms, 2 1/2 baths, 2-car garage
- Basement foundation
- 1,085 square feet on the first floor and 1,110 square feet on the second floor

Price Code C

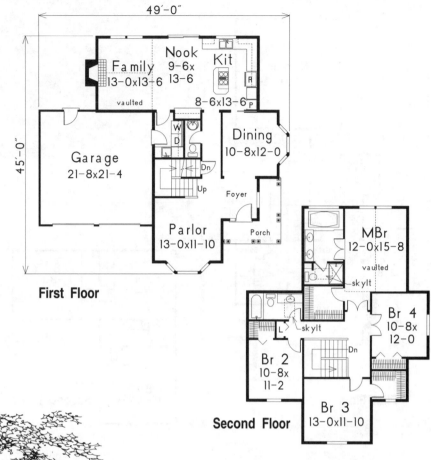

49'-0"

45'-0"

Family 13-0x13-6 vaulted

Nook 9-6x 13-6

Kit 8-6x13-6

Garage 21-8x21-4

W D

Dn

Up

Dining 10-8x12-0

Foyer

Parlor 13-0x11-10

Porch

First Floor

MBr 12-0x15-8 vaulted skylt

Br 4 10-8x 12-0

skylt

L

Br 2 10-8x 11-2

Dn

Br 3 13-0x11-10

Second Floor

MULTI-STORY
over 2,000 square feet

Plan #X20-0404

To order blueprints use the form on page 322 or call toll-free 1-800-DREAM HOME (373-2646)

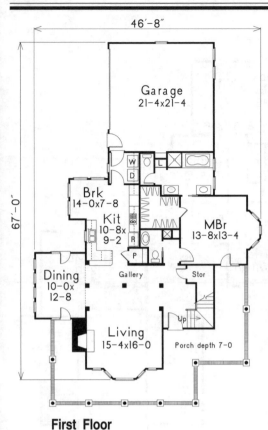

First Floor

46'-8"

67'-0"

Garage
21-4x21-4

Brk
14-0x7-8

Kit
10-8x
9-2

MBr
13-8x13-4

Dining
10-0x
12-8

Gallery

Stor

W D

L

P

R

Living
15-4x16-0

Porch depth 7-0

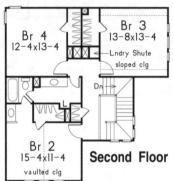

Second Floor

Br 4
12-4x13-4

Br 3
13-8x13-4

Lndry Shute
sloped clg

Dn

Br 2
15-4x11-4
vaulted clg

L

Outside Living Area Created By Veranda

2,213 total square feet of living area

Special features

- Master bedroom features full bath with separate vanities, large walk-in closet and access to veranda

- Living room enhanced by a fireplace, bay window and columns framing the gallery

- 9' ceilings throughout home add to open feeling

- 4 bedrooms, 2 1/2 baths, 2-car side entry garage

- Slab foundation

- 1,351 square feet on the first floor and 862 square feet on the second floor

Price Code E

MULTI-STORY over 2,000 square feet

Plan #X20-0231

AUGUSTA

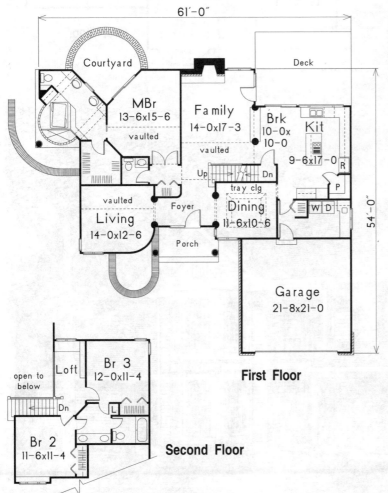

61'-0"

Courtyard

Deck

MBr
13-6x15-6
vaulted

Family
14-0x17-3
vaulted

Brk
10-0x
10-0

Kit
9-6x17-0

vaulted

Up   Dn
tray clg

Living
14-0x12-6

Foyer

Dining
11-6x10-6

W D

R

P

Porch

54'-0"

Garage
21-8x21-0

First Floor

open to
below

Loft

Br 3
12-0x11-4

Dn

Br 2
11-6x11-4

Second Floor

Master Bath
Features Curved
Glass Block Wall

2,223 total square feet of living area

Special features

■ Vaulted master suite opens to
   courtyard

■ Master bath features curved glass
   block wall around tub and shower

■ Vaulted family room combines
   with breakfast and kitchen to
   create large casual living area

■ Second floor includes two
   additional bedrooms and a
   possible loft/office

■ 3 bedrooms, 2 1/2 baths, 2-car
   garage

■ Basement foundation

■ 1,689 square feet on the first floor
   and 534 square feet on the
   second floor

   Price Code D

MULTI-STORY
over 2,000 square feet

Plan #X20-0345
To order blueprints use the form on page 322 or call toll-free 1-800-DREAM HOME (373-2646)

Two-Story Offers Attractive Exterior

2,262 total square feet of living area

Special features

- Charming exterior features include large front porch, two patios, front balcony and double bay windows

- Den/office area provides impressive entry to sunken family room

- Conveniently located first floor laundry

- Large master bedroom with walk-in closet, dressing area and bath

- 3 bedrooms, 2 1/2 baths, 2-car rear entry garage

- Crawl space foundation, drawings also include basement and slab foundations

- 1,127 square feet on the first floor and 1,135 square feet on the second floor

Price Code D

Br 2
15-2x11-3

Br 3
15-5x10-10

Dn

MBr
13-7x22-9

Balcony

Second Floor

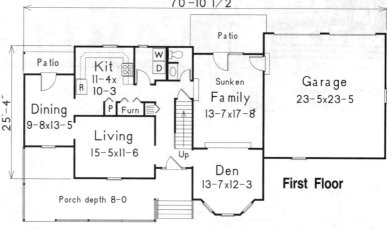

70'-10 1/2"

25'-4"

Patio

Patio

Kit
11-4x
10-3

W
D

Dining
9-8x13-5

Living
15-5x11-6

P   Furn

Sunken
Family
13-7x17-8

Garage
23-5x23-5

Up

Den
13-7x12-3

Porch depth 8-0

First Floor

MULTI-STORY over 2,000 square feet

Plan #X20-0526

VANDOVER

Living And Family Rooms Share A Fireplace

2,274 total square feet of living area

Special features

- Exciting angled stairs lead up to second floor bedrooms
- Family room features media center and bookshelves
- Living and family rooms directly off foyer which has built-in niches
- 3 bedrooms, 2 1/2 baths, 2-car garage
- Crawl space foundation, drawings also include slab foundation
- 1,208 square feet on the first floor and 1,066 square feet on the second floor

Price Code D

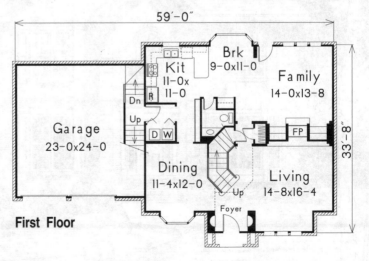

Second Floor

Br 3
12-4x10-4

Br 2
11-4x11-8

coffered clg

open to below

Dn

MBr
14-4x13-8

Sitting

First Floor

59'-0"

33'-8"

Brk
9-0x11-0

Kit
11-0x11-0

Dn

Up

R

Garage
23-0x24-0

DW

Family
14-0x13-8

FP

Dining
11-4x12-0

Living
14-8x16-4

Up

Foyer

MULTI-STORY over 2,000 square feet

Plan #X20-0317

To order blueprints use the form on page 322 or call toll-free 1-800-DREAM HOME (373-2646)

Exterior Accents Complement Front Facade

2,282 total square feet of living area

Special features

- Balcony and two-story foyer add spaciousness to this compact plan

- First floor master suite has corner tub in large master bath

- Out-of-the-way kitchen is open to the full-windowed breakfast room

- 4 bedrooms, 2 1/2 baths, 2-car drive under garage

- Basement foundation

- 1,431 square feet on the first floor and 851 square feet on the second floor

Price Code E

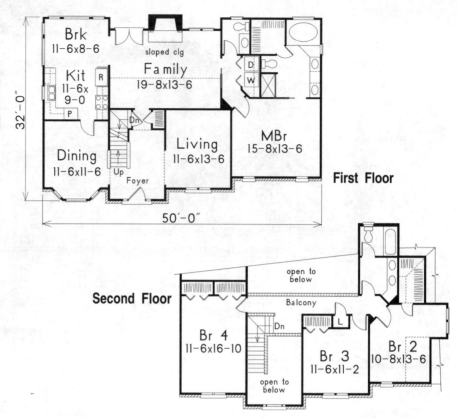

First Floor

Second Floor

MULTI-STORY over 2,000 square feet

Plan #X20-0137

WINSTON

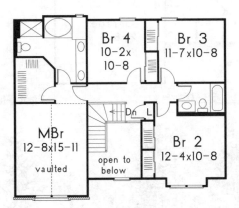

Br 4
10-2x
10-8

Br 3
11-7x10-8

MBr
12-8x15-11
vaulted

Dn L

open to below

Br 2
12-4x10-8

Second Floor

Impressive Victorian Blends Charm And Efficiency

| 2,286 total square feet of living area |

Special features

- Fine architectural detail makes this home a showplace with its large windows, intricate brickwork and fine woodwork and trim

- Stunning two-story entry with attractive wood railing and balustrades in foyer

- Convenient wrap-around kitchen with window view, planning center and pantry

- Oversized master suite with walk-in closet and master bath

- 4 bedrooms, 2 1/2 baths, 2-car garage

- Basement foundation, drawings also include crawl space and slab foundations

- 1,283 square feet on the first floor and 1,003 square feet on the second floor

Price Code E

MULTI-STORY over 2,000 square feet

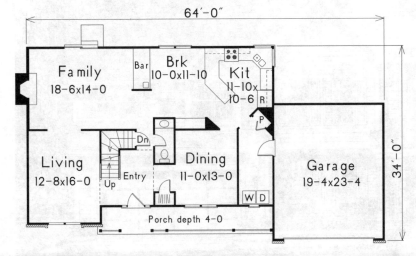

64'-0"

Family
18-6x14-0

Bar

Brk
10-0x11-10

Kit
11-10x
10-6

R

P

Living
12-8x16-0

Dn

Up

Entry

Dining
11-0x13-0

W D

Garage
19-4x23-4

34'-0"

Porch depth 4-0

First Floor

BELLINGHAM

Front Facade Brightened By Windows

2,321 total square feet of living area

Special features

- Fully appointed kitchen high-lighted by convenient center island with snack counter
- Spacious, yet cozy, family room
- Second floor open to living areas below
- 4 bedrooms, 2 1/2 baths, 2-car garage
- Basement foundation
- 1,185 square feet on the first floor and 1,136 square feet on the second floor

Price Code D

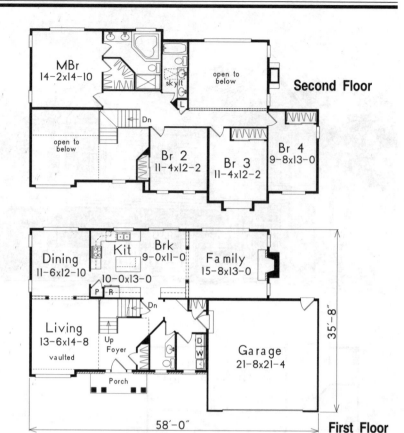

Second Floor

MBr 14-2x14-10
open to below
skylt
Dn
open to below
Br 2 11-4x12-2
Br 3 11-4x12-2
Br 4 9-8x13-0

First Floor

Dining 11-6x12-10
Kit 10-0x13-0
Brk 9-0x11-0
Family 15-8x13-0
Living 13-6x14-8 vaulted
Up Foyer
Dn
Garage 21-8x21-4
Porch

58'-0" 35'-8"

MULTI-STORY over 2,000 square feet

Plan #X20-0380

To order blueprints use the form on page 322 or call toll-free 1-800-DREAM HOME (373-2646)

WHITFIELD

Second Floor

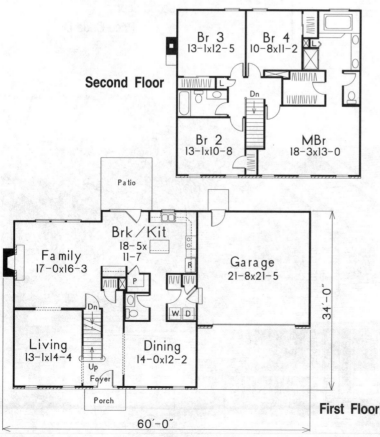

Br 3
13-1x12-5

Br 4
10-8x11-2

L

Dn

Br 2
13-1x10-8

MBr
18-3x13-0

Patio

Brk / Kit
18-5x
11-7

R

Family
17-0x16-3

P

Garage
21-8x21-5

Dn

W D

Living
13-1x14-4

Dining
14-0x12-2

Up
Foyer

Porch

34'-0"

60'-0"

First Floor

Clean, Practical Colonial

2,328 total square feet of living area

Special features

- Formal living and dining rooms feature floor-to-ceiling windows

- Kitchen with island counter and pantry makes cooking a delight

- Expansive master suite has luxury bath with double vanity and walk-in closet

- 4 bedrooms, 2 1/2 baths, 2-car garage

- Basement foundation, drawings also include slab and crawl space foundations

- 1,188 square feet on the first floor and 1,140 square feet on the second floor

Price Code D

MULTI-STORY over 2,000 square feet

Plan #X20-0223

To order blueprints use the form on page 322 or call toll-free 1-800-DREAM HOME (373-2646)

Second Floor

Br 2
11-0x10-0

MBr
13-0x17-8
vaulted

Br 3
11-0x11-0

open to
below

Br 4
10-6x11-0

vaulted

Impressive Two-Story Entry Boasts Popular T-Stair

2,336 total square feet of living area

Special features

- Stately sunken living room with partially vaulted ceiling and classic arched transom windows

- Family room features plenty of windows and fireplace with flanking bookshelves

- 4 bedrooms, 2 1/2 baths, 2-car garage

- Basement foundation

- 1,291 square feet on the first floor and 1,045 square feet on the second floor

Price Code D

First Floor

Family
20-2x16-8

Brk
10-0x16-8

Kitchen
10-8x11-6

Living
11-0x14-8
Sunken
vaulted

Dining
10-6x13-3

Entry

Up

Garage
19-4x21-4

Porch
17-4x5-0

42'-0"

49'-0"

Plan #X20-0365

KEATON

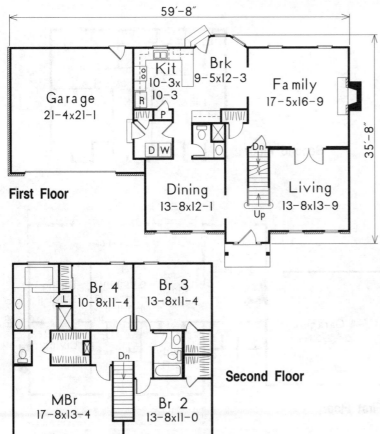

First Floor

Garage
21-4x21-1

Kit
10-3x
10-3

Brk
9-5x12-3

Family
17-5x16-9

Dining
13-8x12-1

Living
13-8x13-9

Up
Dn

R
P
DW

59'-8"

35'-8"

Second Floor

Br 4
10-8x11-4

Br 3
13-8x11-4

Dn
L

MBr
17-8x13-4

Br 2
13-8x11-0

Traditional Styling At Its Best

[2,358 total square feet of living area]

- U-shaped kitchen provides an ideal layout, adjoining breakfast room allows for casual dining

- Formal dining and living rooms have attractive floor-to-ceiling windows

- Master bedroom includes deluxe bath

- 4 bedrooms, 2 1/2 baths, 2-car garage

- Basement foundation, drawings also include crawl space and slab foundations

- 1,218 square feet on the first floor and 1,140 square feet on the second floor

Price Code D

MULTI-STORY
over 2,000 square feet

Plan #X20-0222

Classic Rural Farmhouse

2,363 total square feet of living area

Special features

- Covered porches provide outdoor seating areas
- Corner fireplace becomes focal point of family room
- Kitchen features include island cooktop and adjoining nook
- Energy efficient home with 2" x 6" exterior walls
- 3 bedrooms, 2 1/2 baths, 2-car garage
- Partial basement/crawl space foundation
- 1,500 square feet on the first floor and 863 square feet on the second floor

Price Code D

MULTI-STORY over 2,000 square feet

Second Floor

Br 2
11-9x 11-11

MBr
13-1x13-7

open to below

Dn

Br 3
13-0x10-8

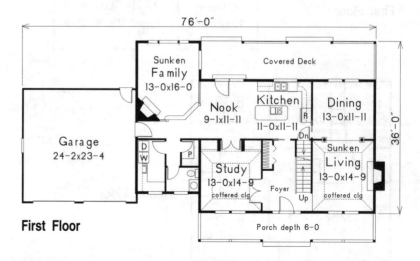

76'-0"

Sunken Family
13-0x16-0

Covered Deck

Nook
9-1x11-11

Kitchen
11-0x11-11

Dining
13-0x11-11

Garage
24-2x23-4

Study
13-0x14-9
coffered clg

Foyer

Up

Dn

Sunken Living
13-0x14-9
coffered clg

36'-0"

First Floor

Porch depth 6-0

Plan #X20-0310

HAMPSHIRE

Stately Facade Features Impressive Front Balcony

2,411 total square feet of living area

Special features

- Elegant entrance features a two-story vaulted foyer
- Large family room enhanced by masonry fireplace and wet bar
- Master bedroom suite includes walk-in closet, oversized tub and separate shower
- Second floor study or 4th bedroom
- 3 bedrooms, 2 1/2 baths, 2-car garage
- Basement foundation, drawings also include slab and crawl space foundations
- 1,293 square feet on the first floor and 1,118 square feet on the second floor

Price Code D

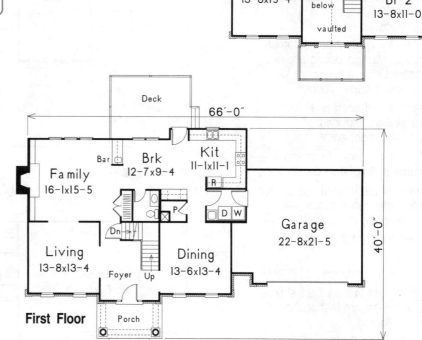

Second Floor

Study 11-5x11-8

Br 3 11-11x10-0

MBr 13-8x15-4

Dn

open to below

vaulted

Br 2 13-8x11-0

Deck

66'-0"

Bar

Brk 12-7x9-4

Kit 11-1x11-1

R

Family 16-1x15-5

P

D W

Garage 22-8x21-5

40'-0"

Living 13-8x13-4

Dn

Foyer

Up

Dining 13-6x13-4

First Floor

Porch

Plan #X20-0184

To order blueprints use the form on page 322 or call toll-free 1-800-DREAM HOME (373-2646)

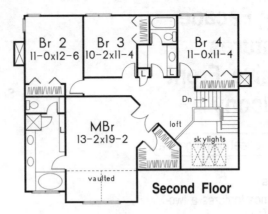

Second Floor

Charming Home With Great Privacy

2,445 total square feet of living area

Special features

- Sunken living room has a corner fireplace, vaulted ceiling and is adjacent to the dining room for entertaining large groups

- Large vaulted open foyer with triple skylight provides an especially bright entry

- Loft area overlooks foyer and features a decorative display area

- Bedrooms are located upstairs for privacy and convenience, with a vaulted ceiling in the master suite

- 4 bedrooms, 2 1/2 baths, 3-car garage

- Basement foundation

- 1,290 square feet on the first floor and 1,155 square feet on the second floor

Price Code E

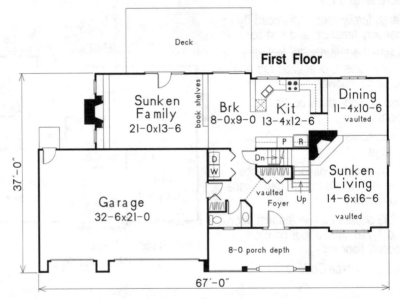

First Floor

CLAREMONT

Bright, Vaulted Spaces

2,459 total square feet of living area

Special features

- Open-feeling kitchen with angled counter to enjoy views through family and breakfast rooms

- Secluded master suite includes dressing area, access to outdoors, and private bath with tub and shower

- Stylish, open stairway overlooks two-story foyer

- Energy efficient home with 2" x 6" exterior walls

- 4 bedrooms, 2 1/2 baths, 2-car garage

- Basement foundation

- 1,861 square feet on the first floor and 598 square feet on the second floor

Price Code D

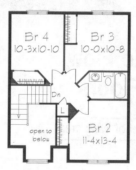

Br 4 10-3x10-10

Br 3 10-0x10-8

Br 2 11-4x13-4

open to below

Second Floor

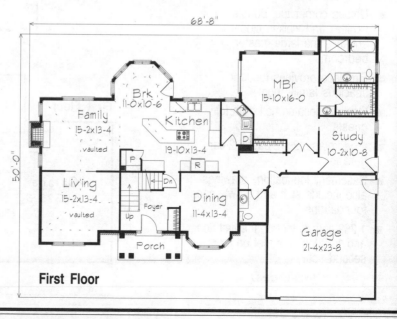

68'-8"

50'-0"

Brk 11-0x10-6

Family 15-2x13-4 vaulted

Kitchen 19-10x13-4

MBr 15-10x16-0

Study 10-2x10-8

Living 15-2x13-4 vaulted

Foyer

Up

Dining 11-4x13-4

Garage 21-4x23-8

Porch

First Floor

MULTI-STORY over 2,000 square feet

Plan #X20-0377

To order blueprints use the form on page 322 or call toll-free 1-800-DREAM HOME (373-2646)

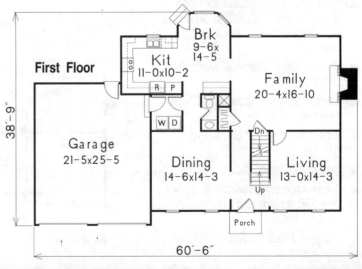

Second Floor

Br 4
12-2x11-1

Br 3
13-0x11-1

L

L

Dn

MBr
18-4x14-3

Br 2
13-0x12-2

Great Traffic Flow On Both Floors

2,461 total square feet of living area

Special features

- Unique corner tub, double vanities and walk-in closet enhance the large master bedroom

- Fireplace provides focus in spacious family room

- Centrally located half bath for guests

- 4 bedrooms, 2 1/2 baths, 2-car garage

- Basement foundation, drawings also include slab and crawl space foundations

- 1,252 square feet on the first floor and 1,209 square feet on the second floor

Price Code D

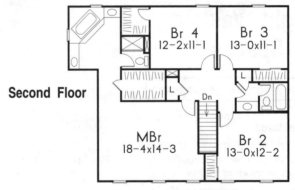

First Floor

Brk
9-6x
14-5

Kit
11-0x10-2

R P

Family
20-4x16-10

W D

38'-9"

Garage
21-5x25-5

Dn

Dining
14-6x14-3

Up

Living
13-0x14-3

Porch

60'-6"

Plan #X20-0224

To order blueprints use the form on page 322 or call toll-free 1-800-DREAM HOME (373-2646)

SWEETBRIAR

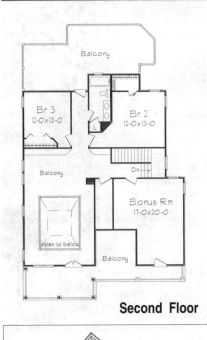

Second Floor

Balcony
Br 3 12-0x13-0
Br 2 12-0x13-0
Balcony
Dn
Bonus Rm 17-0x20-0
open to below
Balcony

40'-0"
62'-0"

MBr 20-0x16-0
Porch
Kit 12-0x 13-0
plant shelf
Dining 15-0x11-0 raised ceiling
Up
Up
Living 18-0x15-0 open to above
Garage 19-8x20-8
Porch

First Floor

Living Room Has Balcony Overlook

2,498 total square feet of living area

Special features

- 10' ceilings on first floor and 9' ceilings on second floor
- Dining room with raised ceiling and convenient wet bar
- Master suite features oversized walk-in closet and bath with garden tub
- 3 bedrooms, 2 1/2 baths, 2-car garage
- Crawl space foundation, drawings also include slab and basement foundations
- 1,530 square feet on the first floor and 968 square feet on the second floor

Price Code D

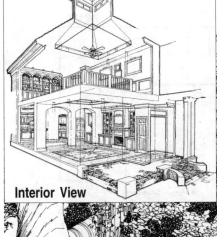

Interior View

MULTI-STORY over 2,000 square feet

Plan #X20-0408

To order blueprints use the form on page 322 or call toll-free 1-800-DREAM HOME (373-2646)

CARRINGTON

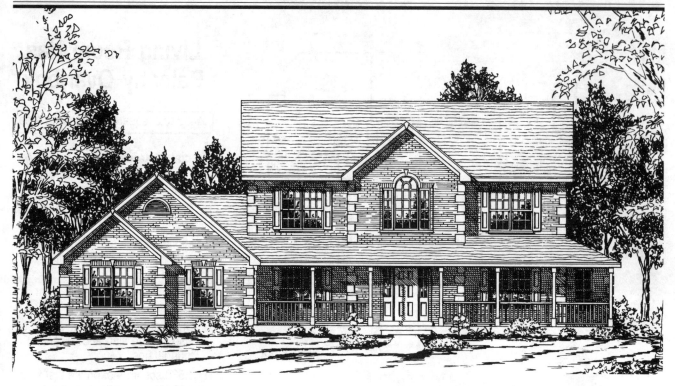

Charming House, Spacious And Functional

2,505 total square feet of living area

Special features

- Garage features extra storage area and ample work space
- Laundry room accessible from outside and garage
- Deluxe raised tub and immense walk-in closet grace master bath
- 3 bedrooms, 2 1/2 baths, 2-car side entry garage
- Basement foundation, drawings also include crawl space foundation
- 1,436 square feet on the first floor and 1,069 square feet on the second floor

Price Code D

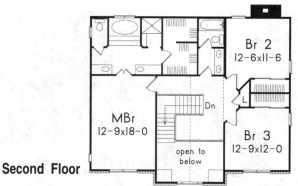

Second Floor

Br 2
12-6x11-6

MBr
12-9x18-0

Dn

open to below

Br 3
12-9x12-0

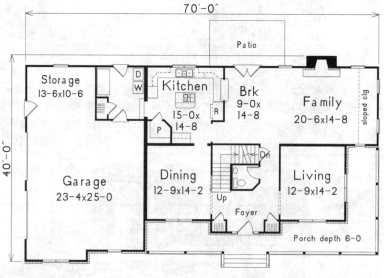

70'-0"

Patio

Storage
13-6x10-6

D
W

Kitchen
15-0x
14-8

Brk
9-0x
14-8

Family
20-6x14-8

sloped clg

40'-0"

Garage
23-4x25-0

Dining
12-9x14-2

Up

Dn

Living
12-9x14-2

Foyer

Porch depth 6-0

First Floor

Plan #X20-0449

To order blueprints use the form on page 322 or call toll-free 1-800-DREAM HOME (373-2646)

BELMONT

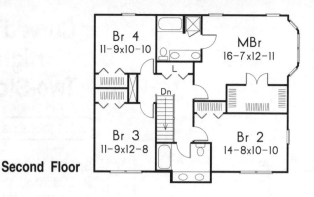

Br 4
11–9x10–10

MBr
16–7x12–11

Br 3
11–9x12–8

Br 2
14–8x10–10

Dn

L

Second Floor

68'–0"

38'–0"

Garage
23–5x35–5

Stor.

Kit
11–4x
12–9

Brk
8–10x
12–9

Family
16–11x13–6

R

P

Furn

Stor.

W
D

Dining
11–9x13–6

Up

Living
12–0x15–7

dropped clg

Porch

First Floor

Impressive Exterior, Spacious Interior

2,511 total square feet of living area

Special features

- Both kitchen/breakfast area and living room feature tray ceilings
- Various architectural elements combine to create impressive exterior
- Master bedroom includes large walk-in closet, oversized bay window and private bath with shower and tub
- Large utility room with convenient workspace
- 4 bedrooms, 2 1/2 baths, 3-car side entry garage
- Basement foundation, drawings also include crawl space and slab foundations
- 1,337 square feet on the first floor and 1,174 square feet on the second floor

Price Code D

MULTI-STORY
over 2,000 square feet

Plan #X20-0528

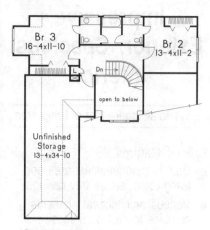

Second Floor

Br 3
16-4x11-10

Br 2
13-4x11-2

Dn

open to below

Unfinished
Storage
13-4x34-10

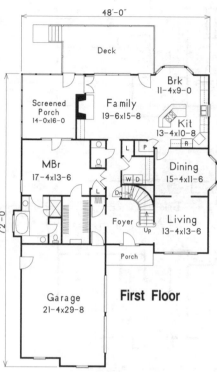

48'-0"

72'-0"

Deck

Brk
11-4x9-0

Screened
Porch
14-0x16-0

Family
19-6x15-8

Kit
13-4x10-8

MBr
17-4x13-6

L   P
R

Dining
15-4x11-6

W D

L

Dn

Foyer

Up

Living
13-4x13-6

Porch

Garage
21-4x29-8

First Floor

Curved Stairway Highlights Two-Story Foyer

2,511 total square feet of living area

Special features

- Unfinished storage area above garage provides room for future expansion

- Screened porch is accessible from three different living areas

- Feeling of spaciousness created by vaulted kitchen and family area

- 3 bedrooms, 2 1/2 baths, 2-car garage

- Basement foundation, drawings also include crawl space and slab foundations

- 1,852 square feet on the first floor and 659 square feet on the second floor

Price Code D

Plan #X20-0599

ROSECROFT

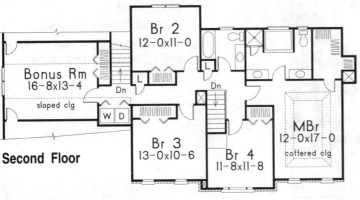

Bonus Rm
16-8x13-4
sloped clg

Dn

W D

Br 2
12-0x11-0

L

L

Dn

Br 3
13-0x10-6

Br 4
11-8x11-8

MBr
12-0x17-0
coffered clg

Second Floor

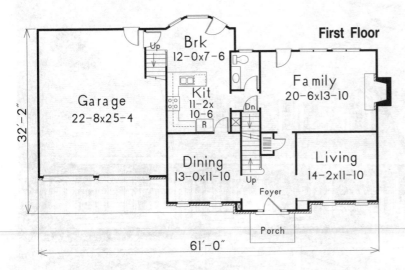

32'-2"

Garage
22-8x25-4

Up

Brk
12-0x7-6

Kit
11-2x
10-6
R

Dining
13-0x11-10

Dn

Up

Foyer

Family
20-6x13-10

First Floor

Living
14-2x11-10

Porch

61'-0"

Handsome Traditional With Gabled Entrance

> 2,529 total square feet of living area

Special features

- Distinguished appearance enhances this home's classic interior arrangement
- Bonus room over the garage with access directly from the outside and from second floor hall
- Garden tub, walk-in closet and coffered ceiling in the master bedroom suite
- 4 bedrooms, 2 1/2 baths, 2-car garage
- Basement foundation
- 1,119 square feet on the first floor and 1,410 square feet on the second floor, including the bonus room above the garage

Price Code E

MULTI-STORY
over 2,000 square feet

Plan #X20-0135

To order blueprints use the form on page 322 or call toll-free 1-800-DREAM HOME (373-2646)

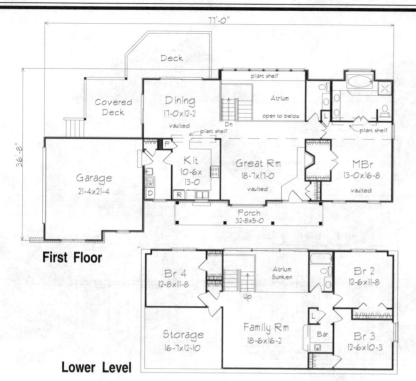

First Floor

Deck

Covered Deck

Dining 17-0x12-2 vaulted

plant shelf

Atrium open to below

Garage 21-4x21-4

Kit 10-6x 13-0

Great Rm 18-7x17-0 vaulted

MBr 13-0x16-8 vaulted

plant shelf

Porch 32-8x5-0

11'-0"

36'-8"

Lower Level

Br 4 12-8x11-8

Atrium Sunken

Br 2 12-6x11-8

up

Storage 16-7x12-10

Family Rm 18-6x16-2

Bar

Br 3 12-6x10-3

Traditional Exterior Boasts Exciting Interior

2,531 total square feet of living area

Special features

- Charming porch with dormers leads into vaulted great room with atrium

- Well-designed kitchen and breakfast bar adjoins extra large laundry/mud room

- Double sinks, windowed tub and plant shelf complete vaulted master suite

- 4 bedrooms, 2 1/2 baths, 2-car side entry garage

- Walk-out basement foundation

- 1,297 square feet on the first floor and 1,234 square feet on the lower floor

  Price Code D

Rear View

MULTI-STORY over 2,000 square feet

Plan #X20-0364

To order blueprints use the form on page 322 or call toll-free 1-800-DREAM HOME (373-2646)

MERAMEC

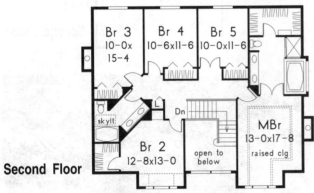

Second Floor

- Br 3
  10-0x 15-4
- Br 4
  10-6x11-6
- Br 5
  10-0x11-6
- skylt
- Dn
- Br 2
  12-8x13-0
- open to below
- MBr
  13-0x17-8
  raised clg

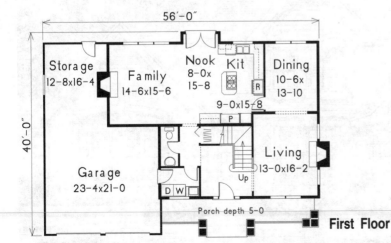

56'-0"

40'-0"

- Storage
  12-8x16-4
- Family
  14-6x15-6
- Nook
  8-0x 15-8
- Kit
- Dining
  10-6x 13-10
- 9-0x15-8
- P
- Garage
  23-4x21-0
- Living
  13-0x16-2
- Up
- D W
- Porch depth 5-0

First Floor

Gabled Front Entrance, Columned Porch

2,539 total square feet of living area

Special features

- Master bedroom features a tray ceiling and deluxe bath with walk-in closet
- Kitchen with island cooktop, desk, and nook area accesses outside
- Bedroom 2 includes walk-in closet and unique angled wall
- Living room includes a fireplace and opens to dining room
- 5 bedrooms, 2 1/2 baths, 2-car garage
- Crawl space foundation
- 1,200 square feet on the first floor and 1,339 square feet on the second floor

Price Code D

MULTI-STORY
over 2,000 square feet

Plan #X20-0326

To order blueprints use the form on page 322 or call toll-free 1-800-DREAM HOME (373-2646)

Outstanding Floor Plan For Year-Round Entertaining

2,597 total square feet of living area

Special features

- Large U-shaped kitchen features island cooktop and breakfast bar
- Entry and great room enhanced by sweeping balcony
- Bedrooms 2 and 3 share a bath; the 4th has a private bath
- Vaulted great room with transomed arch windows
- 4 bedrooms, 3 1/2 baths, 2-car garage
- Walk-out basement foundation
- 1,742 square feet on the first floor and 855 square feet on the second floor

Price Code D

First Floor

Second Floor

MULTI-STORY over 2,000 square feet

Plan #X20-0354

To order blueprints use the form on page 322 or call toll-free 1-800-DREAM HOME (373-2646)

CLAYMONT

Separate Living Areas Lend Privacy

2,562 total square feet of living area

Special features

- Large, open foyer creates a grand entrance
- Convenient open breakfast area includes peninsula counter, bay window and easy access to the sundeck
- Dining and living rooms flow together for expanded entertaining space
- 3 bedrooms, 2 1/2 baths, 2-car side entry garage
- Basement foundation, drawings also include slab and crawl space foundations
- 1,128 square feet on the first floor and 1,434 square feet on the second floor, including the bonus room above the garage

Price Code D

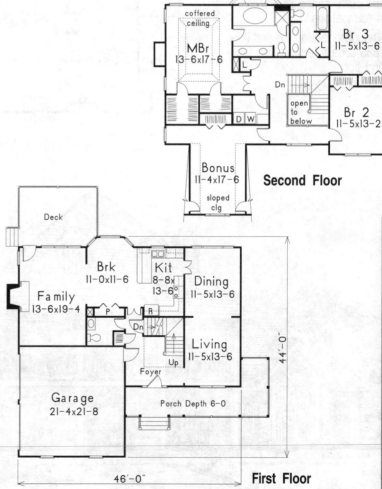

MULTI-STORY
over 2,000 square feet

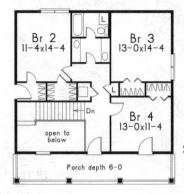

Second Floor

Distinctive Two Level Porch

2,605 total square feet of living area

Special features

- Master bedroom boasts vaulted ceiling and transom picture window which lights sitting area

- Country kitchen features appliances set in between brick dividers and beamed ceiling

- Living room features built-in bookcases, fireplace and raised tray ceiling

- 4 bedrooms, 2 1/2 baths, 2-car side entry garage

- Slab foundation, drawings also include crawl space and basement foundations

- 1,750 square feet on the first floor and 855 square feet on the second floor

Price Code E

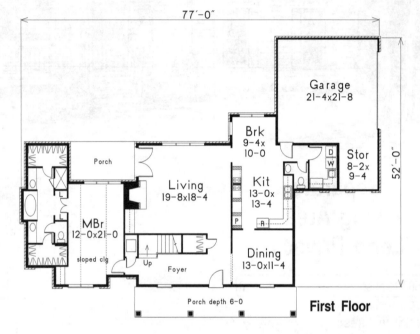

First Floor

MULTI-STORY
over 2,000 square feet

Plan #X20-0305
To order blueprints use the form on page 322 or call toll-free 1-800-DREAM HOME (373-2646)

BERKELEY

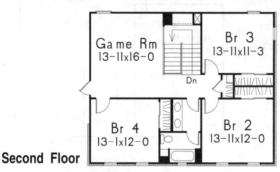

Second Floor

- Game Rm 13-11x16-0
- Br 3 13-11x11-3
- Dn
- Br 4 13-1x12-0
- Br 2 13-11x12-0

58'-0"

51'-0"

First Floor

- Family 21-4x14-0 vaulted
- Brk 11-0x12-0
- Kitchen 14-0x11-9
- MBr 13-11x16-0
- D W
- P
- Up
- Dn
- R
- Garage 21-4x22-0
- Dining 13-10x12-0
- Foyer

Distinguished Exterior And Interior

| 2,613 total square feet of living area |

Special features

- 9' ceilings throughout first floor
- Spacious family room with fireplace, sloped ceiling and wet bar
- Open stairs lead up to large game room
- Kitchen with island work area and pantry is adjacent to breakfast room
- 3 bedrooms, 2 1/2 baths, 2-car garage
- Basement foundation
- 1,625 square feet on the first floor and 988 square feet on the second floor

Price Code E

MULTI-STORY over 2,000 square feet

Plan #X20-0361
To order blueprints use the form on page 322 or call toll-free 1-800-DREAM HOME (373-2646)

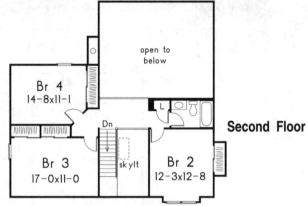

open to below

Br 4
14-8x11-1

L

Second Floor

Br 3
17-0x11-0

Dn

skylt

Br 2
12-3x12-8

Handsome Home With Spacious Living Areas

2,618 total square feet of living area

Special features

- Stylish front facade with covered porch and distinctive window treatment

- Great room features vaulted ceiling, skylights and large fireplace

- Master bedroom and bath with two large walk-in closets, separate oversized tub and shower, first floor convenience and privacy

- Kitchen overlooks the deck and features circle-top windows and corner window view from the sink

- 4 bedrooms, 2 1/2 baths, 2-car garage

- Basement foundation

- 1,804 square feet on the first floor and 814 square feet on the second floor

Price Code E

61'-0"

skylts

Deck

Great Rm
22-1x18-2
vaulted

Brk
10-8x15-1
vaulted

Kit
9-10x12-2

R

W D

P

Bar

Dn

Dining
12-3x12-5

49'-4"

MBr
17-0x16-0

Up

Entry

Porch depth 4-0

Garage
20-8x20-1

First Floor

MULTI-STORY
over 2,000 square feet

Plan #X20-0170

To order blueprints use the form on page 322 or call toll-free 1-800-DREAM HOME (373-2646)

VANDEMARK

First Floor

MBr
17-0x17-8
vaulted
plant shelf

Great Rm
20-6x15-10

Brk
14-10x10-0

Kitchen
14-10x10-6

Garage
21-4x20-4

Dining
14-10x12-4

Foyer

Dn

Up

69'-8"

46'-0"

Second Floor

Br 4
12-6x12-0

open to below

Dn

Br 2
11-8x10-4

open to below

Br 3
12-6x12-0

Irresistible Grandeur

2,624 total square feet of living area

Special features

- Dramatic two-story entry opens to bayed dining room through classic colonnade
- Magnificent great room with 18' ceiling brightly lit with three palladian windows
- Master suite includes bay window, walk-in closets, plant shelves and sunken bath
- 4 bedrooms, 2 1/2 baths, 2-car side entry garage
- Basement foundation
- 1,774 square feet on the first floor and 850 square feet on the second floor

Price Code E

Interior View - Master Bath

MULTI-STORY over 2,000 square feet

Plan #X20-0366
To order blueprints use the form on page 322 or call toll-free 1-800-DREAM HOME (373-2646)

95

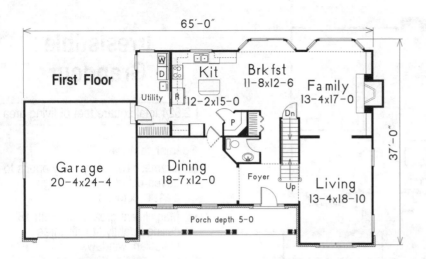

First Floor

65'-0"

Brk fst
11-8x12-6

Kit
12-2x15-0

Family
13-4x17-0

Utility

W
D

R

P

Dn

37'-0"

Garage
20-4x24-4

Dining
18-7x12-0

Foyer

Up

Living
13-4x18-10

Porch depth 5-0

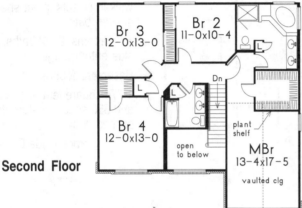

Br 3
12-0x13-0

Br 2
11-0x10-4

L

L

L

Dn

plant
shelf

Br 4
12-0x13-0

open
to below

MBr
13-4x17-5

vaulted clg

Second Floor

Great Looks Accentuated By Elliptical Brick Arches

2,521 total square feet of living area

Special features

- Spacious living and dining rooms are a plus for formal entertaining or large family gatherings

- Informal kitchen, breakfast and family rooms feature a 37' vista and double bay windows

- Generous-sized master bedroom suite and three secondary bedrooms grace the second floor

- 4 bedrooms, 2 1/2 baths, 2-car garage

- Basement foundation

- 1,375 square feet on the first floor and 1,146 square feet on the second flooor

Price Code D

MULTI-STORY
over 2,000 square feet

J.N. HANSEN S.D.G.

Plan #X20-0709

To order blueprints use the form on page 322 or call toll-free 1-800-DREAM HOME (373-2646)

Fireplaces Accent Gathering Rooms

2,659 total square feet of living area

Special features

- 9' ceilings throughout first floor
- Balcony overlooks large family room
- Private first floor master suite features double walk-in closets, sloped ceilings and luxury bath
- Double french doors in dining room open onto porch
- 4 bedrooms, 3 1/2 baths, 2-car garage
- Basement foundation
- 1,627 square feet on the first floor and 1,032 square feet on the second floor

Price Code E

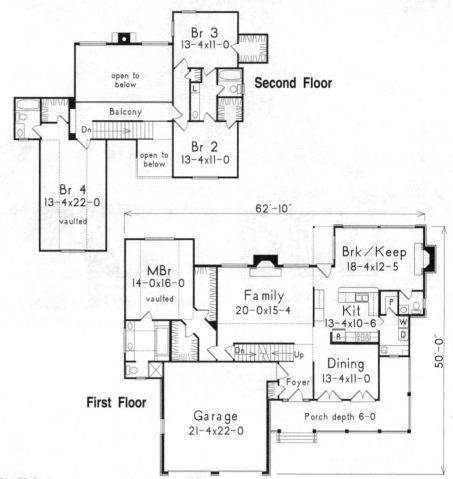

Second Floor

Br 3
13-4x11-0

open to below

Balcony

Dn

Br 2
13-4x11-0

open to below

Br 4
13-4x22-0
vaulted

62'-10"

MBr
14-0x16-0
vaulted

Family
20-0x15-4

Brk/Keep
18-4x12-5

Kit
13-4x10-6

Dn   Up

Dining
13-4x11-0

Foyer

First Floor

Garage
21-4x22-0

Porch depth 6-0

50'-0"

MULTI-STORY over 2,000 square feet

Plan #X20-0359

To order blueprints use the form on page 322 or call toll-free 1-800-DREAM HOME (373-2646)

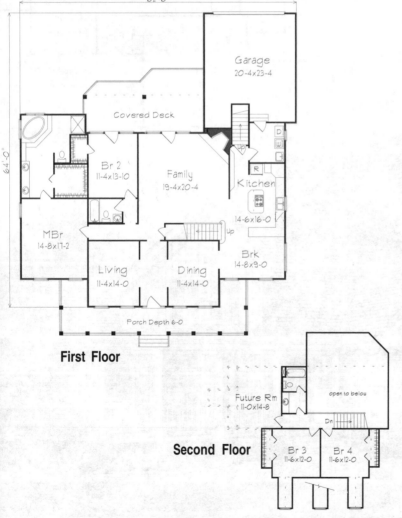

62'-6"

64'-0"

Garage
20-4x23-4

Covered Deck

Br 2
11-4x13-10

Family
19-4x20-4

Kitchen

14-6x16-0

MBr
14-8x17-2

Living
11-4x14-0

Dining
11-4x14-0

Brk
14-8x9-0

Up

Up

Porch Depth 6-0

First Floor

Future Rm
11-0x14-8

open to below

Dn

Second Floor

Br 3
11-6x12-0

Br 4
11-6x12-0

Cozy Porches, Front And Back

2,673 total square feet of living area

Special features

- 9' ceilings on first floor
- Combined breakfast and kitchen areas
- Large family room is graced by corner fireplace
- Convenient storage above garage
- Rear covered porch adjacent to bedroom two and family room
- 4 bedrooms, 3 baths, 2-car rear entry garage
- Slab foundation, drawings also include crawl space foundation
- 2,135 square feet on the first floor and 538 square feet on the second floor

Price Code E

Plan #X20-0433

To order blueprints use the form on page 322 or call toll-free 1-800-DREAM HOME (373-2646)

SHADYOAK

Second Floor

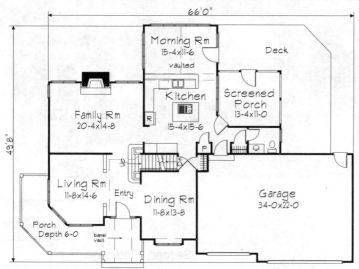

First Floor

Outdoor Exposure Front And Back

2,685 total square feet of living area

Special features

- 9' ceilings throughout first floor
- Vaulted master suite, isolated for privacy, boasts magnificent bath with garden tub, separate shower and two closets
- Laundry area near bedrooms
- Screened porch and morning room both located off well-planned kitchen
- 4 bedrooms, 2 1/2 baths, 3-car garage
- Basement foundation
- 1,360 square feet on the first floor and 1,325 square feet on the second floor

Price Code E

MULTI-STORY over 2,000 square feet

Plan #X20-0391

To order blueprints use the form on page 322 or call toll-free 1-800-DREAM HOME (373-2646)

Varied Exterior Finishes Enrich Facade

2,696 total square feet of living area

Special features

- Magnificent master suite with private covered porch and luxurious bath

- Second floor game room with balcony access and adjacent loft

- Well-planned kitchen includes walk-in pantry, island cooktop and nearby spacious breakfast room

- 4 bedrooms, 3 baths, 2-car side entry garage

- Slab foundation, drawings also include crawl space foundation

- 1,904 square feet on the first floor and 792 square feet on the second floor

  Price Code E

Second Floor

First Floor

Plan #X20-0411

To order blueprints use the form on page 322 or call toll-free 1-800-DREAM HOME (373-2646)

Attractive Bay Kitchen

2,716 total square feet of living area

Special features

- 9' ceilings throughout first floor
- All bedrooms boast walk-in closets
- Great room and hearth room share see-through fireplace
- Balcony overlooks large great room
- 4 bedrooms, 4 1/2 baths, 2-car side entry garage
- Basement foundation
- 1,754 square feet on the first floor and 962 square feet on the second floor

Price Code E

First Floor

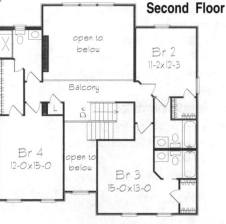

Second Floor

Plan #X20-0369

To order blueprints use the form on page 322 or call toll-free 1-800-DREAM HOME (373-2646)

Second Floor

Br 2
11-8x13-4

open to below

MBr
16-8x15-8
recessed clg

Dn

open to below

shower

Br 3
10-8x12-0

High-Style With Great Function

2,723 total square feet of living area

Special features

- Entry and stairwell create two-story space opening into formal dining room

- Large island cooktop with breakfast bar, corner sink and built-in desk in kitchen

- Two-story dining nook adjacent to kitchen visually enlarges area

- Double-doors open into master suite with tray ceiling and large master bath with glass block shower

- 3 bedrooms, 2 1/2 baths, 3-car garage

- Crawl space foundation

- 1,600 square feet on the first floor and 1,123 square feet on the second floor

Price Code E

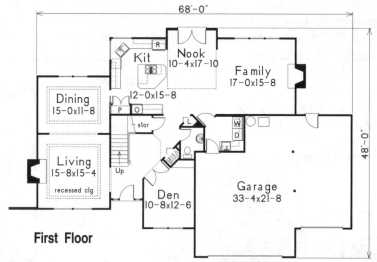

68'-0"

48'-0"

Kit
12-0x15-8

Nook
10-4x17-10

Family
17-0x15-8

Dining
15-0x11-8

stor

Living
15-8x15-4
recessed clg

Up

Den
10-8x12-6

Garage
33-4x21-8

First Floor

Plan #X20-0333

BELLEWOOD

Entry Porch And Parlor Adds Distinctive Touch

2,730 total square feet of living area

Special features

■ Dining room opens to wrap-around front porch

■ Master bedroom features double-door entrance, deluxe master bath and walk-in closet with stacked washer and dryer

■ Vaulted ceiling, fireplace and built-in bookshelves in family room

■ Kitchen includes corner sink, island cooktop, breakfast bar and pantry

■ 3 bedrooms, 2 1/2 baths, 2-car garage

■ Crawl space foundation

■ 1,587 square feet on the first floor and 1,143 square feet on the second floor including the bonus room

Price Code E

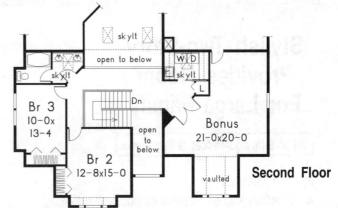

skylt skylt

open to below

W D

skylt

Br 3
10-0x
13-4

Dn

open to below

Bonus
21-0x20-0

Br 2
12-8x15-0

vaulted

Second Floor

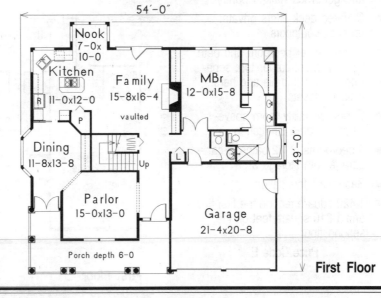

54'-0"

Nook
7-0x
10-0

Kitchen
11-0x12-0

Family
15-8x16-4

vaulted

MBr
12-0x15-8

R

P

Dining
11-8x13-8

Up

Parlor
15-0x13-0

Garage
21-4x20-8

Porch depth 6-0

49'-0"

First Floor

MULTI-STORY over 2,000 square feet

Plan #X20-0331

Stylish Two-Story Provides Room For Large Family

> 2,730 total square feet of living area

Special features

- Spacious kitchen features island and generous walk-in pantry

- Covered deck offers private retreat to outdoors

- Large master bedroom and bath with whirlpool corner tub, separate shower and his and hers walk-in closets

- Oversized utility room conveniently located off kitchen

- 4 bedrooms, 2 1/2 baths, 3-car garage with storage area

- Basement foundation

- 1,420 square feet on the first floor and 1,310 square feet on the second floor

Price Code E

Second Floor

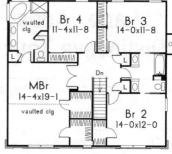

Br 4
11-4x11-8

Br 3
14-0x11-8

vaulted clg

MBr
14-4x19-1

vaulted clg

Br 2
14-0x12-0

Dn

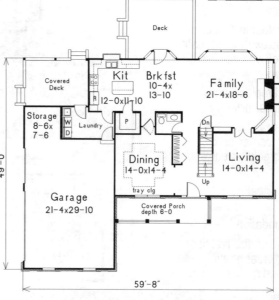

Deck

Covered
Deck

Kit
12-0x11-10

Brk fst
10-4x
13-10

Family
21-4x18-6

Storage
8-6x
7-6

Laundry

W
D

P

Dn

Dining
14-0x14-4

tray clg

Living
14-0x14-4

Up

Garage
21-4x29-10

Covered Porch
depth 6-0

49'-0"

59'-8"

First Floor

Plan #X20-0691

ASHINGTON

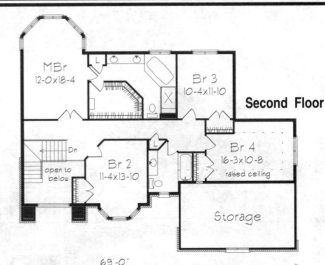

Second Floor

Living And Dining Rooms Frame The Two-Story Foyer

| 2,733 total square feet of living area |

Special features

- 9' ceilings throughout first floor
- Master bedroom features double-door entry, large bay window and master bath with walk-in closet and separate tub and shower
- Efficiently designed kitchen adjoins an octagonal breakfast nook, which opens to outdoors
- 4 bedrooms, 2 1/2 baths, 2-car garage
- Basement foundation
- 1,514 square feet on the first floor and 1,219 square feet on the second floor

Price Code E

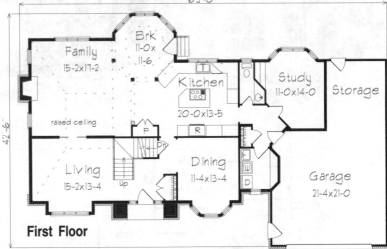

First Floor

Plan #X20-0371

To order blueprints use the form on page 322 or call toll-free 1-800-DREAM HOME (373-2646)

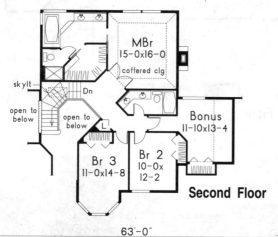

Second Floor

MBr
15-0x16-0

coffered clg

skylt

Dn

open to below

open to below

Bonus
11-10x13-4

Br 3
11-0x14-8

Br 2
10-0x
12-2

Distinctive Bay Windows Flank Entrance

2,744 total square feet of living area

Special features

- Large master bedroom features vaulted ceiling and elegant master bath with large walk-in closet
- Formal living room with tray ceiling, bay windows and prominent fireplace
- Kitchen features island cooktop, corner sink and built-in desk area
- Family room boasts fireplace and full view windows
- 3 bedrooms, 2 1/2 baths, 3-car garage
- Crawl space foundation
- 1,592 square feet on the first floor and 1,152 square feet on the second floor including the bonus room

Price Code E

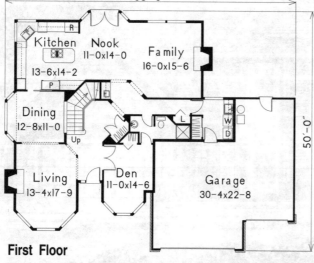

63'-0"

Kitchen
13-6x14-2

Nook
11-0x14-0

Family
16-0x15-6

Dining
12-8x11-0

Up

50'-0"

Living
13-4x17-9

Den
11-0x14-6

Garage
30-4x22-8

First Floor

MULTI-STORY over 2,000 square feet

Plan #X20-0323

To order blueprints use the form on page 322 or call toll-free 1-800-DREAM HOME (373-2646)

OAKVILLE

Unique Features Create Style And Sophistication

2,772 total square feet of living area

Special features

- 10' ceilings on first floor and 9' ceilings on second floor create spacious atmosphere
- Large bay windows accent study and master bath
- Breakfast room features dramatic curved wall with direct view and access onto porch
- 4 bedrooms, 3 1/2 baths, 2-car side entry garage
- Slab foundation
- 1,354 square feet on the first floor and 1,418 square feet on the second floor

Price Code E

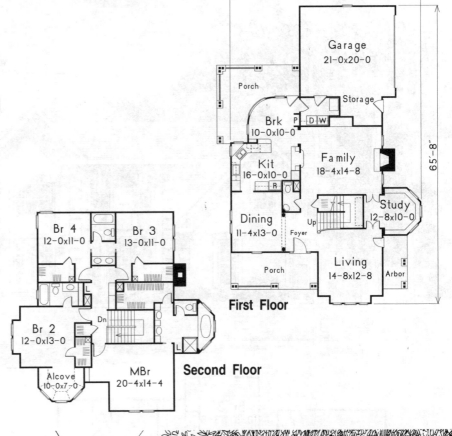

First Floor

43'-6"
65'-8"

Garage 21-0x20-0
Porch
Storage
Brk 10-0x10-0
Kit 16-0x10-0
Family 18-4x14-8
Dining 11-4x13-0
Foyer
Up
Study 12-8x10-0
Living 14-8x12-8
Porch
Arbor

Second Floor

Br 4 12-0x11-0
Br 3 13-0x11-0
Br 2 12-0x13-0
Dn
Alcove 10-0x7-0
MBr 20-4x14-4

MULTI-STORY over 2,000 square feet

Plan #X20-0233

To order blueprints use the form on page 322 or call toll-free 1-800-DREAM HOME (373-2646)

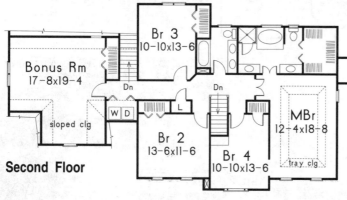

Bonus Rm
17-8x19-4

sloped clg

Second Floor

Br 3
10-10x13-6

Dn   Dn

W D   L

Br 2
13-6x11-6

Br 4
10-10x13-6

MBr
12-4x18-8

tray clg

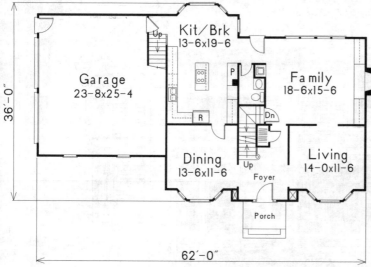

Up

Kit/Brk
13-6x19-6

Garage
23-8x25-4

P

Family
18-6x15-6

R   Dn

Dining
13-6x11-6

Up

Foyer

Living
14-0x11-6

Porch

36'-0"

62'-0"

First Floor

MULTI-STORY
over 2,000 square feet

Traditional With Attention To Detail

2,773 total square feet of living area

Special features

- Extensive use of bay and other large windows front and rear adds brightness and space

- Master bedroom suite features double-door entrance, oversized walk-in closet and tray ceiling

- Rear stairway leads to bonus room, laundry and the second floor

- 4 bedrooms, 2 1/2 baths, 2-car side entry garage

- Basement foundation

- 1,208 square feet on the first floor and 1,565 square feet on the second floor, including the bonus room above the garage

Price Code F

Plan #X20-0139

BAKERSTON

HD

Spectacular Five Bedroom Home

2,801 total square feet of living area

Special features

- 9' ceilings on first floor
- Full view dining bay with elegant circle-top windows
- Wrap-around porches provide outdoor exposure in all directions
- Secluded master bedroom with double vanities and walk-in closets
- Convenient game room
- 5 bedrooms, 3 baths, 2-car side entry garage
- Slab foundation
- 1,651 square feet on the first floor and 1,150 square feet on the second floor

Price Code E

First Floor

45'-6"

78'-3"

Garage
23-4x23-4

Covered Porch

Living
18-0x17-3

MBr
17-0x16-0

Brk
10-0x10-0

Kit
10-8x 12-0

Br 2
13-0x10-6

Up

Dining
10-8x13-4

Porch Depth 4-0

Second Floor

Br 3
13-3x13-3

Game Rm
17-0x10-10

Br 4
14-4x13-0

Br 5
17-2x12-0

Dn

Plan #X20-0436

To order blueprints use the form on page 322 or call toll-free 1-800-DREAM HOME (373-2646)

109

Balcony Enjoys Spectacular Views In Atrium Home

2,806 total square feet of living area

Special features

- Harmonious charm throughout
- Sweeping balcony and vaulted ceiling soar above spacious great room and walk-in bar
- 4 bedrooms, 2 1/2 baths, 2-car garage
- Walk-out basement foundation
- 1,473 square feet on the first floor, 785 square feet on the second floor, and 548 square feet on the lower level

Price Code E

First Floor

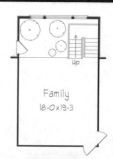

Lower Level

Second Floor

Rear View

MULTI-STORY over 2,000 square feet

Plan #X20-0356

To order blueprints use the form on page 322 or call toll-free 1-800-DREAM HOME (373-2646)

110

CASCADE

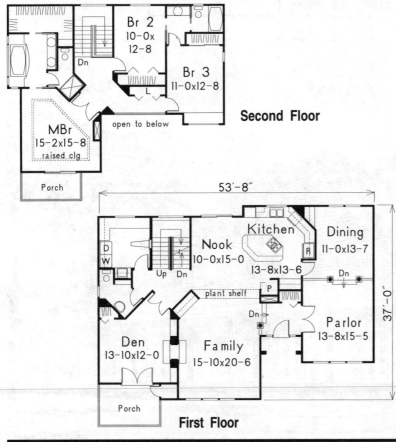

Second Floor

Br 2
10-0x12-8

Br 3
11-0x12-8

Dn

MBr
15-2x15-8
raised clg

open to below

Porch

Great Plan For Sloping Lots

$\boxed{\text{2,813 total square feet of living area}}$

Special features

- Entrance foyer opens into parlor and two-story family room
- Double-doors lead into den, which accesses deck
- Double-doors lead into master suite with deluxe bath and walk-in closet
- 3 bedrooms, 2 1/2 baths, 3-car garage
- Partial basement/crawl space foundation
- 102 square feet on the garage level, 1,713 square feet on the first floor and 998 square feet on the second floor

Price Code E

MULTI-STORY
over 2,000 square feet

53'-8"

37'-0"

Kitchen
13-8x13-6

Nook
10-0x15-0

Dining
11-0x13-7

Dn

Up Dn

plant shelf

Dn

Parlor
13-8x15-5

Den
13-10x12-0

Family
15-10x20-6

Porch

D
W

R

P

First Floor

Sweeping Elegant Front Colonade

2,824 total square feet of living area

Special features

- 9' ceilings on first floor
- Second floor bedrooms feature private dressing areas and share a bath
- Large great room includes fireplace flanked by french doors leading to rear patio
- Kitchen conveniently serves formal dining room and breakfast room with large bay window
- 4 bedrooms, 3 baths, 2-car side entry garage
- Slab foundation, drawings also include crawl space foundation
- 2,120 square feet on the first floor and 704 square feet on the second floor

Price Code E

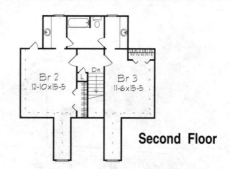

Second Floor

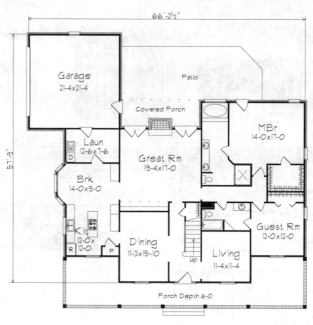

First Floor

MULTI-STORY over 2,000 square feet

Plan #X20-0431

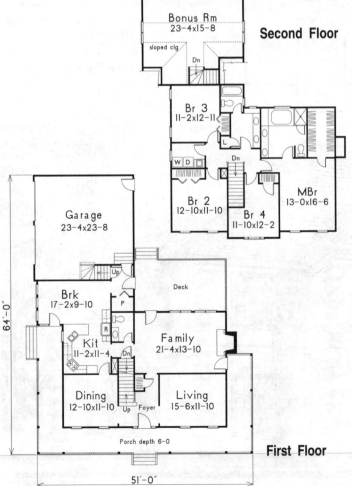

Second Floor

Bonus Rm
23-4x15-8

sloped clg.

Dn

Br 3
11-2x12-11

L

W D

Dn

Br 2
12-10x11-10

Br 4
11-10x12-2

MBr
13-0x16-6

Garage
23-4x23-8

64'-0"

Brk
17-2x9-10

Deck

P

Kit
11-2x11-4

R

Dn

Family
21-4x13-10

Up

Dining
12-10x11-10

Up Foyer

Living
15-6x11-10

Porch depth 6-0

First Floor

51'-0"

Country-Style Comfort

2,826 total square feet of living area

Special features

- Wrap-around covered porch is accessible from family room and breakfast room in addition to front entrance

- Bonus room with separate entrance suitable for an office or private accommodations

- Large, full-windowed breakfast room

- 4 bedrooms, 2 1/2 baths, 2-car side entry garage

- Basement foundation

- 1,252 square feet on the first floor and 1,574 square feet on the second floor, including the bonus room above the garage

Price Code E

MULTI-STORY
over 2,000 square feet

Plan #X20-0141

First Floor

Garage
21-4x25-8

Covered Porch

Kit
12-8x17-0

Family
22-2x17-0

Brk
12-8x10-0

Dining
11-4x14-0

Living
11-4x10-6

MBr
12-8x16-0

Porch

60'-6"

74'-0"

Second Floor

Br 2
12-6x10-10

Dn

Br 3
11-4x16-0

open to below

Br 4
11-4x16-0

plant shelf

Elegant Home Provides Formal And Informal Areas

2,826 total square feet of living area

Special features

- 9' ceilings throughout
- Fully appointed master bedroom with luxurious bath
- Second floor bedrooms include private dressing areas and walk-in closets
- Large, well-planned kitchen features center island
- 4 bedrooms, 3 1/2 baths, 2-car side entry garage
- Slab foundation, drawings also include crawl space foundation
- 1,904 square feet on the first floor and 922 square feet on the second floor

Price Code F

MULTI-STORY over 2,000 square feet

Plan #X20-0432

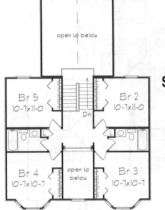

Second Floor

Br 5
10-7x11-0

Br 2
10-7x11-0

Br 4
10-7x10-7

open to below

Br 3
10-7x10-7

open to below

First Floor

Family
16-4x19-4
vaulted

Patio

Bar

Kitchen
13-0x12-8

Brk
13-2x10-9

Up Dn

Garage
20-4x21-10

Dining
12-2x13-0

Foyer

Study
13-5x13-0

MBr
15-0x16-11
vaulted

Porch Depth 6-0

55'-6"

70'-6"

Five Bedroom Home Embraces Large Family

2,828 total square feet of living area

Special features

- Popular wrap-around porch gives home country charm
- Secluded oversized family room with vaulted ceiling and wet bar features many windows
- Any chef would be delighted to cook in this smartly designed kitchen with island and corner windows
- Spectacular master suite
- 5 bedrooms, 3 1/2 baths, 2-car side entry garage
- Basement foundation
- 2,006 square feet on the first floor and 822 square feet on the second floor

Price Code E

MULTI-STORY over 2,000 square feet

Plan #X20-0417

To order blueprints use the form on page 322 or call toll-free 1-800-DREAM HOME (373-2646)

ASHBERRY

Vaulted Ceiling In Living Room Adds Spaciousness

2,838 total square feet of living area

Special features

- 10' ceilings throughout first floor
- Dining room enhanced with large corner bay windows
- Master bath boasts double sinks and oversized tub
- Kitchen features an island and corner double sink which overlooks dinette and family room
- 4 bedrooms, 2 1/2 baths, 3-car garage
- Basement foundation
- 1,602 square feet on the first floor and 1,236 square feet on the second floor

Price Code E

MULTI-STORY
over 2,000 square feet

Second Floor

MBr
13-6x17-0

Br 3
13-10x11-6

Br 4
12-0x10-0

Br 2
11-0x9-6

open to below

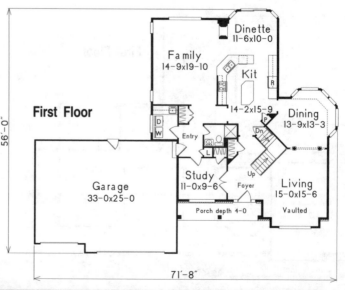

First Floor

56'-0"

Dinette
11-6x10-0

Family
14-9x19-10

Kit
14-2x15-9

Dining
13-9x13-3

Garage
33-0x25-0

Entry

Study
11-0x9-6

Up

Foyer

Living
15-0x15-6

Vaulted

Porch depth 4-0

71'-8"

Plan #X20-0373

To order blueprints use the form on page 322 or call toll-free 1-800-DREAM HOME (373-2646)

WESTBROOKE

Second Floor

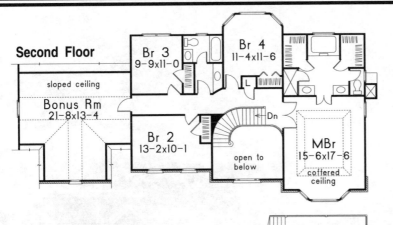

sloped ceiling

Bonus Rm
21-8x13-4

Br 3
9-9x11-0

Br 4
11-4x11-6

Br 2
13-2x10-1

open to
below

Dn

MBr
15-6x17-6
coffered
ceiling

First Floor

W D

Kit
11-0x11-6

Brk
11-4x11-6

Deck

P

O R

Family
15-6x15-6

Garage
21-8x25-4

Dining
15-6x11-6

Up

Foyer

Dn

Living
15-6x11-6

Porch

34'-0"

68'-0"

Elegant Two-Story Exterior And Entry

2,846 total square feet of living area

Special features

- 9' ceilings on first floor and 8' ceilings on second floor
- Bonus room over garage
- Prominent double-bay windows and foyer add brightness and space to both floors
- Master suite with double-door entry and coffered ceiling includes an elaborate bath with large tub, separate shower and individual walk-in closets
- 4 bedrooms, 2 1/2 baths, 2-car side entry garage
- Basement foundation, drawings also include slab and crawl space foundations
- 1,277 square feet on the first floor and 1,569 square feet on the second floor, including the bonus room above the garage

Price Code E

MULTI-STORY
over 2,000 square feet

Plan #X20-0178

To order blueprints use the form on page 322 or call toll-free 1-800-DREAM HOME (373-2646)

117

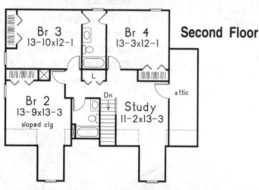

Second Floor

Br 3 13-10x12-1

Br 4 13-3x12-1

Br 2 13-9x13-3 sloped clg

Study 11-2x13-3

Dn

attic

L

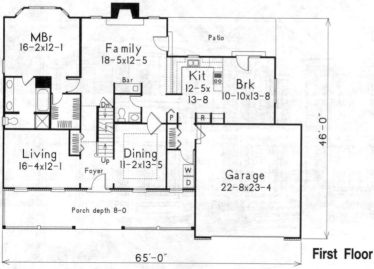

MBr 16-2x12-1

Family 18-5x12-5

Patio

Bar

Kit 12-5x 13-8

Brk 10-10x13-8

Living 16-4x12-1

Dn

Dining 11-2x13-5

Up

Foyer

P

R

W D

Garage 22-8x23-4

Porch depth 8-0

46'-0"

65'-0"

First Floor

MULTI-STORY over 2,000 square feet

Compact Design Offers Privacy

2,847 total square feet of living area

Special features

- Secluded first floor master bedroom suite includes an oversized window and a large walk-in closet

- Extensive attic storage and closet space

- Spacious second floor bedrooms, two of which share a private bath

- Great starter home with option to finish the second floor as needed

- 4 bedrooms, 3 1/2 baths, 2-car garage

- Basement foundation, drawings also include slab and crawl space foundations

- 1,745 square feet on the first floor and 1,102 square feet on the second floor

Price Code E

Plan #X20-0183

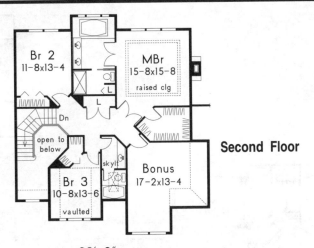

Second Floor

63'-0"

47'-0"

First Floor

Distinctive Front Facade Welcomes Guests

2,871 total square feet of living area

Special features

- Living room and dining rooms feature tray ceilings and round-top windows

- Den isolated with double-door entrance and bay window with transom above

- Nook and family room adjacent to kitchen, which includes island cooktop and desk

- Master suite with deluxe bath, walk-in closet and tray ceiling

- 3 bedrooms, 2 1/2 baths, 3-car garage

- Crawl space foundation

- 1,465 square feet on the first floor and 1,406 square feet on the second floor including the bonus room

Price Code E

MULTI-STORY over 2,000 square feet

Plan #X20-0324

Magnificent Facade

2,887 total square feet of living area

Special features

- Columned foyer opens into living room with sunken wet bar extending into pool area

- Stunning master suite offers view of pool through curved window wall and accesses patio

- Dining room boasts window walls

- Second floor includes two bedrooms, bath and shared balcony deck overlooking pool area

- 4 bedrooms, 2 1/2 baths, 2-car garage

- Slab foundation

- 2,212 square feet on the first floor and 675 square feet on the second floor

Price Code F

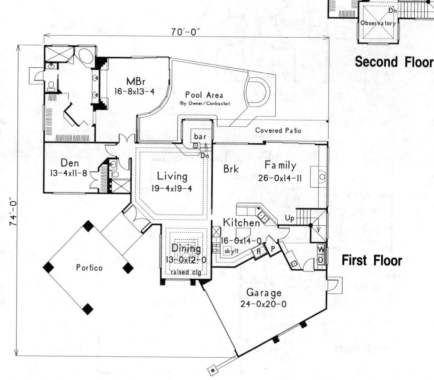

Second Floor

First Floor

J.N. HANSEN RTL.

MULTI-STORY over 2,000 square feet

Fireplaces Add Warm Cozy Feeling

2,932 total square feet of living area

Special features

- 9' ceilings throughout home
- Rear stairs create convenient access to second floor from living area
- Spacious kitchen has pass-through to the family room, a convenient island and pantry
- Cozy built-in table in breakfast area
- Secluded master suite with luxurious bath and patio access
- 4 bedrooms, 3 1/2 baths, 2-car side entry garage
- Slab foundation
- 1,999 square feet on the first floor and 933 square feet on the second floor

Price Code F

Second Floor

Br 4 16-0x11-4

Br 2 11-4x16-0

Br 3 11-4x15-0

open to below

Garage 21-4x22-4

Porch

Living 16-0x21-0

Porch

Brk 11-0x10-0

MBr 15-8x16-4

Kit 13-0x13-0

Gallery

First Floor

Study 11-4x 14-0

Foyer

Dining 11-0x 14-0

Porch depth 8-0

79'-4"

51'-0"

MULTI-STORY over 2,000 square feet

Arch Windows Grace Magnificent Facade

2,993 total square feet of living area

Special features

- 10' ceilings on first floor, 9' ceilings on second floor
- Second floor bedrooms include private dressing areas, walk-in closets and share a bath
- Generous family room and kitchen combine for activity center
- 4 bedrooms, 3 baths, 2-car side entry garage
- Slab foundation, drawings also include crawl space foundation
- 2,369 square feet on the first floor and 624 square feet on the second floor

Price Code E

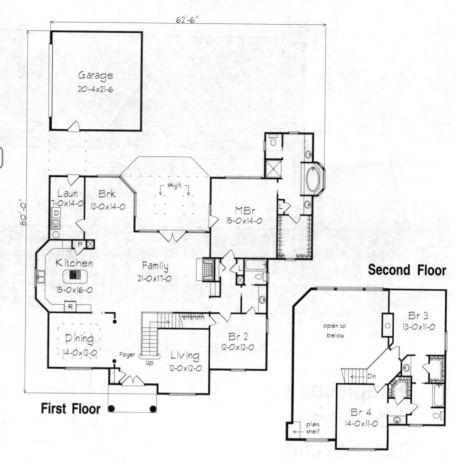

62'-6"

80'-0"

Garage
20-4x21-6

Laun
7-0x14-0

Brk
12-0x14-0

skylt

MBr
15-0x14-0

Kitchen
15-0x16-0

Family
21-0x17-0

Dining
14-0x12-0

Foyer

Up

Living
12-0x12-0

Br 2
12-0x12-0

First Floor

Second Floor

Br 3
13-0x11-0

open to below

Dn

Br 4
14-0x11-0

plant shelf

Plan #X20-0435

To order blueprints use the form on page 322 or call toll-free 1-800-DREAM HOME (373-2646)

ELLIE

Spacious Room Around A Central Foyer

3,006 total square feet of living area

Special features

- Energy efficient home with 2" x 6" exterior walls

- Large all purpose room and bath on third floor

- Efficient U-shaped kitchen includes a pantry and adjacent planning desk

- 4 bedrooms, 2 1/2 baths, 2-car side entry garage

- Basement foundation, drawings also include slab foundation

- 1,293 square feet on the first floor, 1,138 square feet on the second floor and 575 square feet on the third floor

Price Code E

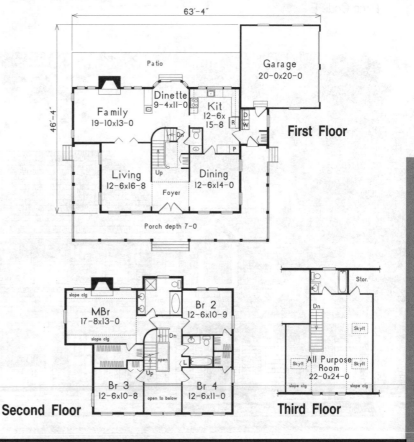

First Floor

63'-4"

46'-4"

Patio

Garage
20-0x20-0

Dinette
9-4x11-0

Kit
12-6x
15-8

Family
19-10x13-0

Living
12-6x16-8

Dining
12-6x14-0

Foyer

Up

Porch depth 7-0

Second Floor

slope clg

MBr
17-8x13-0

Br 2
12-6x10-9

slope clg

Dn

Up

open

Br 3
12-6x10-8

Br 4
12-6x11-0

open to below

L

Third Floor

Stor.

Dn

Skylt

Skylt

All Purpose
Room
22-0x24-0

Skylt

slope clg

slope clg

MULTI-STORY over 2,000 square feet

Plan #X20-0677

To order blueprints use the form on page 322 or call toll-free 1-800-DREAM HOME (373-2646)

123

Deluxe Master Suite Provides Ultimate Style

3,019 total square feet of living area

Special features

- Master suite features double-doors, dramatic vaulted ceiling and spacious master bath with large bay window

- Bonus room accented by dormer windows and ceiling vaults

- Handy additional storage in secondary bath

- 4 bedrooms, 2 1/2 baths, 3-car side entry garage

- Basement foundation

- 1,360 square feet on the first floor and 1,659 square feet on the second floor, including the bonus room above the garage

Price Code E

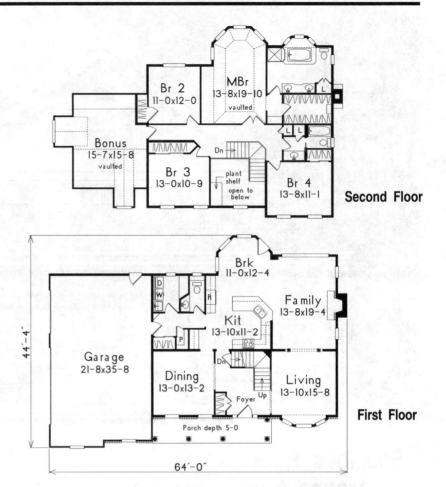

Second Floor

Br 2
11-0x12-0

MBr
13-8x19-10
vaulted

Bonus
15-7x15-8
vaulted

Br 3
13-0x10-9

Dn

plant shelf

open to below

Br 4
13-8x11-1

First Floor

Brk
11-0x12-4

Family
13-8x19-4

Kit
13-10x11-2

Garage
21-8x35-8

Dining
13-0x13-2

Dn

Living
13-10x15-8

Up

Foyer

Porch depth 5-0

44'-4"

64'-0"

Plan #X20-0376

LEVINSON

Curved Stairway Graces Large Foyer

3,072 total square feet of living area

Special features

- Master bedroom boasts fireplace, large dressing area and a garden bath

- Kitchen includes a walk-in pantry

- Sunroom breakfast area accesses rear porch

- Great room with vaulted ceiling and a fireplace

- 4 bedrooms, 2 1/2 baths, 2-car side entry garage

- Basement foundation

- 2,229 square feet on the first floor and 843 square feet on the second floor

Price Code E

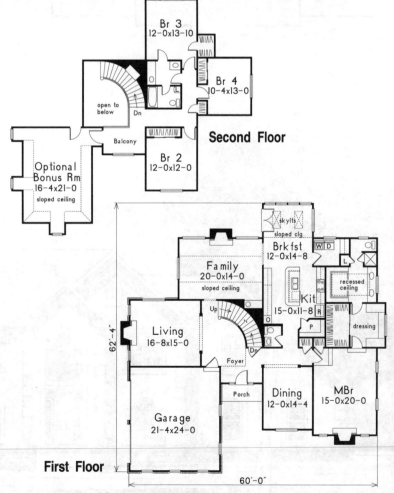

Second Floor

Br 3
12-0x13-10

Br 4
10-4x13-0

open to below

Dn

Optional Bonus Rm
16-4x21-0
sloped ceiling

Balcony

Br 2
12-0x12-0

First Floor

62'-4"

60'-0"

skylts
sloped clg

Brk fst
12-0x14-8

W D

Family
20-0x14-0
sloped ceiling

recessed ceiling

Kit
15-0x11-8

Up

Living
16-8x15-0

Dn

P

dressing

Foyer

Porch

Dining
12-0x14-4

MBr
15-0x20-0

Garage
21-4x24-0

MULTI-STORY
over 2,000 square feet

Plan #X20-0300

To order blueprints use the form on page 322 or call toll-free 1-800-DREAM HOME (373-2646)

125

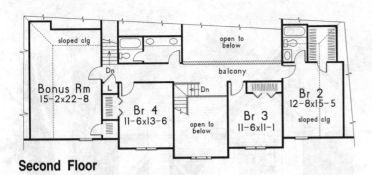

Second Floor

Bonus Rm
15-2x22-8

Br 4
11-6x13-6

Br 3
11-6x11-1

Br 2
12-8x15-5

sloped clg

open to below

balcony

Dn

open to below

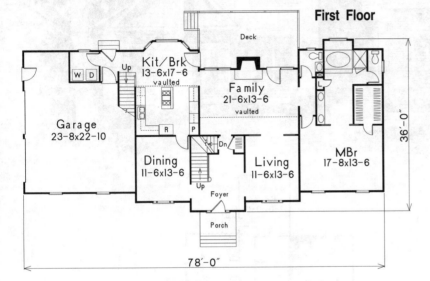

First Floor

Deck

Kit/Brk
13-6x17-6
vaulted

Family
21-6x13-6
vaulted

Up

W D

Garage
23-8x22-10

Dining
11-6x13-6

Living
11-6x13-6

MBr
17-8x13-6

Up

Foyer

Porch

Dn

R

P

36'-0"

78'-0"

Impressive Elegance In A Rambling Two-Story

3,116 total square feet of living area

Special features

- Arched mullioned windows provide balance across the impressive facade

- First floor master bedroom and one upstairs bedroom have private baths and walk-in closets

- Large area above the garage available for future use

- Vaulted ceiling and balcony add to spaciousness

- 4 bedrooms, 3 1/2 baths, 2-car side entry garage

- Basement foundation

- 1,741 square feet on the first floor and 1,375 square feet on the second floor, including the bonus room above the garage

  Price Code F

MULTI-STORY over 2,000 square feet

Plan #X20-0146

RIDGEMONT

Two-Story Foyer With Grand Curved Stairway

3,144 total square feet of living area

Special features

- 9' ceilings on first floor
- Kitchen offers large pantry, island cooktop and close proximity to laundry room and dining room
- Expansive family room includes bar, fireplace and attractive bay window
- 4 bedrooms, 4 1/2 baths, 3-car side entry garage
- Basement foundation
- 1,724 square feet on the first floor and 1,420 square feet on the second floor

Price Code E

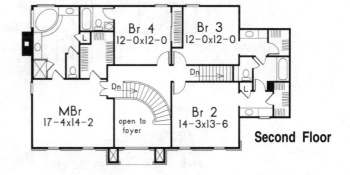

Br 4 12-0x12-0
Br 3 12-0x12-0
MBr 17-4x14-2
open to foyer
Br 2 14-3x13-6

Second Floor

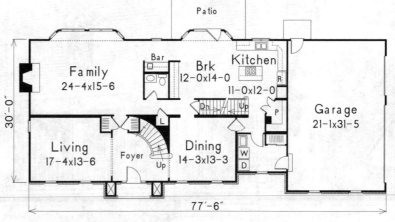

Patio
Family 24-4x15-6
Bar
Brk 12-0x14-0
Kitchen 11-0x12-0
Garage 21-1x31-5
30'-0"
Living 17-4x13-6
Foyer
Dining 14-3x13-3
W D
77'-6"

First Floor

MULTI-STORY
over 2,000 square feet

Outdoor Living Created By Decks And Porches

3,149 total square feet of living area

Special features

- 10' ceilings on first floor and 9' ceilings on second floor
- All bedrooms include walk-in closets
- Formal living and dining rooms flank two-story foyer
- 4 bedrooms, 3 1/2 baths, 2-car detached garage
- Slab foundation, drawings also include crawl space foundation
- 2,033 square feet on the first floor and 1,116 square feet on the second floor

Price Code E

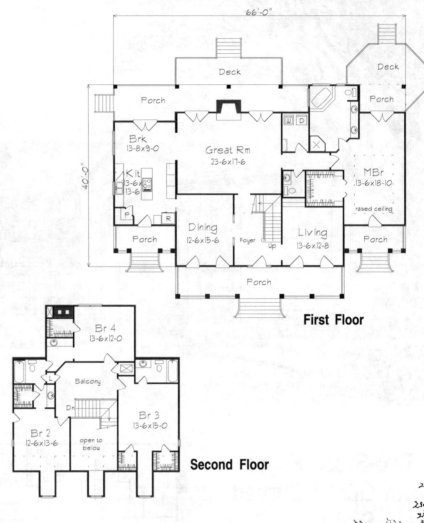

First Floor

Second Floor

MULTI-STORY over 2,000 square feet

Plan #X20-0429

To order blueprints use the form on page 322 or call toll-free 1-800-DREAM HOME (373-2646)

Large Porches Bring In The Outdoors

3,153 total square feet of living area

Special features

- Master suite with full amenities
- Energy efficient design with 2" x 6" exterior walls
- Covered breezeway and front and rear porches
- Full-size workshop and storage with garage below, a unique combination
- 4 bedrooms, 3 1/2 baths, 2-car drive under garage
- Basement foundation, drawings also include crawl space and slab foundations
- 2,040 square feet on the first floor and 1,113 square feet on the second floor

Price Code E

Second Floor

Balcony

Br 4
15-0x12-0

skylt

Dn

Br 3
13-0x13-0
vaulted

Br 2
13-0x13-0
vaulted

First Floor

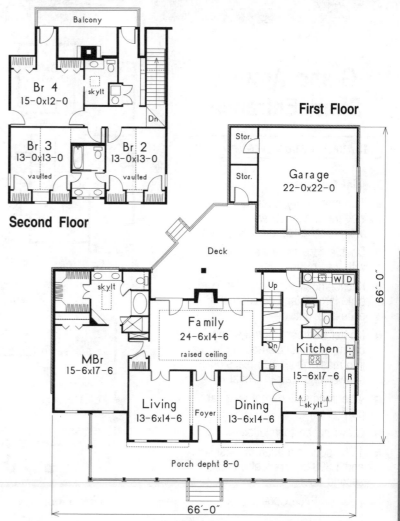

Stor.

Stor.

Garage
22-0x22-0

Deck

skylt

MBr
15-6x17-6

Family
24-6x14-6
raised ceiling

Up

Dn

W D

Kitchen
15-6x17-6

Living
13-6x14-6

Foyer

Dining
13-6x14-6

skylt

R

Porch depth 8-0

66'-0"

66'-0"

MULTI-STORY over 2,000 square feet

Grand Arched Front Entrance

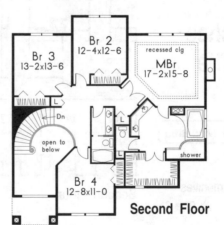

Br 3
13-2x13-6

Br 2
12-4x12-6

recessed clg

MBr
17-2x15-8

L

Dn

L

L

open to below

L

shower

Br 4
12-8x11-0

Second Floor

3,157 total square feet of living area

Special features

- Two-story entry foyer features elegant curved stairway and arched entrance into living room

- Double-door entrance into den with wall of built-ins

- Kitchen/nook area includes corner sink, large island cooktop and accesses outside

- Master bedroom features tray ceiling and double-door entrance into master bath with glass block shower and walk-in closet

- 4 bedrooms, 2 1/2 baths, 3-car garage

- Crawl space foundation

- 1,764 square feet on the first floor and 1,393 square feet on the second floor

Price Code E

Nook
12-4x14-0

Kitchen
R

Family
20-8x15-8

Dining
13-8x11-8
P
O
B

13-6x15-8

W
D

Living
13-8x15-4
recessed clg
Up

L

Den
12-8x12-6

Garage
33-4x21-8

50'-0"

First Floor

70'-0"

Plan #X20-0329

To order blueprints use the form on page 322 or call toll-free 1-800-DREAM HOME (373-2646)

MULTI-STORY over 2,000 square feet

KENSINGTON

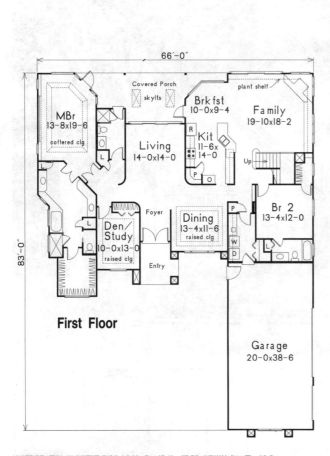

First Floor

66'-0"

83'-0"

MBr
13-8x19-6
coffered clg

Covered Porch
skylts

Brk fst
10-0x9-4

plant shelf

Family
19-10x18-2

Living
14-0x14-0

Kit
11-6x
14-0

R

Up

P   O

Den/
Study
10-0x13-0
raised clg

Foyer

Dining
13-4x11-6
raised clg

P

W
D

Br 2
13-4x12-0

Entry

L

Garage
20-0x38-6

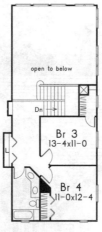

Second Floor

open to below

Dn

Br 3
13-4x11-0

Br 4
11-0x12-4

Arches Grace
Classic Facade

3,164 total square feet of living area

Special features

- Double-door front entry leads into central living area with unique curved walls
- Family room features two-story ceiling, corner fireplace and built-in media center
- Master suite accesses covered patio
- Double-doors lead into master bath with a large walk-in closet
- Varied ceiling heights throughout
- 4 bedrooms, 4 baths, 3-car side entry garage
- Slab foundation
- 2,624 square feet on the first floor and 540 square feet on the second floor

Price Code E

HOME DESIGN SERVICES, INC.

Plan #X20-0337

To order blueprints use the form on page 322 or call toll-free 1-800-DREAM HOME (373-2646)

Curved Features Create Flowing Layout

3,169 total square feet of living area

Special features

- 9' ceilings throughout first floor
- Second floor bedrooms boast private baths
- Spacious game room includes deck/balcony
- Master bedroom features private patio and ideal bath
- 4 bedrooms, 4 baths, 2-car side entry garage
- Slab foundation, drawings also include crawl space foundation
- 2,109 square feet on the first floor and 1,060 square feet on the second floor

Price Code E

MULTI-STORY over 2,000 square feet

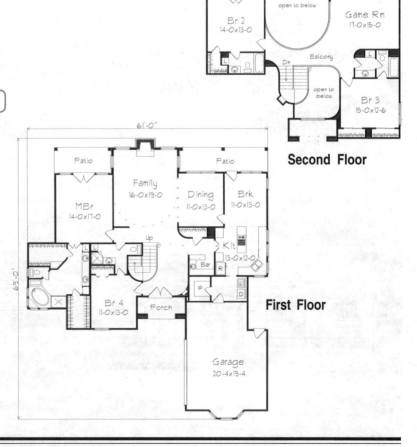

Second Floor

First Floor

Plan #X20-0406

WINDSOR

Rounded Entry Adds Distinctive Touch

3,175 total square feet of living area

Special features

- 9' ceilings on first floor
- Dining and living rooms open to sun-drenched solarium and patio
- Family room with fireplace immersed in light from windows
- Double-door entry into den with built-in cabinets and shelves
- 4 bedrooms, 2 1/2 baths, 3-car garage
- Basement foundation
- 1,937 square feet on the first floor and 1,238 square feet on the second floor

Price Code E

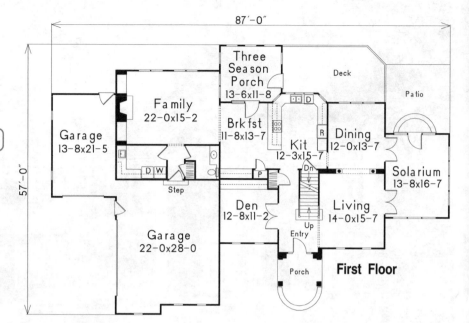

First Floor

- 87'-0"
- 57'-0"
- Garage 13-8x21-5
- Family 22-0x15-2
- Three Season Porch 13-6x11-8
- Deck
- Patio
- Brkfst 11-8x13-7
- Kit 12-3x15-7
- Dining 12-0x13-7
- Solarium 13-8x16-7
- Garage 22-0x28-0
- Den 12-8x11-2
- Living 14-0x15-7
- Step
- Up Entry
- Porch

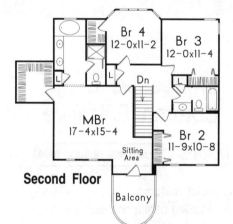

Second Floor

- Br 4 12-0x11-2
- Br 3 12-0x11-4
- MBr 17-4x15-4
- Br 2 11-9x10-8
- Sitting Area
- Balcony

Plan #X20-0446

To order blueprints use the form on page 322 or call toll-free 1-800-DREAM HOME (373-2646)

BRITTANY

Impressive Large Column Entrance

| 3,206 total square feet of living area |

Special features

- Vaulted ceiling and fireplace in living room

- Kitchen/nook area features island cooktop with breakfast bar, desk and accesses outside

- Step up double-door entrance to master suite featuring large walk-in closet and elegant bath

- Sizable bonus room with a vaulted ceiling on second level

- 3 bedrooms, 2 1/2 baths, 3-car side entry garage

- Crawl space foundation

- 1,618 square feet on the first floor and 1,588 square feet on the second floor including the bonus room above the garage

Price Code F

MULTI-STORY over 2,000 square feet

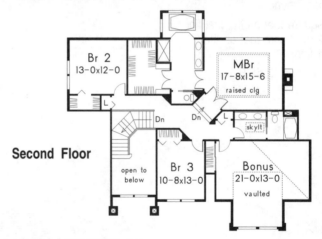

Second Floor

Br 2
13-0x12-0

MBr
17-8x15-6
raised clg

skylt

open to below

Dn   Dn

Br 3
10-8x13-0

Bonus
21-0x13-0
vaulted

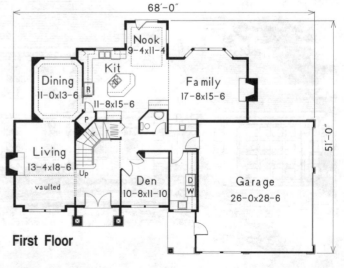

68'-0"

51'-0"

Nook
9-4x11-4

Dining
11-0x13-6

Kit
11-8x15-6

Family
17-8x15-6

Living
13-4x18-6
vaulted

Up

Den
10-8x11-10

Garage
26-0x28-6

First Floor

Plan #X20-0330

BRIARCREST

Second Floor

Br 2
12-11x12-7

open to
below

Br 3
12-0x13-3

Dn

open to
below

Br 4
12-1x12-4

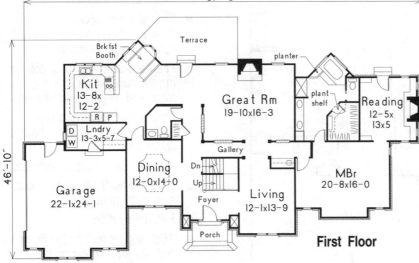

87'-8"

46'-10"

Brkfst
Booth

Terrace

planter

Kit
13-8x
12-2

Great Rm
19-10x16-3

plant
shelf

Reading
12-5x
13x5

Lndry
13-3x5-7

R P

D
W

Gallery

Dining
12-0x14-0

Dn
Up

Foyer

Living
12-1x13-9

MBr
20-8x16-0

Garage
22-1x24-1

Porch

First Floor

Arched Elegance

3,234 total square feet of living area

Special features

- Two-story foyer features central staircase and views to upper level, dining and living rooms
- Built-in breakfast booth surrounded by windows
- Gourmet kitchen with view to the great room
- Two-story great room features large fireplace and arched openings to the upper level
- Elegant master suite has separate reading room with bookshelves and fireplace
- 4 bedrooms, 3 1/2 baths, 2-car side entry garage
- Basement foundation, drawings also include crawl space and slab foundations
- 2,273 square feet on the first floor and 961 square feet on the second floor

Price Code F

MULTI-STORY
over 2,000 square feet

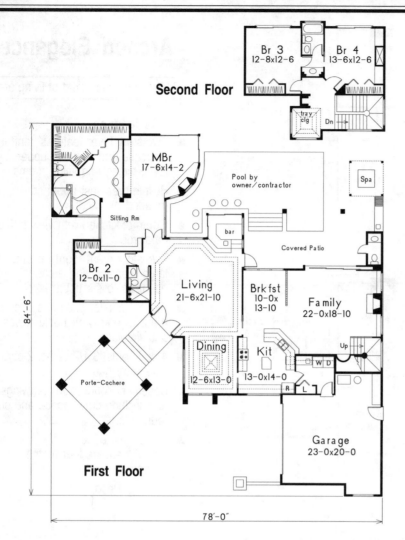

Second Floor

Br 3
12-8x12-6

Br 4
13-6x12-6

tray clg

Dn

First Floor

MBr
17-6x14-2

Pool by owner/contractor

Spa

Sitting Rm

bar

Covered Patio

Br 2
12-0x11-0

Living
21-6x21-10

Brkfst
10-0x
13-10

Family
22-0x18-10

Up

Dining
12-6x13-0

Kit
13-0x14-0

W D

R L

Porte-Cochere

Garage
23-0x20-0

84'-6"

78'-0"

Large Patio And Pool For Entertaining

3,290 total square feet of living area

Special features

- Patio area surrounds pool with swim-up bar and spa
- Formal dining room features dramatic drop down ceiling and easy access to kitchen
- Fireplace provides focal point in master suite which includes sitting room and elegant master bath
- Observation room and two bedrooms with adjoining bath on upper level
- Varied ceiling heights throughout
- 4 bedrooms, 3 1/2 baths, 2-car side entry garage
- Slab foundation
- 2,669 square feet on the first floor and 621 square feet on the second floor

Price Code F

MULTI-STORY over 2,000 square feet

Plan #X20-0341

To order blueprints use the form on page 322 or call toll-free 1-800-DREAM HOME (373-2646)

LAVISTA

Two-Story Sunken Family Room

3,315 total square feet of living area

Special features

- Island kitchen, breakfast room and two-story sunken family room combine for convenient family dining or entertaining

- Two-story foyer opens onto bay windowed formal dining and living rooms

- Master suite features sitting area, his and her walk-in closet and deluxe bath

- 4 bedrooms, 3 1/2 baths, 2-car side entry garage

- Basement foundation

- 1,695 square feet on the first floor and 1,620 square feet on the second floor

Price Code F

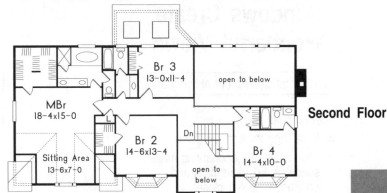

Second Floor

Br 3
13-0x11-4

open to below

MBr
18-4x15-0

Sitting Area
13-6x7-0

Br 2
14-6x13-4

Dn

open to below

Br 4
14-4x10-0

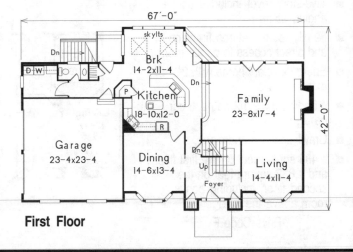

First Floor

67'-0"

skylts

Brk
14-2x11-4

Dn

Kitchen
18-10x12-0

Family
23-8x17-4

42'-0"

Garage
23-4x23-4

Dining
14-6x13-4

Dn

Up

Living
14-4x11-4

Foyer

MULTI-STORY
over 2,000 square feet

Plan #X20-0351

To order blueprints use the form on page 322 or call toll-free 1-800-DREAM HOME (373-2646)

Lots Of Windows Create Wonderful Views

3,316 total square feet of living area

Special features

- 9' ceilings throughout home
- Step down into enchanting master suite with luxurious bath and enormous walk-in closet
- Two-story foyer includes unique angled stairs
- Family room features fireplace and direct access to bonus room
- Energy efficient home with 2" x 6" exterior walls
- 4 bedrooms, 2 1/2 baths, 3-car garage
- Crawl space foundation
- 1,484 square feet on the first floor and 1,832 square feet on the second floor, including bonus room above the garage

Price Code F

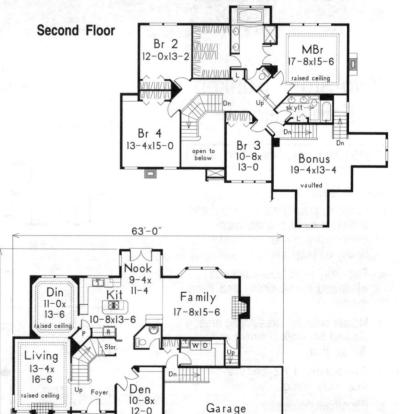

Second Floor

Br 2
12-0x13-2

MBr
17-8x15-6
raised ceiling

Br 4
13-4x15-0

open to below

Br 3
10-8x 13-0

Bonus
19-4x13-4
vaulted

skylt

Dn Up

63'-0"

51'-0"

Din
11-0x 13-6
raised ceiling

Kit
10-8x13-6

Nook
9-4x 11-4

Family
17-8x15-6

Living
13-4x 16-6
raised ceiling

Up Foyer

Den
10-8x 12-0

Stor.

W D

Dn

Garage
27-4x23-10

Porch

First Floor

Plan #X20-0403

BRENTWOOD

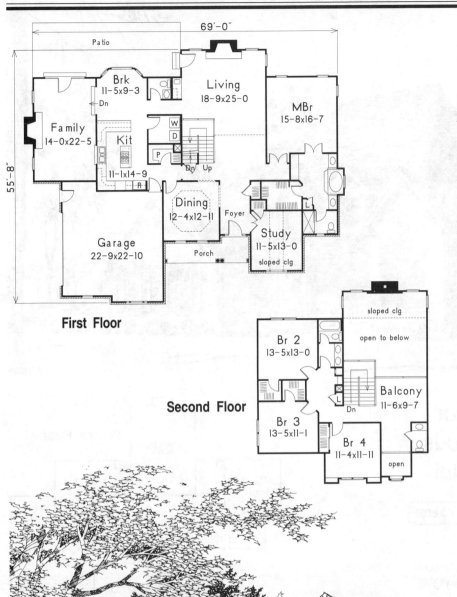

First Floor

69'-0"

Patio

Brk
11-5x9-3

Living
18-9x25-0

MBr
15-8x16-7

Family
14-0x22-5

Kit

55'-8"

W
D

P

Dn Up

Dining
12-4x12-11

Foyer

Garage
22-9x22-10

Study
11-5x13-0
sloped clg

Porch

11-1x14-9

R

Second Floor

sloped clg

open to below

Br 2
13-5x13-0

Balcony
11-6x9-7

Dn

Br 3
13-5x11-1

Br 4
11-4x11-11

open

Elegant Entrance

| 3,357 total square feet of living area |

Special features

- Attractive balcony overlooks entry foyer and living area
- Balcony area could easily convert to a fifth bedroom
- Spacious kitchen also opens into sunken family room with a fireplace
- First floor master suite boasts large walk-in closet and dressing area
- Central laundry room with laundry chute from second floor
- 4 bedrooms, 2 baths, 2 half baths, 2-car side entry garage
- Basement foundation, drawings also include crawl space and slab foundations
- 2,374 square feet on the first floor and 983 square feet on the second floor

Price Code F

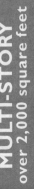

MULTI-STORY
over 2,000 square feet

Plan #X20-0236

To order blueprints use the form on page 322 or call toll-free 1-800-DREAM HOME (373-2646)

MANOR HOUSE

A Great Manor House, Spacious Inside And Out

3,368 total square feet of living area

Special features

- Sunken great room with cathedral ceiling, wooden beams, skylights, and a masonry fireplace
- Octagonal shaped breakfast room has domed ceiling with beams, large windows and door to patio
- Master bedroom in a private wing with deluxe bath and dressing area
- Oversized walk-in closets and storage areas in each bedroom
- 4 bedrooms, 3 baths, 2 half baths, 2-car side entry garage
- Basement foundation
- 2,150 square feet on the first floor and 1,218 square feet on the second floor

Price Code F

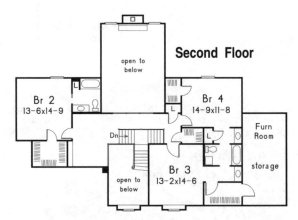

Second Floor

Br 2
13-6x14-9

open to below

Br 4
14-9x11-8

Furn Room

storage

Dn

Br 3
13-2x14-6

open to below

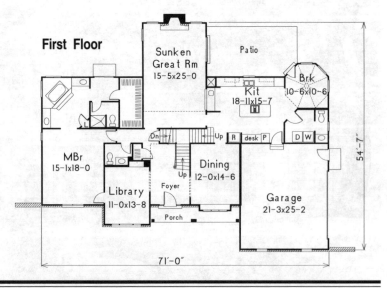

First Floor

Sunken Great Rm
15-5x25-0

Patio

Brk
10-6x10-6

Kit
18-11x15-7

MBr
15-1x18-0

Dn   Up   R   desk   P   D   W

Dining
12-0x14-6

Up

Library
11-0x13-8

Foyer

Garage
21-3x25-2

Porch

54'-7"

71'-0"

MULTI-STORY over 2,000 square feet

Plan #X20-0159

To order blueprints use the form on page 322 or call toll-free 1-800-DREAM HOME (373-2646)

140

FAIRFIELD

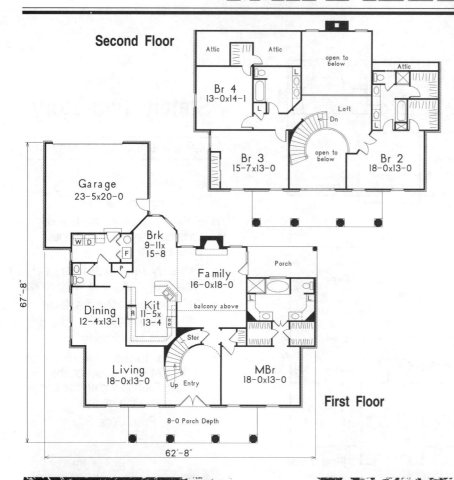

Second Floor

Attic · Attic
open to below
Attic

Br 4
13-0x14-1

Loft
Dn

open to below

Br 3
15-7x13-0

Br 2
18-0x13-0

Garage
23-5x20-0

Brk
9-11x
15-8

Family
16-0x18-0

Porch

W D
F
P

Dining
12-4x13-1

Kit
11-5x
13-4

balcony above

R

Stor

Living
18-0x13-0

Up Entry

MBr
18-0x13-0

First Floor

67'-8"

8-0 Porch Depth

62'-8"

Dramatic Entry With Soaring Staircase

3,391 total square feet of living area

Special features

■ Magnificent first floor master suite has two walk-in closets and double vanities

■ Generous secondary bedrooms

■ Bedroom 2 has private bath and plenty of closet space

■ Two-story family room with fireplace and balcony above

■ 4 bedrooms, 3 1/2 baths, 2-car rear entry garage

■ Crawl space foundation, drawings also include slab foundation

■ 1,958 square feet on the first floor and 1,433 square feet on the second floor

Price Code F

Plan #X20-0220

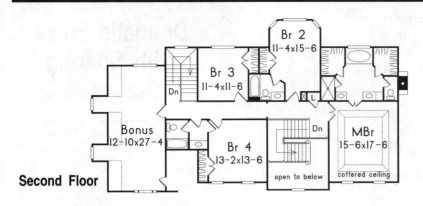

Second Floor

Br 2
11-4x15-6

Br 3
11-4x11-6

Dn

Bonus
12-10x27-4

Br 4
13-2x13-6

Dn

MBr
15-6x17-6

open to below

coffered ceiling

Stately Two-Story

| 3,427 total square feet of living area |

Special features

- 10' ceilings on first floor
- Elaborate master suite features coffered ceiling and luxurious private bath
- Two-story showplace foyer flanked by dining and living rooms
- 4 bedrooms, 3 1/2 baths, 2-car side entry garage
- Basement foundation
- 1,553 square feet on the first floor and 1,874 square feet on the second floor, including the bonus room above the garage

Price Code F

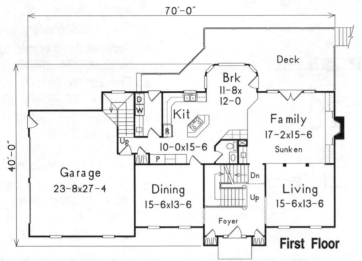

70'-0"

40'-0"

Deck

Brk
11-8x
12-0

Kit

Family
17-2x15-6

Sunken

Garage
23-8x27-4

10-0x15-6

P

Dining
15-6x13-6

Dn

Up

Living
15-6x13-6

Foyer

First Floor

Plan #X20-0445

To order blueprints use the form on page 322 or call toll-free 1-800-DREAM HOME (373-2646)

CANTERBURY

Striking Double Arched Entry

> 3,494 total square feet of living area

Special features

- Majestic two-story foyer opens into living and dining rooms, both framed by arched columns
- Balcony overlooks large living area featuring french doors to covered porch
- Luxurious master suite
- Convenient game room supports lots of activities
- 4 bedrooms, 3 1/2 baths, 3-car side entry garage
- Slab foundation, drawings also include crawl space foundation
- 2,469 square feet on the first floor and 1,025 square feet on the second floor

Price Code F

First Floor

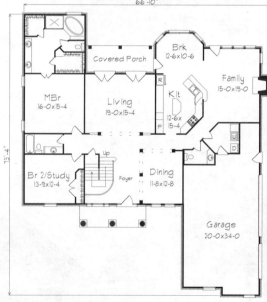

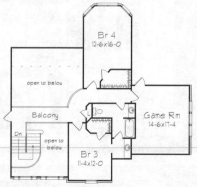

Second Floor

MULTI-STORY over 2,000 square feet

Plan #X20-0405

Elegant Family Room With Arched Top Windows

[3,503 total square feet of living area]

Special features

- Entry foyer leads to elegant curved stairway
- Family room features 14' ceiling and a fireplace flanked on both sides by windows
- Study, tucked away from the traffic area, features one full wall of built-in bookcases
- 5 bedrooms, 3 1/2 baths
- Slab foundation
- 2,157 square feet on the first floor and 1,346 square feet on the second floor

Price Code F

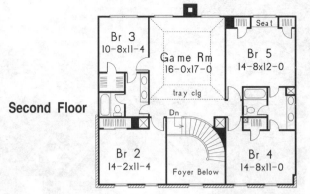

Second Floor

Br 3
10-8x11-4

Game Rm
16-0x17-0
tray clg

Br 5
14-8x12-0

Seat

Dn

Br 2
14-2x11-4

Foyer Below

Br 4
14-8x11-0

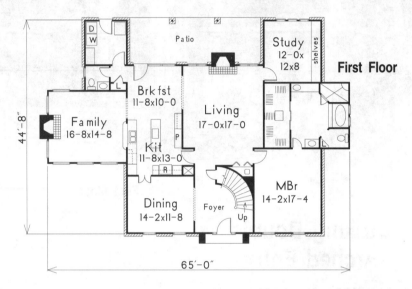

First Floor

D W

Patio

Study
12-0x 12x8
shelves

Brkfst
11-8x10-0

Living
17-0x17-0

Family
16-8x14-8

Kit
11-8x13-0

P

R

Dining
14-2x11-8

Foyer

Up

MBr
14-2x17-4

44'-8"

65'-0"

MULTI-STORY over 2,000 square feet

Plan #X20-0313

Dramatic Shape And Features

3,646 total square feet of living area

Special features

- 9' ceilings on first floor
- Secluded first floor master suite features double-door access to the side veranda, walk-in closet and private bath with separate tub and shower and enclosed stool and sink
- Magnificent two-story foyer with curved stairway
- Family room and kitchen/breakfast area create central room with fireplace, wet bar and access to veranda
- Large laundry room includes two sinks and extra work space
- 5 bedrooms, 3 1/2 baths, 1-car and 2-car side entry garage
- Slab foundation
- 2,142 square feet on the first floor and 1,504 square feet on the second floor

Price Code F

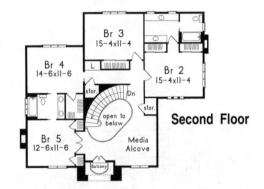

Second Floor

Br 3
15-4x11-4

Br 4
14-6x11-6

Br 2
15-4x11-4

stor.

Dn

open to below

stor.

Br 5
12-6x11-6

Media Alcove

Balcony

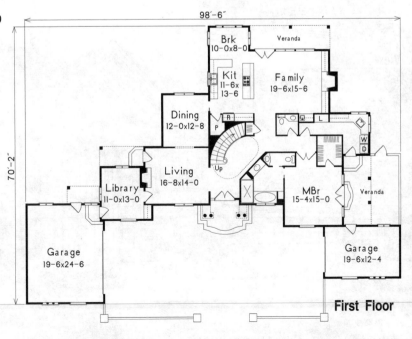

First Floor

98'-6"

70'-2"

Brk
10-0x8-0

Veranda

Kit
11-6x 13-6

Family
19-6x15-6

Dining
12-0x12-8

Living
16-8x14-0

Up

Library
11-0x13-0

MBr
15-4x15-0

Veranda

Garage
19-6x24-6

Garage
19-6x12-4

MULTI-STORY over 2,000 square feet

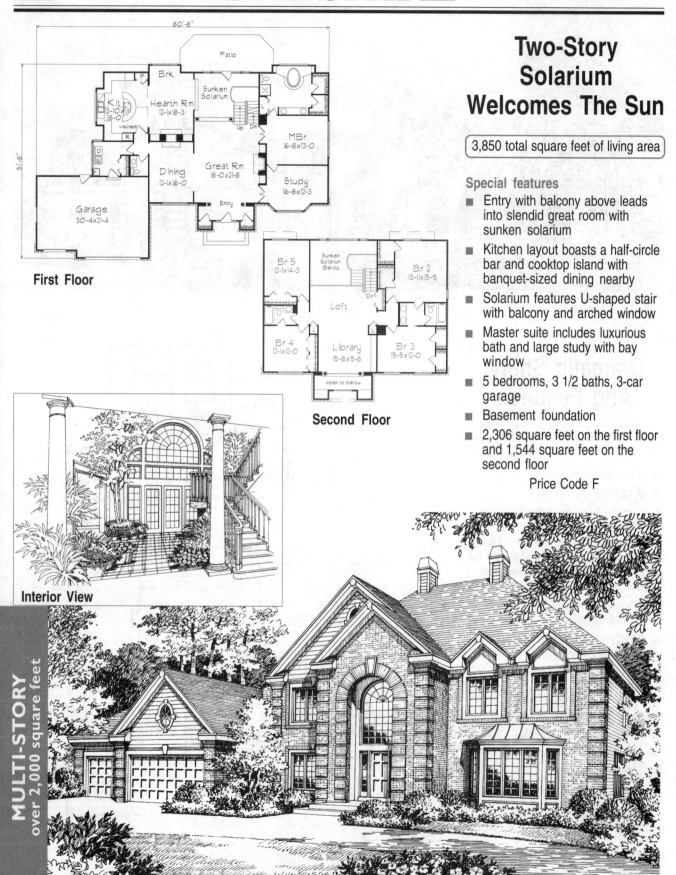

First Floor

Second Floor

Interior View

Two-Story Solarium Welcomes The Sun

> 3,850 total square feet of living area

Special features

- Entry with balcony above leads into slendid great room with sunken solarium

- Kitchen layout boasts a half-circle bar and cooktop island with banquet-sized dining nearby

- Solarium features U-shaped stair with balcony and arched window

- Master suite includes luxurious bath and large study with bay window

- 5 bedrooms, 3 1/2 baths, 3-car garage

- Basement foundation

- 2,306 square feet on the first floor and 1,544 square feet on the second floor

Price Code F

MULTI-STORY over 2,000 square feet

Plan #X20-0418

To order blueprints use the form on page 322 or call toll-free 1-800-DREAM HOME (373-2646)

CROSSWOOD

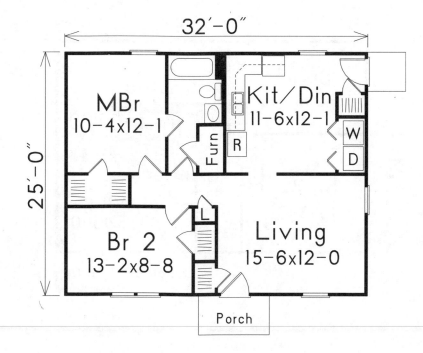

32'-0"

25'-0"

MBr
10-4x12-1

Kit/Din
11-6x12-1

Furn

R

W

D

Br 2
13-2x8-8

L

Living
15-6x12-0

Porch

Ideal For Starter Home

800 total square feet of living area

Special features

- Master bedroom with walk-in closet and private access to bath
- Large living room features handy coat closet
- Kitchen includes side entrance, closet and convenient laundry area
- 2 bedrooms, 1 bath
- Crawl space foundation, drawings also include basement and slab foundations

Price Code AA

SINGLE-STORY under 2,000 square feet

Plan #X20-0582

Perfect Home For A Small Family

| 864 total square feet of living area |

Special features

- L-shaped kitchen with convenient pantry is adjacent to dining area
- Easy access to laundry area, linen closet and storage closet
- Both bedrooms include ample closet space
- 2 bedrooms, 1 bath
- Crawl space foundation, drawings also include basement and slab foundations

    Price Code AA

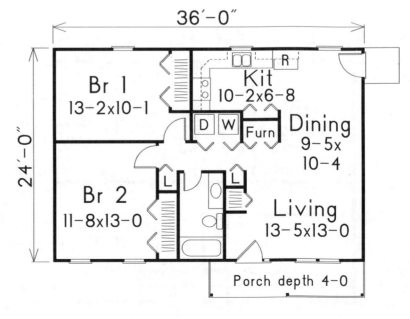

36'-0"

24'-0"

Br 1
13-2x10-1

Kit
10-2x6-8

D W Furn

Dining
9-5x
10-4

Br 2
11-8x13-0

L L

Living
13-5x13-0

R

Porch depth 4-0

Plan #X20-0502

To order blueprints use the form on page 322 or call toll-free 1-800-DREAM HOME (373-2646)

Cozy Ranch Home

950 total square feet of living area

Special features

- Deck adjacent to kitchen/breakfast area for outdoor dining
- Vaulted ceiling, open stairway and fireplace compliment great room
- Secondary bedroom with sloped ceiling and box bay window can convert to den
- Master bedroom with walk-in closet, plant shelf, separate dressing area and private access to bath master suite
- Kitchen has garage access and opens to great room
- 2 bedrooms, 1 bath, 1-car garage
- Basement foundation

Price Code A

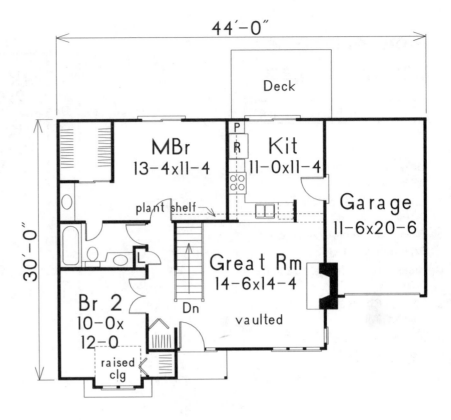

SINGLE-STORY under 2,000 square feet

Compact Home Maximizes Space

987 total square feet of living area

Special features

- Galley kitchen opens into the cozy breakfast room
- Convenient coat closets located by both entrances
- Dining/living room combined for expansive open area
- Breakfast room has access to the outdoors
- Front porch great for enjoying outdoor living
- 3 bedrooms, 1 bath
- Basement foundation

Price Code A

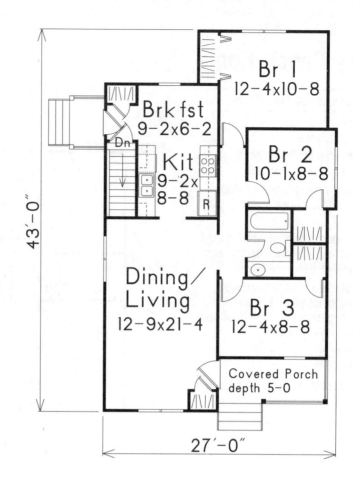

SINGLE-STORY under 2,000 square feet

Plan #X20-0495

To order blueprints use the form on page 322 or call toll-free 1-800-DREAM HOME (373-2646)

TIMBERLAND

Compact Ranch An Ideal Starter Home

988 total square feet of living area

Special features

- Great room features corner fireplace
- Vaulted ceiling and corner windows add space and light in great room
- Eat-in kitchen with vaulted ceiling accesses deck for outdoor living
- Master bedroom features separate vanity and private access to the bathroom
- 2 bedrooms, 1 bath, 2-car garage
- Basement foundation

Price Code A

SINGLE-STORY under 2,000 square feet

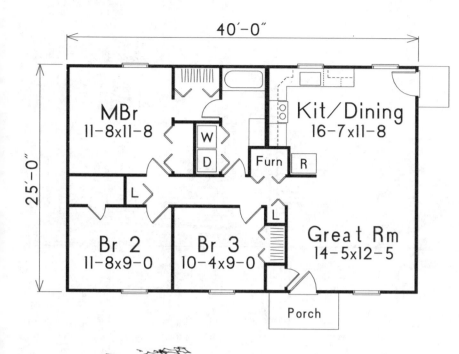

Open Living Space Creates Comfortable Atmosphere

1,000 total square feet of living area

Special features

- Bath includes convenient closeted laundry area
- Master bedroom includes double closets and private access to bath
- Foyer features handy coat closet
- L-shaped kitchen provides easy outside access
- 3 bedrooms, 1 bath
- Crawl space foundation, drawings also include basement and slab foundations

Price Code A

SINGLE-STORY under 2,000 square feet

Plan #X20-0503

To order blueprints use the form on page 322 or call toll-free 1-800-DREAM HOME (373-2646)

HATHAWAY

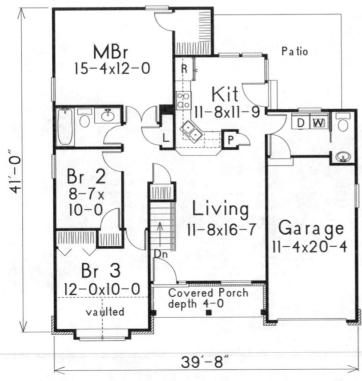

MBr
15-4x12-0

Patio

Kit
11-8x11-9

R

L

P

D W

Br 2
8-7x
10-0

Living
11-8x16-7

Dn

Garage
11-4x20-4

Br 3
12-0x10-0
vaulted

Covered Porch
depth 4-0

41'-0"

39'-8"

Innovative Ranch Has Cozy Corner Patio

1,092 total square feet of living area

Special features

- Box window and inviting porch with dormers creates a charming facade

- Eat-in kitchen offers a pass-through breakfast bar, corner window wall to patio, pantry and convenient laundry with half bath

- Master bedroom features double entry doors and walk-in closet

- 3 bedrooms, 1 1/2 baths, 1-car garage

- Basement foundation

  Price Code A

SINGLE-STORY under 2,000 square feet

Plan #X20-0478

To order blueprints use the form on page 322 or call toll-free 1-800-DREAM HOME (373-2646)

Spacious Dining And Living Areas

1,104 total square feet of living area

Special features

- Master bedroom includes private bath
- Convenient side entrance to kitchen/dining area
- Laundry area located near kitchen
- Large living area creates comfortable atmosphere
- 3 bedrooms, 2 baths
- Crawl space foundation, drawings also include basement and slab foundations

Price Code A

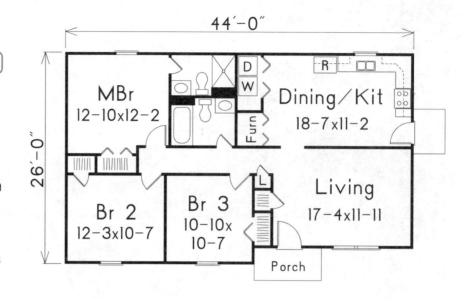

44'-0"

26'-0"

MBr
12-10x12-2

D
W

Furn

Dining/Kit
18-7x11-2

R

Br 2
12-3x10-7

Br 3
10-10x 10-7

L

Living
17-4x11-11

Porch

SINGLE-STORY
under 2,000 square feet

Plan #X20-0505

To order blueprints use the form on page 322 or call toll-free 1-800-DREAM HOME (373-2646)

GREENRIDGE

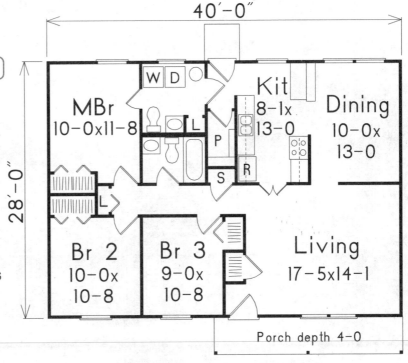

Convenient Ranch

1,120 total square feet of living area

Special features

- Master bedroom includes a half bath with laundry area, linen closet and kitchen access
- Kitchen has charming double-door entry, breakfast bar and a convenient walk-in pantry
- Welcoming front porch opens to large living room with coat closet
- 3 bedrooms, 1 1/2 baths
- Crawl space foundation, drawings also include basement and slab foundations

Price Code A

40'-0"

28'-0"

MBr
10-0x11-8

W D

Kit
8-1x
13-0

Dining
10-0x
13-0

L

P

S

R

Br 2
10-0x
10-8

Br 3
9-0x
10-8

Living
17-5x14-1

Porch depth 4-0

SINGLE-STORY
under 2,000 square feet

Plan #X20-0587

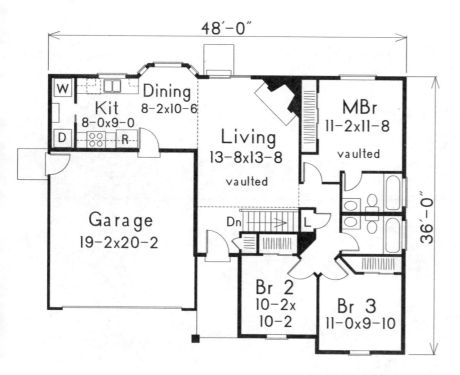

48'-0"

W
Kit
8-0x9-0
D
R

Dining
8-2x10-6

Living
13-8x13-8
vaulted

MBr
11-2x11-8
vaulted

Garage
19-2x20-2

Dn
L

36'-0"

Br 2
10-2x
10-2

Br 3
11-0x9-10

Vaulted Ceilings Show Off This Ranch

1,135 total square feet of living area

Special features

- Living and dining rooms feature vaulted ceilings and a corner fireplace
- Energy efficient home with 2" x 6" exterior walls
- Master bedroom offers vaulted ceilings, private bathroom and generous closet space
- Compact but functional kitchen complete with pantry and adjacent utility room
- 3 bedrooms, 2 baths, 2-car garage
- Basement foundation, drawings also include crawl space foundation

Price Code A

SINGLE-STORY under 2,000 square feet

Plan #X20-0268

Enchanting Country Cottage

1,140 total square feet of living area

Special features

- Open and spacious living and dining area for family gatherings
- Well-organized kitchen with abundance of cabinetry and built-in pantry
- Roomy master bath features double-bowl vanity
- 3 bedrooms, 2 baths, 2-car drive under garage
- Basement foundation

    Price Code A

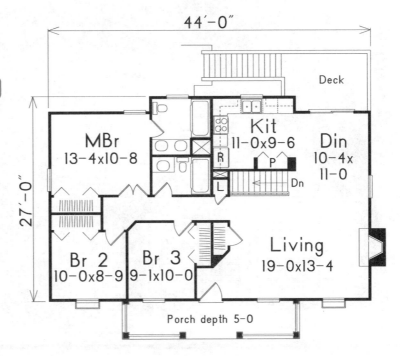

44′-0″

Deck

MBr
13-4x10-8

Kit
11-0x9-6

Din
10-4x
11-0

R

P

L

Dn

27′-0″

Br 2
10-0x8-9

Br 3
9-1x10-0

Living
19-0x13-4

Porch depth 5-0

SINGLE-STORY
under 2,000 square feet

Plan #X20-0477

HD®

Brick And Siding Enhance This Traditional Home

1,170 total square feet of living area

Special features

- Master bedroom enjoys privacy at the rear of this home
- Kitchen has angled bar that overlooks great room and breakfast area
- Living areas combine to create a greater sense of spaciousness
- Great room with cozy fireplace
- 3 bedrooms, 2 baths, 2-car garage
- Slab foundation

Price Code A

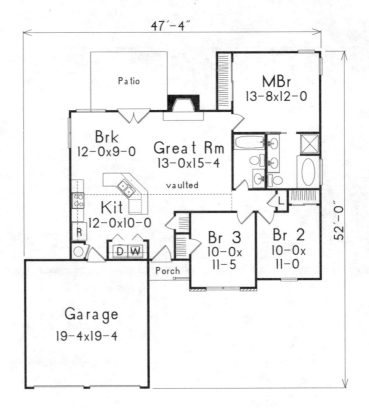

SINGLE-STORY under 2,000 square feet

Plan #X20-0670

To order blueprints use the form on page 322 or call toll-free 1-800-DREAM HOME (373-2646)

DAYTON

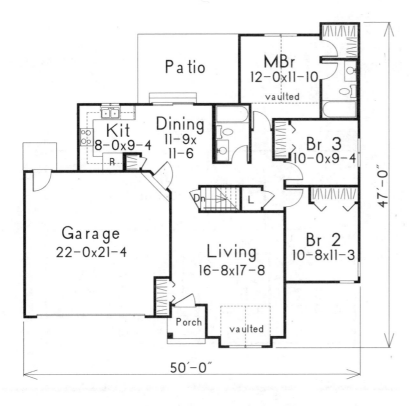

Vaulted Ceiling Frames Circle-Top Window

1,195 total square feet of living area

Special features

- Kitchen/dining room opens onto the patio
- Master bedroom features vaulted ceiling, private bath and walk-in closet
- Coat closets located by both the entrances
- Convenient secondary entrance at the back of the garage
- 3 bedrooms, 2 baths, 2-car garage
- Basement foundation

Price Code A

SINGLE-STORY under 2,000 square feet

Plan #X20-0485

To order blueprints use the form on page 322 or call toll-free 1-800-DREAM HOME (373-2646)

Country-Style With Spacious Rooms

1,197 total square feet of living area

Special features

- U-shaped kitchen includes ample work space, breakfast bar, laundry area and direct access to outside

- Large living room with convenient coat closet

- Master bedroom features large walk-in closet

- 3 bedrooms, 1 bath

- Crawl space foundation, drawings also include basement and slab foundations

    Price Code A

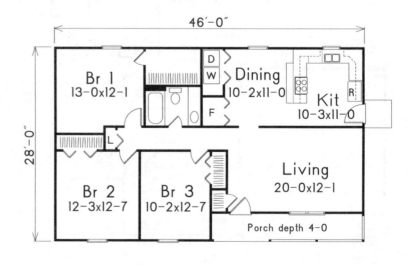

46'-0"

28'-0"

Br 1
13-0x12-1

D
W

Dining
10-2x11-0

F

Kit
10-3x11-0

R

L

Br 2
12-3x12-7

Br 3
10-2x12-7

Living
20-0x12-1

Porch depth 4-0

Plan #X20-0507

To order blueprints use the form on page 322 or call toll-free 1-800-DREAM HOME (373-2646)

DUNWOOD

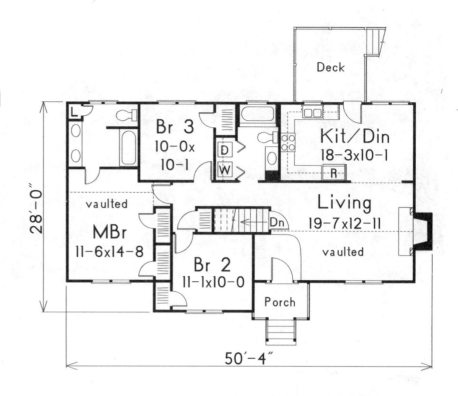

Compact Home For Functional Living

1,220 total square feet of living area

Special features

- Vaulted ceilings add luxury to living room and master suite
- Spacious living room accented with a large fireplace and hearth
- Gracious dining area is adjacent to the convenient wrap-around kitchen
- Washer and dryer handy to the bedrooms
- Covered porch entry adds appeal
- Rear sundeck adjoins dining area
- 3 bedrooms, 2 baths, 2-car drive under garage
- Basement foundation
  Price Code A

Deck

Br 3
10-0x
10-1

Kit/Din
18-3x10-1

28'-0"

vaulted

MBr
11-6x14-8

Living
19-7x12-11

vaulted

Br 2
11-1x10-0

Porch

Dn

50'-4"

SINGLE-STORY under 2,000 square feet

Plan #X20-0173
To order blueprints use the form on page 322 or call toll-free 1-800-DREAM HOME (373-2646)

Central Fireplace Brightens Family Living

1,260 total square feet of living area

Special features

- Spacious kitchen and dining area features large pantry, storage area, easy access to garage and laundry room

- Pleasant covered front porch adds a practical touch

- Master bedroom with a private bath adjoins two other bedrooms, all with plenty of closet space

- 3 bedrooms, 2 baths, 2-car garage

- Basement foundation, drawings also include crawl space and slab foundations

Price Code A

SINGLE-STORY under 2,000 square feet

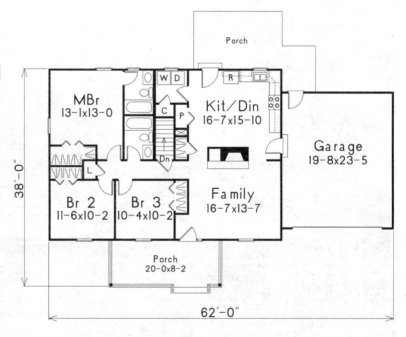

FOXBRIAR

Compact, Convenient And Charming

1,266 total square feet of living area

Special features

- Narrow frontage is perfect for small lots
- Energy efficient home with 2" x 6" exterior walls
- Prominent central hall provides a convenient connection for all main rooms
- Design incorporates full-size master bedroom complete with dressing room, bath and walk-in closet
- Angled kitchen includes handy laundry facilities and is adjacent to an oversized storage area
- 3 bedrooms, 2 baths, 2-car rear entry garage
- Crawl space foundation, drawings also include slab foundation

Price Code A

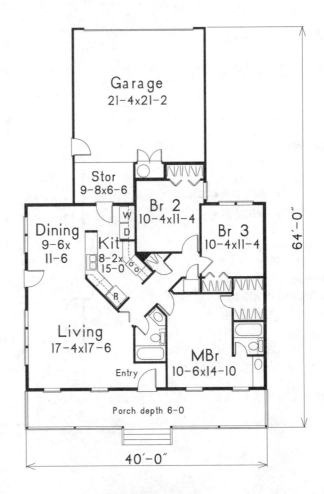

Garage
21-4x21-2

Stor
9-8x6-6

Br 2
10-4x11-4

Br 3
10-4x11-4

Dining
9-6x
11-6

Kit
8-2x
15-0

Living
17-4x17-6

MBr
10-6x14-10

Entry

Porch depth 6-0

64'-0"

40'-0"

Plan #X20-0192

Perfect Fit For A Narrow Site

1,270 total square feet of living area

Special features

- Spacious living area features angled stairs, vaulted ceiling, exciting fireplace and deck access
- Master bedroom with walk-in closet and private bath
- Dining room and living room join to create open atmosphere
- Eat-in kitchen with convenient pass-through to dining room
- 3 bedrooms, 2 baths, 2-car garage
- Basement foundation

Price Code A

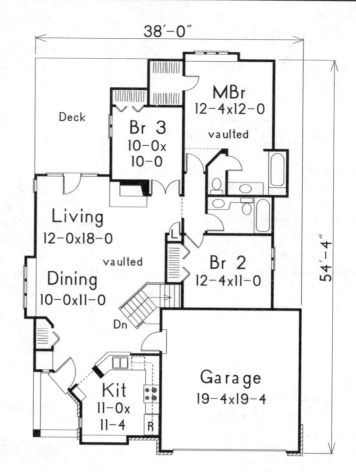

Deck

Br 3
10-0x
10-0

MBr
12-4x12-0
vaulted

Living
12-0x18-0
vaulted

Dining
10-0x11-0

Br 2
12-4x11-0

Dn

Kit
11-0x
11-4

Garage
19-4x19-4

38'-0"

54'-4"

Plan #X20-0275

Large Corner Deck Lends Way To Outside Living Area

1,283 total square feet of living area

Special features

- Vaulted breakfast room with sliding doors that open onto deck
- Kitchen features convenient corner sink and pass-through to dining room
- Open living atmosphere in dining area and great room
- Vaulted great room features a fireplace
- 3 bedrooms, 2 baths, 2-car garage
- Basement foundation

    Price Code A

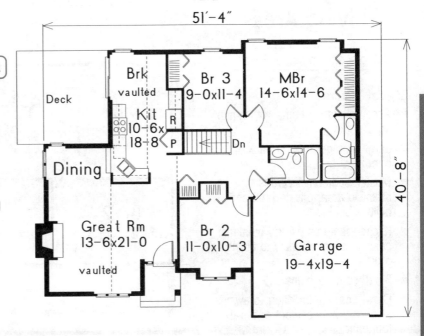

SINGLE-STORY under 2,000 square feet

Layout Creates Large Open Living Area

1,285 total square feet of living area

Special features

- Accommodating home with ranch style porch
- Large storage area on back of home
- Master bedroom includes dressing area, private bath and built-in bookcase
- Kitchen features pantry, breakfast bar and complete view to dining room
- 3 bedrooms, 2 baths
- Crawl space foundation, drawings also include basement and slab foundations

  Price Code B

SINGLE-STORY under 2,000 square feet

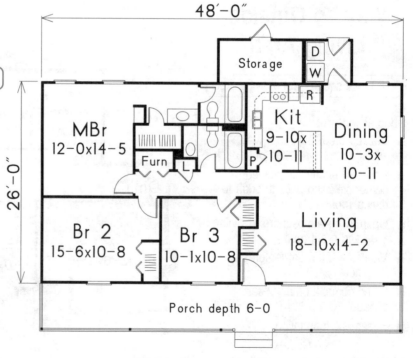

48'-0"

26'-0"

Storage

D
W
R

MBr
12-0x14-5

Furn
L

Kit
9-10x
10-11

P

Dining
10-3x
10-11

Br 2
15-6x10-8

Br 3
10-1x10-8

Living
18-10x14-2

Porch depth 6-0

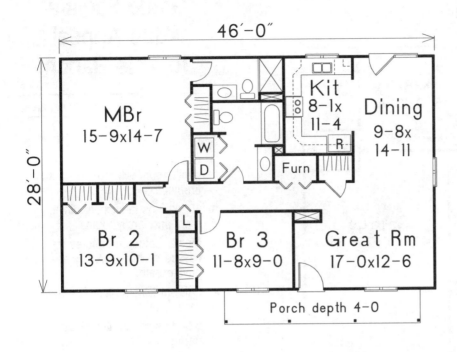

46'-0"

28'-0"

MBr
15-9x14-7

Kit
8-1x
11-4

Dining
9-8x
14-11

W
D

Furn

R

Br 2
13-9x10-1

L

Br 3
11-8x9-0

Great Rm
17-0x12-6

Porch depth 4-0

Peaceful Shaded Front Porch

1,288 total square feet of living area

Special features

- Kitchen, dining, and great rooms join to create open living space
- Master bedroom includes private bath
- Secondary bedrooms include ample closet space
- Hall bath features convenient laundry closet
- Dining room accesses outdoors
- 3 bedrooms, 2 baths
- Crawl space foundation, drawings also include basement and slab foundations

Price Code A

SINGLE-STORY under 2,000 square feet

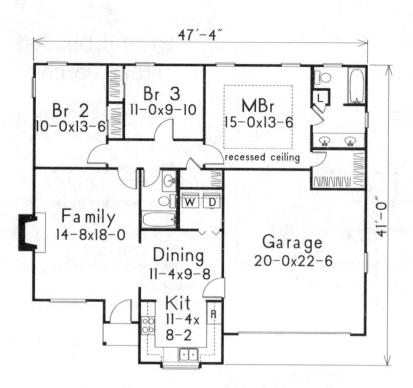

47'-4"

Br 2
10-0x13-6

Br 3
11-0x9-10

MBr
15-0x13-6
recessed ceiling

41'-0"

Family
14-8x18-0

W D

Dining
11-4x9-8

Garage
20-0x22-6

Kit
11-4x
8-2

Gable Facade Adds Appeal To This Ranch

1,304 total square feet of living area

Special features

- Covered entrance leads into family room with 10' ceiling and fireplace
- 10' ceilings in kitchen, dining room and family rooms
- Master bedroom features recessed ceiling, walk-in closet and private bath
- Efficient kitchen includes large window over the sink
- 3 bedrooms, 2 baths, 2-car garage
- Slab foundation

Price Code A

SINGLE-STORY under 2,000 square feet

Plan #X20-0292

To order blueprints use the form on page 322 or call toll-free 1-800-DREAM HOME (373-2646)

OREGON

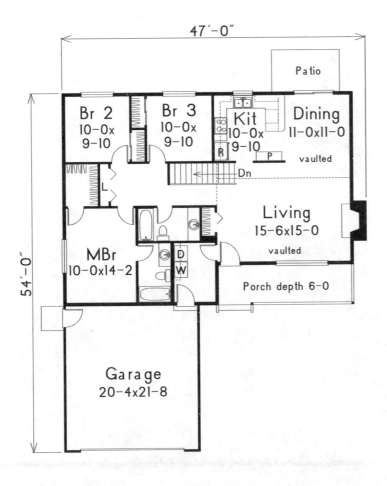

Economical Ranch For Easy Living

1,314 total square feet of living area

Special features

- Energy efficient home with 2" x 6" exterior walls
- Covered porch adds immediate appeal and welcoming charm
- Open floor plan combined with vaulted ceiling offers spacious living
- Functional kitchen complete with pantry and eating bar
- Cozy fireplace in the living room
- Private master bedroom features a large walk-in closet and bath
- 3 bedrooms, 2 baths, 2-car garage
- Basement foundation

Price Code A

SINGLE-STORY under 2,000 square feet

Plan #X20-0265

To order blueprints use the form on page 322 or call toll-free 1-800-DREAM HOME (373-2646)

Gabled, Covered Front Porch

1,320 total square feet of living area

Special features

- Functional U-shaped kitchen features pantry
- Large living and dining areas join to create open atmosphere
- Secluded master bedroom includes private full bath
- Covered front porch opens into large living area with convenient coat closet
- Utility/laundry room located near the kitchen
- 3 bedrooms and 2 baths
- Crawl space foundation

    Price Code A

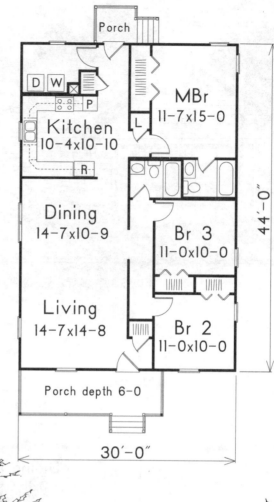

Porch

Kitchen
10-4x10-10

MBr
11-7x15-0

Dining
14-7x10-9

Br 3
11-0x10-0

Living
14-7x14-8

Br 2
11-0x10-0

Porch depth 6-0

44'-0"

30'-0"

SINGLE-STORY under 2,000 square feet

Plan #X20-0297

Open Living Area Adds Drama To Home

> 1,340 total square feet of living area

Special features

- Master bedroom with private bath and walk-in closet
- Recessed entry leads to vaulted family room with see-through fireplace to dining area
- Garage includes handy storage area
- Convenient laundry closet in the kitchen
- 3 bedrooms, 2 baths, 2-car side entry garage
- Slab foundation, drawings also include crawl space foundation

Price Code A

48'-0"

Deck

tray clg

MBr
13-6x13-6

Family
13-10x17-5

vaulted

Kit/Din
17-1x
17-5

W D P R

42'-0"

F W

Br 3
10-0x11-0

L

Garage
19-5x19-8

Br 2
11-1x11-0

Storage

Plan #X20-0255

SINGLE-STORY under 2,000 square feet

SAXONY II

Stylish Ranch With Rustic Charm

| 1,344 total square feet of living area |

Special features

- Family/dining room with sliding door
- Master bedroom and private bath with shower
- Hall bath includes double vanity for added convenience
- Kitchen features U-shaped design, large pantry and laundry area
- 3 bedrooms, 2 baths, 2-car garage
- Crawl space foundation, drawings also include basement and slab foundations

Price Code A

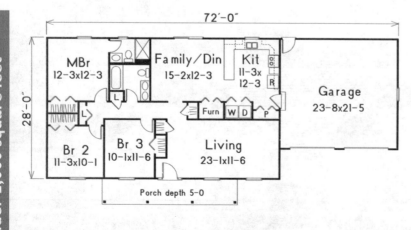

72'-0"

28'-0"

MBr
12-3x12-3

Family/Din
15-2x12-3

Kit
11-3x
12-3

Garage
23-8x21-5

Furn W D P

Br 2
11-3x10-1

Br 3
10-1x11-6

Living
23-1x11-6

Porch depth 5-0

Plan #X20-0515

To order blueprints use the form on page 322 or call toll-free 1-800-DREAM HOME (373-2646)

ASHLAND

Layout Features All The Essentials For Comfortable Living

1,344 total square feet of living area

Special features

- Kitchen has side entry, laundry area, pantry and joins family/dining area
- Master bedroom includes private bath
- Linen and storage closets in hall
- Covered porch opens to spacious living room with handy coat closet
- 3 bedrooms, 2 baths
- Crawl space foundation, drawings also include basement and slab foundations

    Price Code A

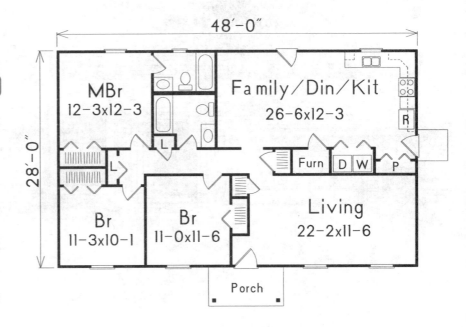

48'-0"

28'-0"

MBr
12-3x12-3

Family/Din/Kit
26-6x12-3

R

L

L

Furn | D | W | P

Br
11-3x10-1

Br
11-0x11-6

Living
22-2x11-6

Porch

SINGLE-STORY
under 2,000 square feet

Plan #X20-0585

Distinctive Ranch Has A Larger Look

| 1,360 total square feet of living area |

Special features

- Double-gabled front facade frames large windows

- Through-view from entry area to vaulted great room, fireplace and rear deck

- Vaulted ceiling and large windows add openness to kitchen/breakfast room

- Convenient den convertible to third bedroom

- Plan easily adapts to crawl space or slab construction, with the utilities replacing the stairs

- 3 bedrooms, 2 baths, 2-car garage

- Basement foundation

    Price Code A

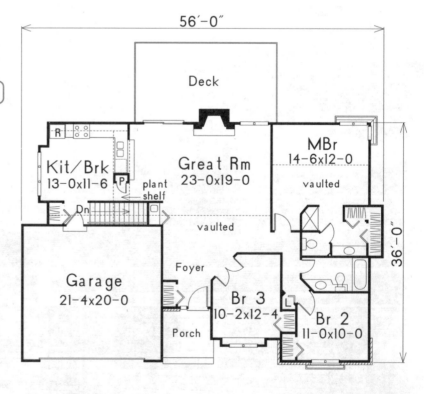

56'-0"

Deck

R

Kit/Brk
13-0x11-6

Great Rm
23-0x19-0
vaulted

MBr
14-6x12-0
vaulted

plant shelf

Dn

vaulted

36'-0"

Garage
21-4x20-0

Foyer

Br 3
10-2x12-4

Br 2
11-0x10-0

Porch

Plan #X20-0105

To order blueprints use the form on page 322 or call toll-free 1-800-DREAM HOME (373-2646)

Functional Layout For Comfortable Living

1,360 total square feet of living area

Special features

- Kitchen/dining room features island work space and plenty of dining area
- Master bedroom with large walk-in closet and private bath
- Laundry room adjacent to the kitchen for easy access
- Convenient workshop in garage
- Large closets in secondary bedrooms
- 3 bedrooms, 2 baths, 2-car side entry garage
- Basement foundation, drawings also include crawl space and slab foundations

Price Code A

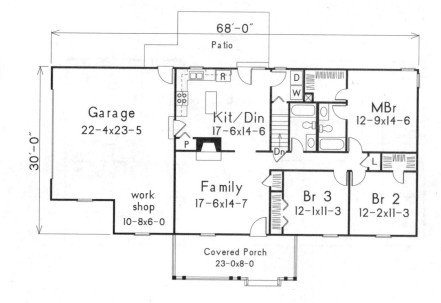

68'-0"

Patio

Garage 22-4x23-5

Kit/Din 17-6x14-6

MBr 12-9x14-6

30'-0"

work shop 10-8x6-0

Family 17-6x14-7

Br 3 12-1x11-3

Br 2 12-2x11-3

Covered Porch 23-0x8-0

Plan #X20-0217

To order blueprints use the form on page 322 or call toll-free 1-800-DREAM HOME (373-2646)

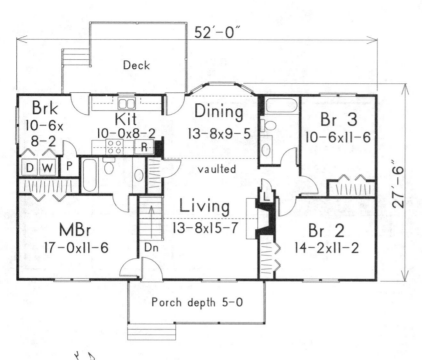

52'-0"

Deck

Brk
10-6x
8-2

Kit
10-0x8-2

D W P

MBr
17-0x11-6

Dn

Dining
13-8x9-5

vaulted

Living
13-8x15-7

L

R

Br 3
10-6x11-6

Br 2
14-2x11-2

27'-6"

Porch depth 5-0

Design Revolves Around Central Living Space

1,364 total square feet of living area

Special features

- Master bedroom includes full bath
- Pass-through kitchen opens into breakfast room with laundry closet and access to deck
- Energy efficient home with 2" x 6" exterior walls
- Joining the dining and living rooms with vaulted ceilings and a fireplace creates open living area
- Dining room features large bay window
- 3 bedrooms, 2 baths, 2-car drive under garage
- Basement foundation

Price Code A

SINGLE-STORY under 2,000 square feet

Plan #X20-0252

To order blueprints use the form on page 322 or call toll-free 1-800-DREAM HOME (373-2646)

FLORENCE

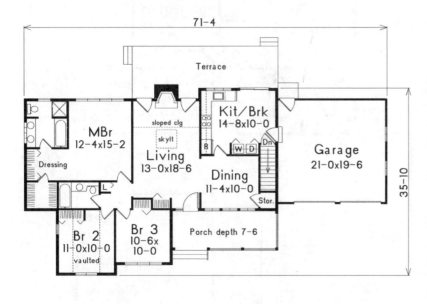

Comfortable One-Story Country Home

1,367 total square feet of living area

Special features

- Neat front porch shelters the entrance
- Dining room has full wall of windows and convenient storage area
- Breakfast area leads to the rear terrace through sliding doors
- Large living room with high ceiling, skylight and fireplace
- 3 bedrooms, 2 baths, 2-car garage
- Basement foundation, drawings also include slab foundation

Price Code A

Plan #X20-0676

To order blueprints use the form on page 322 or call toll-free 1-800-DREAM HOME (373-2646)

Great Room Window Adds Character Inside And Out

| 1,368 total square feet of living area |

Special features

- Entry foyer steps down to open living area which combines great room and formal dining area
- Vaulted master suite includes box bay window, large vanity, separate tub and shower
- Cozy breakfast area features direct access to the patio and pass-through kitchen
- Handy linen closet located in hall
- 3 bedrooms, 2 baths, 2-car garage
- Basement foundation

Price Code A

SINGLE-STORY under 2,000 square feet

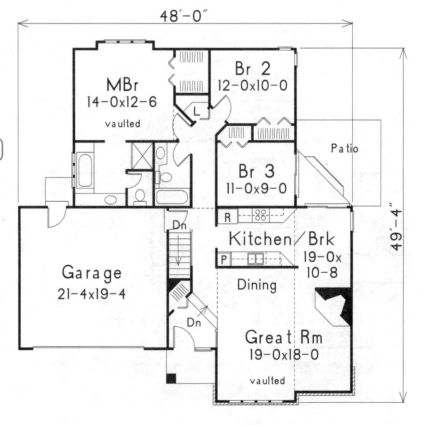

Plan #X20-0271

Distinctive Design, Convenient Floor Plan

1,375 total square feet of living area

Special features

- Attractive gables highlight home's exterior
- Centrally located living room with bay area
- Master suite features patio access, double walk-in-closets and private bath
- Side entry garage includes handy storage area
- 3 bedrooms, 2 baths, 2-car side entry garage
- Crawl space foundation, drawings also include basement and slab foundations

Price Code A

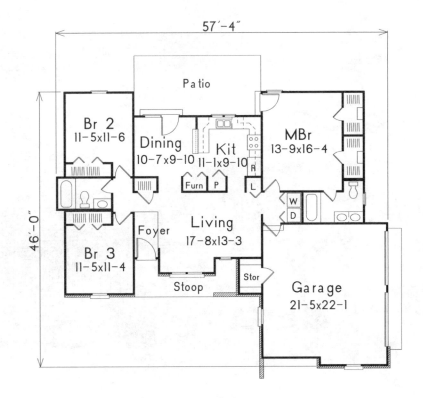

57'-4"

46'-0"

Patio

Br 2
11-5x11-6

Dining
10-7x9-10

Kit
11-1x9-10

MBr
13-9x16-4

Furn P

Living
17-8x13-3

Foyer

Br 3
11-5x11-4

Stoop

Stor

Garage
21-5x22-1

SINGLE-STORY under 2,000 square feet

Cozy Front Porch Welcomes Guests

1,393 total square feet of living area

Special features

- L-shaped kitchen features walk-in pantry, island cooktop and is convenient to laundry room and dining area

- Master bedroom features large walk-in closet and private bath with separate tub and shower

- Convenient storage/coat closet in hall

- View to the patio and garage from dining area

- 3 bedrooms, 2 baths, 2-car detached garage

- Crawl space foundation, drawings also include slab foundation

  Price Code B

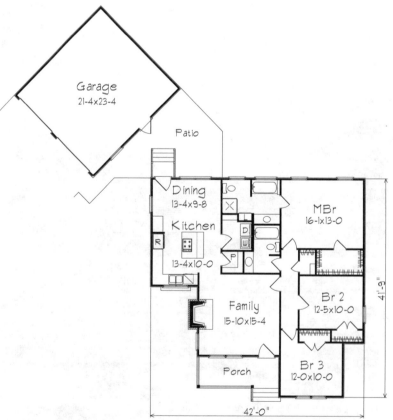

Garage
21-4x23-4

Patio

Dining
13-4x9-8

Kitchen
13-4x10-0

MBr
16-1x13-0

Family
15-10x15-4

Br 2
12-5x10-0

Porch

Br 3
12-0x10-0

41'-9"

42'-0"

FRANKLIN

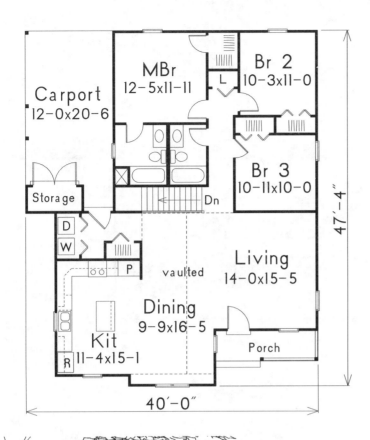

Carport
12-0x20-6

MBr
12-5x11-11

Br 2
10-3x11-0

L

Storage

Dn

Br 3
10-11x10-0

D
W

P

vaulted

Living
14-0x15-5

Dining
9-9x16-5

Kit
11-4x15-1

R

Porch

47'-4"

40'-0"

Compact Home With Functional Design

1,396 total square feet of living area

Special features

- Gabled front adds interest to facade
- Living and dining rooms share a vaulted ceiling
- Master bedroom features a walk-in closet and private bath
- Functional kitchen with a center work island and convenient pantry
- 3 bedrooms, 2 baths, 1-car carport
- Basement foundation, drawings also include crawl space foundation

Price Code A

SINGLE STORY
under 2,000 square feet

Plan #X20-0296

Spacious Interior For Open Living

1,400 total square feet of living area

Special features

- Front porch offers warmth and welcome

- Large great room opens into dining room creating open living atmosphere

- Kitchen features convenient laundry area, pantry and breakfast bar

- 3 bedrooms, 2 baths, 2-car garage

- Crawl space foundation, drawings also include basement and slab foundations

Price Code A

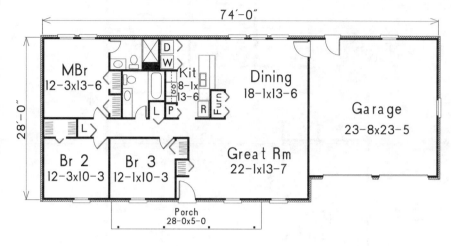

74'-0"

28'-0"

MBr
12-3x13-6

Kit
8-1x13-6

Dining
18-1x13-6

Garage
23-8x23-5

Br 2
12-3x10-3

Br 3
12-1x10-3

Great Rm
22-1x13-7

Porch
28-0x5-0

SINGLE-STORY
under 2,000 square feet

Plan #X20-0510

Classic Ranch Has Grand Appeal With Expansive Porch

1,400 total square feet of living area

Special features

- Master bedroom is secluded for privacy
- Large utility room with additional cabinet space
- Covered porch provides an outdoor seating area
- Roof dormers add great curb appeal
- Vaulted ceilings in living room and master bedroom
- Oversize 2-car garage with storage
- 3 bedrooms, 2 baths, 2-car garage
- Basement foundation, drawings also include crawl space foundation

Price Code A

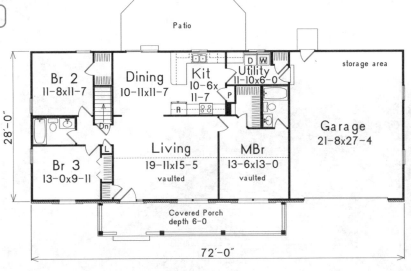

SINGLE-STORY under 2,000 square feet

Central Fireplace Focuses Family Living

1,408 total square feet of living area

Special features

- Handsome see-through fireplace offers a gathering point for the family room and breakfast/kitchen area
- Vaulted ceiling and large bay window in the master bedroom add charm to this room
- A dramatic angular wall and large windows add brightness to the kitchen/breakfast area
- Family room and breakfast/kitchen area have vaulted ceilings, adding to this central living area
- 3 bedrooms, 2 baths, 2-car garage
- Crawl space foundation, drawings also include slab foundation

Price Code A

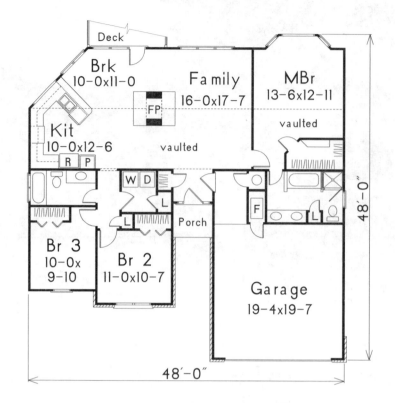

Deck

Brk
10-0x11-0

Family
16-0x17-7

MBr
13-6x12-11

vaulted

FP

Kit
10-0x12-6

vaulted

R   P

W   D

L

F

L

L

Porch

Br 3
10-0x
9-10

Br 2
11-0x10-7

Garage
19-4x19-7

48'-0"

48'-0"

Plan #X20-0181

To order blueprints use the form on page 322 or call toll-free 1-800-DREAM HOME (373-2646)

WYDOWN

Spacious And Open Family Living Area

1,416 total square feet of living area

Special features

- Family room includes fireplace, elevated plant shelf and vaulted ceiling
- Patio is accessible from dining area and garage
- Centrally located laundry area
- Oversized walk-in pantry
- 3 bedrooms, 2 baths, 2-car garage
- Basement foundation, drawings also include crawl space and slab foundations

Price Code A

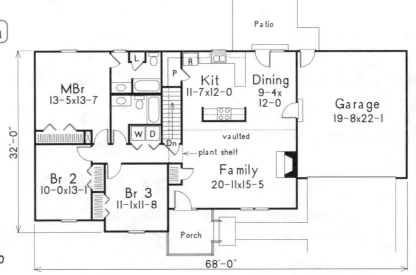

Patio

MBr
13-5x13-7

Kit
11-7x12-0

Dining
9-4x
12-0

Garage
19-8x22-1

32'-0"

W D

Dn

vaulted

plant shelf

Br 2
10-0x13-1

Br 3
11-1x11-8

Family
20-11x15-5

Porch

68'-0"

SINGLE-STORY under 2,000 square feet

Plan #X20-0226

To order blueprints use the form on page 322 or call toll-free 1-800-DREAM HOME (373-2646)

Vaulted Ceilings Throughout Create Dramatic Interior

1,428 total square feet of living area

Special features

- 10' ceiling in entry and hallway
- Vaulted dining room combines a desk area near the see-through fireplace
- Energy efficient home with 2" x 6" exterior walls
- Vaulted secondary bedrooms
- Kitchen loaded with amenities including an island with salad sink and pantry
- Master bedroom with vaulted ceilings includes large walk-in closet and private master bath
- 3 bedrooms, 2 baths, 2-car garage
- Basement foundation, drawings also include crawl space foundation

Price Code A

SINGLE-STORY under 2,000 square feet

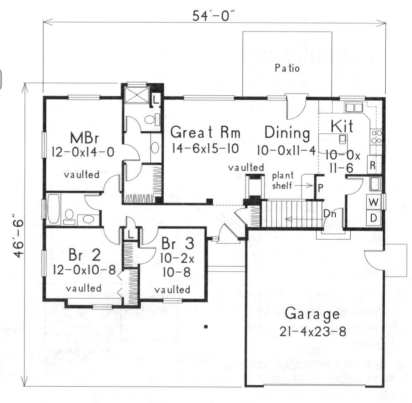

54'-0"

46'-6"

Patio

MBr 12-0x14-0 vaulted

Great Rm 14-6x15-10

Dining 10-0x11-4 vaulted

Kit 10-0x 11-6

plant shelf

P

Dn

R

W D

Br 2 12-0x10-8 vaulted

Br 3 10-2x 10-8 vaulted

Garage 21-4x23-8

Plan #X20-0269

Secluded Master Suite Has Private Patio Area

1,438 total square feet of living area

Special features

- Vaulted living room and dining room unite to provide open space for entertaining
- Secondary bedrooms share full bath
- Compact kitchen
- Vaulted master bedroom includes private bath, large walk-in closet and access to patio
- 3 bedrooms, 2 baths, 2-car side entry garage
- Crawl space foundation, drawings also include slab foundation

Price Code A

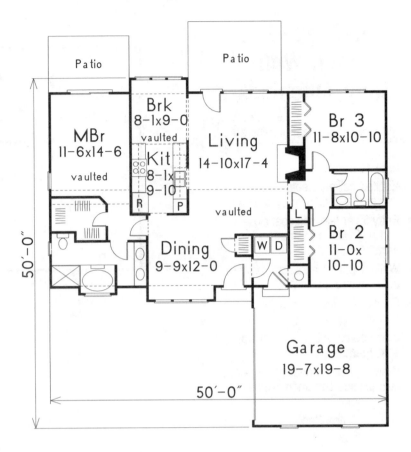

Patio

Patio

MBr
11-6x14-6
vaulted

Brk
8-1x9-0
vaulted

Kit
8-1x
9-10

Living
14-10x17-4

Br 3
11-8x10-10

vaulted

Dining
9-9x12-0

R   P

W D

L

Br 2
11-0x
10-10

50'-0"

50'-0"

Garage
19-7x19-8

SINGLE-STORY
under 2,000 square feet

L-Shaped Ranch With Many Amenities

1,440 total square feet of living area

Special features

- Vaulted ceiling creates an impressive dining/living area
- Entry foyer features coat closet and half wall leading into living area
- Walk-in pantry adds convenience to U-shaped kitchen
- Spacious utility room adjacent to garage
- 3 bedrooms, 2 baths, 2-car side entry garage
- Crawl space foundation, drawings also include basement and slab foundations

Price Code A

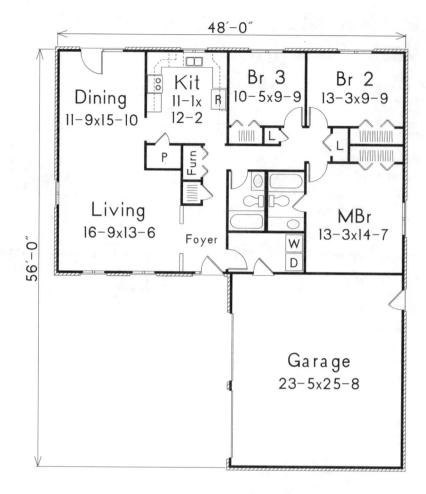

SINGLE-STORY under 2,000 square feet

Plan #X20-0533

To order blueprints use the form on page 322 or call toll-free 1-800-DREAM HOME (373-2646)

MORTLAND

Central Fireplace Warms This Cozy Contemporary

1,442 total square feet of living area

Special features

- Centrally located living room with recessed fireplace and 10' ceiling
- The large U-shaped kitchen offers an eating bar and pantry
- Expanded garage provides extra storage and work area
- Spacious master bedroom with sitting area and large walk-in closet
- 3 bedrooms, 2 baths, 2-car garage
- Slab foundation, drawings also include crawl space foundation

Price Code A

SINGLE-STORY
under 2,000 square feet

STRATTON

High-Style Vaulted Ranch

| 1,453 total square feet of living area |

Special features

- Decorative vents, window trim, shutters, and brick blend to create dramatic curb appeal

- Energy efficient home with 2" x 6" exterior walls

- Kitchen opens to living area and includes salad sink in the island, pantry and handy laundry room

- Exquisite master bedroom highlighted by vaulted ceiling

- Dressing area with walk-in closet, private bath and spa tub/shower

- 3 bedrooms, 2 baths, 2-car garage

- Basement foundation, drawings also include crawl space foundation

    Price Code A

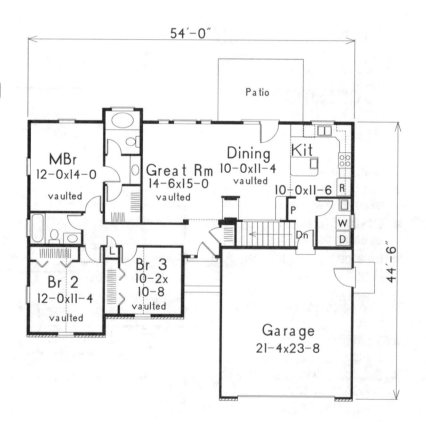

Plan #X20-0267

To order blueprints use the form on page 322 or call toll-free 1-800-DREAM HOME (373-2646)

DAVENPORT

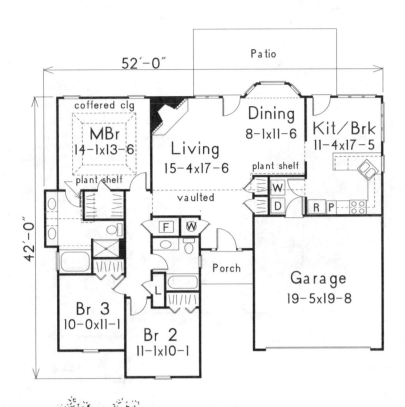

52'-0"

Patio

coffered clg

MBr
14-1x13-6

plant shelf

Living
15-4x17-6

vaulted

Dining
8-1x11-6

plant shelf

Kit/Brk
11-4x17-5

W
D

R P

42'-0"

F W

L

Porch

Br 3
10-0x11-1

Br 2
11-1x10-1

Garage
19-5x19-8

Impressive Corner Fireplace Highlights The Living Area

1,458 total square feet of living area

Special features

- Convenient snack bar joins kitchen with breakfast room
- Large living/dining room with fireplace, plenty of windows, vaulted ceiling and plant shelves
- Master bedroom offers a private bath with vaulted ceiling, walk-in closet, plant shelf and coffered ceiling
- Corner windows provide abundant light in breakfast room
- 3 bedrooms, 2 baths, 2-car garage
- Crawl space foundation, drawings also include slab foundation

Price Code A

SINGLE-STORY under 2,000 square feet

Plan #X20-0253

Rambling Country Bungalow

1,475 total square feet of living area

Special features

- Family room features a high ceiling and prominent corner fireplace
- Kitchen with island counter and garden window makes a convenient connection between the family and dining rooms
- Private hallway leads to the three bedrooms, all with large walk-in closets
- Covered breezeway joins main house and garage
- Full width entry covered porch lends a country touch
- 3 bedrooms, 2 baths, 2-car garage
- Slab foundation, drawings also include crawl space foundation

Price Code B

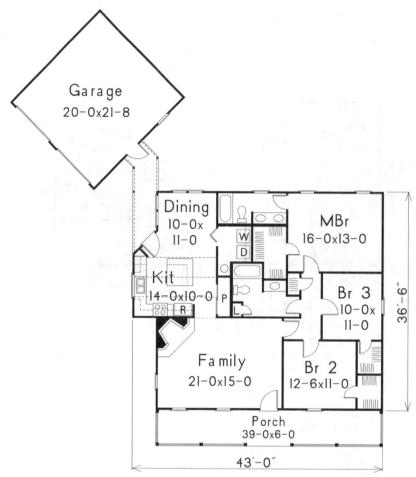

Garage
20-0x21-8

Dining
10-0x
11-0

MBr
16-0x13-0

Kit
14-0x10-0

Br 3
10-0x
11-0

Family
21-0x15-0

Br 2
12-6x11-0

Porch
39-0x6-0

36'-6"

43'-0"

SINGLE-STORY
under 2,000 square feet

Plan #X20-0203

To order blueprints use the form on page 322 or call toll-free 1-800-DREAM HOME (373-2646)

MAYLAND

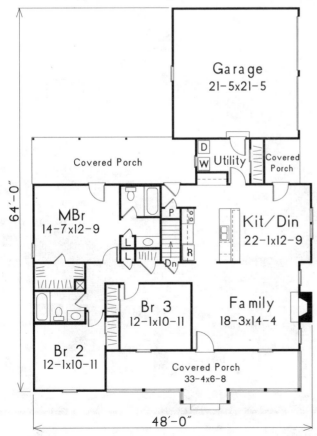

Country-Style Home With Large Front Porch

1,501 total square feet of living area

Special features

- Spacious kitchen with dining area open to outside
- Convenient utility room adjacent to garage
- Master suite with private bath, dressing area and access to large covered porch
- Large family room creates openness
- 3 bedrooms, 2 baths, 2-car side entry garage
- Basement foundation, drawings also include crawl space and slab foundations

Price Code B

SINGLE-STORY under 2,000 square feet

Plan #X20-0249

To order blueprints use the form on page 322 or call toll-free 1-800-DREAM HOME (373-2646)

193

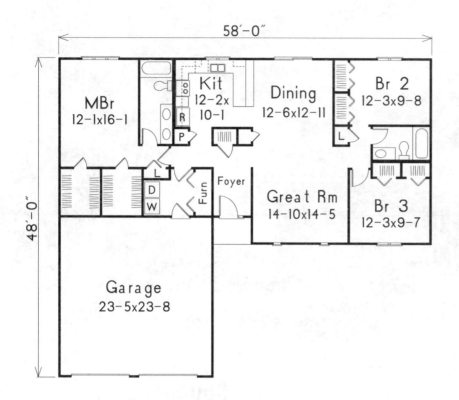

Beauty And Practicality Designed As One

1,504 total square feet of living area

Special features

- Private master bedroom features double walk-in closets, linen closet and bath
- Laundry room conveniently located near garage
- Great room and dining room layout creates open living atmosphere
- Generous closet space in secondary bedrooms
- Kitchen features breakfast bar, pantry and storage closet
- 3 bedrooms, 2 baths, 2-car garage
- Crawl space foundation, drawings also include basement and slab foundations

Price Code B

SINGLE-STORY under 2,000 square feet

Plan #X20-0531

To order blueprints use the form on page 322 or call toll-free 1-800-DREAM HOME (373-2646)

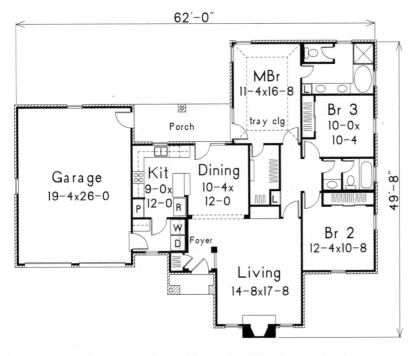

62'-0"

Garage
19-4x26-0

Porch

MBr
11-4x16-8

tray clg

Br 3
10-0x
10-4

Kit
9-0x
12-0

P

R

W
D

Foyer

Dining
10-4x
12-0

L

Br 2
12-4x10-8

Living
14-8x17-8

49'-8"

Built-In Media Center Focal Point In Living Room

1,539 total square feet of living area

Special features

- Standard 9' ceilings
- Master bedroom features 10' tray ceiling, access to porch, ample closet space and full bath
- Serving counter separates kitchen and dining room
- Foyer with handy coat closet opens to living area with fireplace
- Handy utility room near kitchen
- 3 bedrooms, 2 baths, 2-car garage
- Slab foundation

Price Code B

SINGLE-STORY under 2,000 square feet

Plan #X20-0246

Spacious And Centrally Located Family Area

1,539 total square feet of living area

Special features

- Large master suite with private bath has access to patio
- Convenient laundry room located between carport and kitchen
- Bedrooms secluded off living areas for added privacy
- Private dining area with bay window for elegant entertaining
- Attached carport offers additional roomy storage area
- 3 bedrooms, 2 baths, 2-car attached carport
- Slab foundation

        Price Code B

SINGLE-STORY under 2,000 square feet

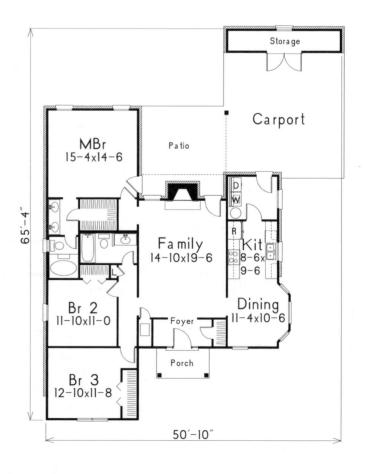

Storage

Carport

MBr
15-4x14-6

Patio

65'-4"

D W

Family
14-10x19-6

Kit
8-6x
9-6

R

Br 2
11-10x11-0

Foyer

Dining
11-4x10-6

Br 3
12-10x11-8

Porch

50'-10"

OAKRIDGE

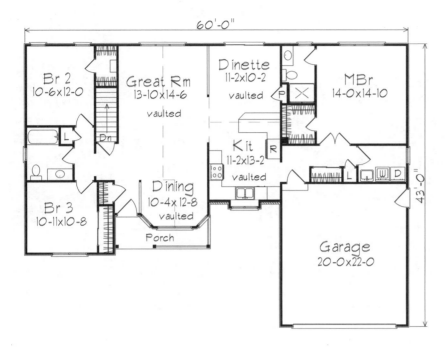

- Br 2
  10-6x12-0
- Great Rm
  13-10x14-6
  vaulted
- Dinette
  11-2x10-2
  vaulted
- MBr
  14-0x14-10
- Dn
- Dining
  10-4x12-8
  vaulted
- Kit
  11-2x13-2
  vaulted
- R
- P
- Br 3
  10-11x10-8
- Porch
- L
- W
- D
- Garage
  20-0x22-0

60'-0"

43'-0"

Central Living Area Keeps Bedrooms Private

1,546 total square feet of living area

Special features

- Spacious open rooms create casual atmosphere
- Master suite secluded for privacy
- Dining room features large bay window
- Kitchen/dinette room combination offers access to the outdoors
- Large laundry room includes convenient sink
- 3 bedrooms, 2 baths, 2-car garage
- Basement foundation

Price Code B

SINGLE-STORY under 2,000 square feet

Plan #X20-0382

To order blueprints use the form on page 322 or call toll-free 1-800-DREAM HOME (373-2646)

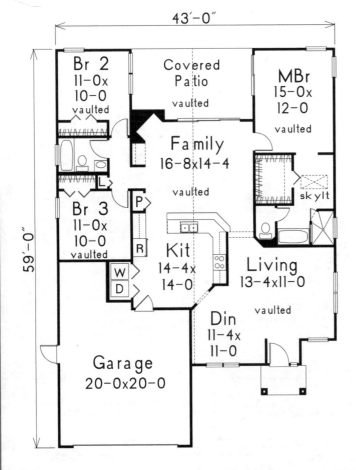

Vaulted Ceilings
Add Dimension

| 1,550 total square feet of living area |

Special features

- Cozy corner fireplace provides focal point in family room
- Master bedroom features large walk-in closet, skylight and separate tub and shower
- Convenient laundry closet
- Kitchen with pantry and breakfast bar connects to family room
- Family room and master bedroom access covered patio
- 3 bedrooms, 2 baths, 2-car garage
- Slab foundation

   Price Code B

Plan #X20-0357

VICKSDALE

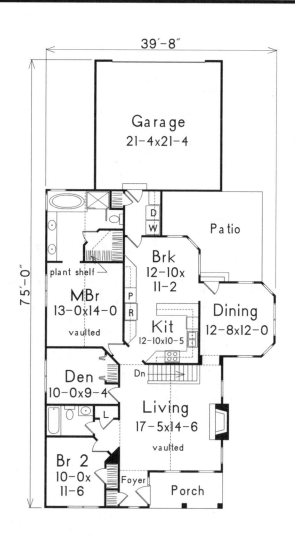

39'-8"

Garage
21-4x21-4

75'-0"

Patio

plant shelf

D
W

Brk
12-10x
11-2

MBr
13-0x14-0
vaulted

P
R

Kit
12-10x10-5

Dining
12-8x12-0

Den
10-0x9-4

Dn

Living
17-5x14-6
vaulted

L

Br 2
10-0x
11-6

Foyer

Porch

Innovative Design For That Narrow Lot

> 1,558 total square feet of living area

Special features

- Illuminated spaces created by visual access to outside living areas
- Vaulted master bedroom features private bath with whirlpool tub, separate shower and large walk-in closet
- Convenient main floor laundry with garage access
- Den or third bedroom
- U-shaped kitchen adjacent to sunny breakfast area
- 2 bedrooms, 2 baths, 2-car rear entry garage
- Basement foundation

Price Code B

SINGLE-STORY under 2,000 square feet

Plan #X20-0394

To order blueprints use the form on page 322 or call toll-free 1-800-DREAM HOME (373-2646)

Lovely, Spacious Floor Plan

1,558 total square feet of living area

Special features

- Spacious utility room located conveniently between garage and kitchen/dining area

- Bedrooms separated off main living areas by hallway adds privacy

- Enormous living area with fireplace and vaulted ceilings opens to kitchen and dining area

- Master suite enhanced with large bay window, walk-in closet and private bath

- 3 bedrooms, 2 baths, 2-car garage

- Basement foundation

  Price Code B

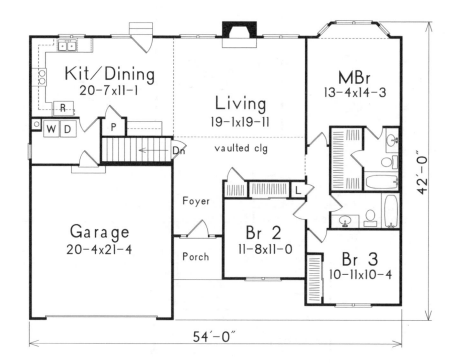

Kit/Dining 20-7x11-1

Living 19-1x19-11
vaulted clg

MBr 13-4x14-3

Garage 20-4x21-4

Foyer

Porch

Br 2 11-8x11-0

Br 3 10-11x10-4

42'-0"

54'-0"

Plan #X20-0702

HILLSBORO

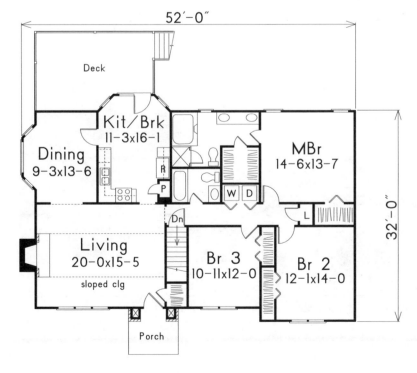

52'-0"

Deck

Kit/Brk
11-3x16-1

Dining
9-3x13-6

MBr
14-6x13-7

R

W D

P

32'-0"

Dn

L

Living
20-0x15-5

sloped clg

Br 3
10-11x12-0

Br 2
12-1x14-0

Porch

Compact Layout, Amenity Full

1,567 total square feet of living area

Special features

- Front gables and extended porch add charm to facade
- Large bay windows add brightness to breakfast and dining rooms
- The master bath boasts an oversized tub, separate shower, double sinks and large walk-in closet
- Living room features a vaulted ceiling and a prominent fireplace
- 3 bedrooms, 2 baths, 2-car garage
- Basement foundation

  Price Code B

SINGLE-STORY under 2,000 square feet

Plan #X20-0180

Circletop Transom Window Graces This Exterior

1,588 total square feet of living area

Special features

- Family and dining rooms access rear patio

- Angled walkway leads guests by an attractive landscape area

- Master bedroom with separate dressing area, walk-in closet and private bath

- Sunken living room features an attractive railing on two sides

- U-shaped kitchen complete with large pantry and eating bar

- 3 bedrooms, 2 baths, 2-car garage

- Basement foundation, drawings also include crawl space and slab foundations

Price Code B

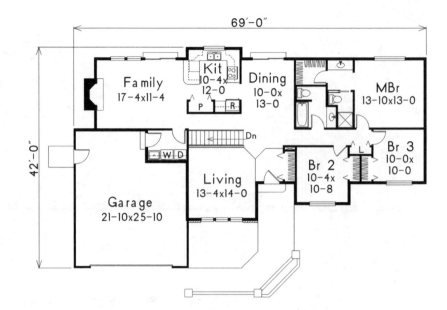

Family 17-4x11-4
Kit 10-4x 12-0
Dining 10-0x 13-0
MBr 13-10x13-0
Br 3 10-0x 10-0
Br 2 10-4x 10-8
Living 13-4x14-0
Garage 21-10x25-10
69'-0"
42'-0"

SINGLE-STORY under 2,000 square feet

Plan #X20-0266

To order blueprints use the form on page 322 or call toll-free 1-800-DREAM HOME (373-2646)

Covered Porch Is Focal Point Of Entry

1,595 total square feet of living area

Special features

- Dining room with convenient built-in desk also provides access to the outdoors
- L-shaped kitchen area features island cook top
- Family room has high ceiling and a fireplace
- Private master suite includes large walk-in closet and bath with separate tub and shower units
- 3 bedrooms, 2 baths, 2-car side entry garage
- Slab foundation, drawings also include crawl space foundation

Price Code B

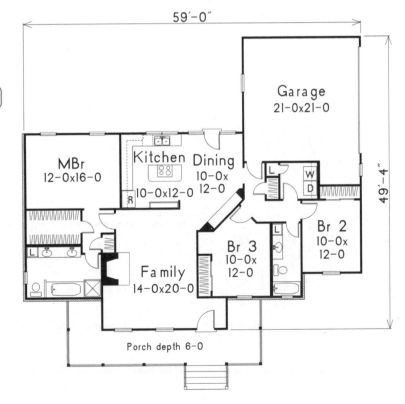

59'-0"

Garage
21-0x21-0

49'-4"

MBr
12-0x16-0

Kitchen
10-0x12-0

Dining
10-0x
12-0

L W
   D

R

L

Br 2
10-0x
12-0

Br 3
10-0x
12-0

Family
14-0x20-0

L

Porch depth 6-0

SINGLE-STORY under 2,000 square feet

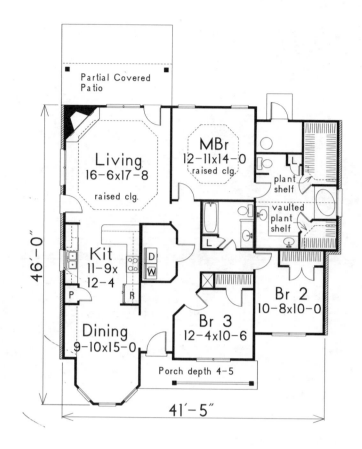

BELCOURT

Spacious Master Suite Adds Luxury

| 1,596 total square feet of living area |

Special features

- Large corner fireplace enhances living area
- Centrally located utility room provides convenient access
- Master bath features double walk-in closets, oversized tub and plant shelves
- Both the living area and master suite are accented with raised ceilings
- Bay window in dining area adds interest and light
- 3 bedrooms, 2 baths
- Slab foundation

Price Code B

Partial Covered Patio

Living 16-6x17-8 raised clg.

MBr 12-11x14-0 raised clg.

plant shelf

vaulted plant shelf

Kit 11-9x 12-4

Br 2 10-8x10-0

Dining 9-10x15-0

Br 3 12-4x10-6

Porch depth 4-5

46'-0"

41'-5"

SINGLE-STORY under 2,000 square feet

Plan #X20-0687

Elegant Contemporary Features Formal Living

1,600 total square feet of living area

Special features

- Impressive sunken living room with massive stone fireplace and 16' vaulted ceilings
- Dining room conveniently located next to kitchen and divided for privacy
- Energy efficient home with 2" x 6" exterior walls
- Special amenities include sewing room, glass shelves in the kitchen and master bath and a large utility area
- The sunken master bedroom features a distinctive sitting room
- 3 bedrooms, 2 baths, 2-car side entry garage
- Slab foundation, drawings also include crawl space and basement foundations

Price Code C

SINGLE-STORY under 2,000 square feet

Floor plan labels:
- Br 2 11-5x11-6
- Sunken Living 18-0x17-6 vaulted
- MBr 11-8x13-6
- Sitting 7-8x 8-1
- Storage 10-8x8-8
- Br 3 11-5x11-3
- Dining 11-0x11-3
- Kit 10-0x 11-3
- Entry
- Garage 21-4x21-8
- Porch depth 7-0
- 30'-0"
- 75'-0"

Vaulted Ceilings Create Spacious Feeling

1,605 total square feet of living area

Special features

- Vaulted ceilings in great room and kitchen/breakfast area

- Spacious great room features large bay window, fireplace, built-in bookshelves and a convenient wet bar

- Dine in formal dining room or breakfast room overlooking rear yard, perfect for entertaining or everyday living

- Master bedroom has a spacious master bath with oval tub and separate shower

- 3 bedrooms, 2 baths, 2-car garage

- Basement foundation, drawings also include slab and crawl space foundations

Price Code B

SINGLE-STORY under 2,000 square feet

64'-0"

40'-0"

Patio

Brk
10-8x8-11

Great Rm
17-9x19-5
vaulted

MBr
12-11x14-11

Kit
10-8x
10-6

W
D

Garage
18-8x21-9

Dining
11-5x10-8

Entry

Dn

Br 3
10-0x
11-9

Br 2
10-11x10-9

Porch

Plan #X20-0110
To order blueprints use the form on page 322 or call toll-free 1-800-DREAM HOME (373-2646)

BAKERSVILLE

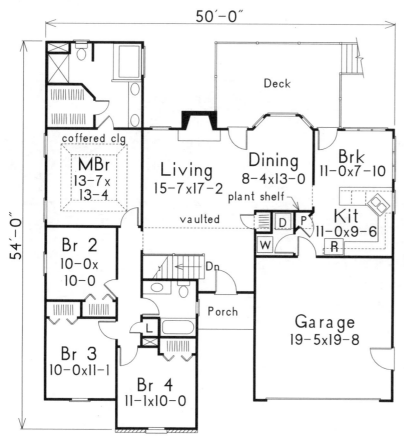

50'-0"

54'-0"

Deck

MBr
13-7x
13-4

coffered clg.

Living
15-7x17-2

vaulted

plant shelf

Dining
8-4x13-0

Brk
11-0x7-10

Kit
11-0x9-6

D P

W R

Br 2
10-0x
10-0

Dn

Porch

Garage
19-5x19-8

Br 3
10-0x11-1

L

Br 4
11-1x10-0

Dormers And Stone Veneer Add Exterior Appeal

| 1,609 total square feet of living area |

Special features

- Efficient kitchen with corner pantry and adjacent laundry room
- Breakfast room boasts plenty of windows and opens onto rear deck
- Master bedroom features tray ceiling and private deluxe bath
- Entry opens into large living area with fireplace
- 4 bedrooms, 2 baths, 2-car garage
- Basement foundation

Price Code B

Plan #X20-0295

To order blueprints use the form on page 322 or call toll-free 1-800-DREAM HOME (373-2646)

SYCAMORE

Open Ranch Design Gives Expansive Look

1,630 total square feet of living area

Special features

- Crisp facade and full windows front and back offer open viewing
- Wrap-around rear deck is accessible from breakfast room, dining room and master bedroom
- Vaulted ceiling in living room and master bedroom
- Sitting area and large walk-in closet complement master bath
- Master bedroom has a private sitting area
- 3 bedrooms, 2 baths, 2-car garage
- Basement foundation

   Price Code B

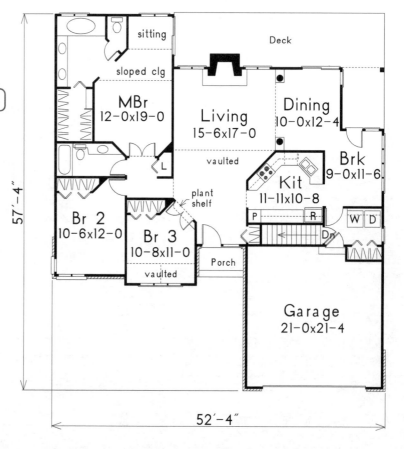

Floor plan labels:

- sitting
- sloped clg
- MBr 12-0x19-0
- Deck
- Living 15-6x17-0 vaulted
- Dining 10-0x12-4
- Brk 9-0x11-6
- L
- plant shelf
- Kit 11-11x10-8
- P   R   W   D
- Br 2 10-6x12-0
- Br 3 10-8x11-0 vaulted
- Porch
- Garage 21-0x21-4
- 57'-4"
- 52'-4"

Plan #X20-0161

To order blueprints use the form on page 322 or call toll-free 1-800-DREAM HOME (373-2646)

BEDFORD

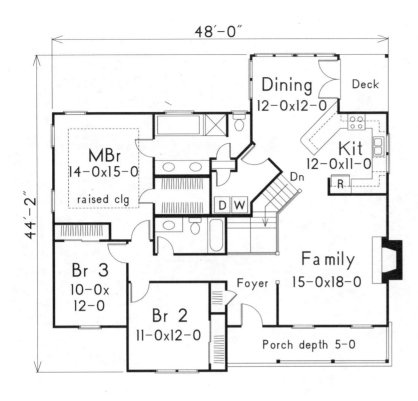

48'-0"

44'-2"

MBr
14-0x15-0
raised clg

Dining
12-0x12-0

Deck

Kit
12-0x11-0

R

Dn

D W

Family
15-0x18-0

Foyer

Br 3
10-0x
12-0

Br 2
11-0x12-0

Porch depth 5-0

Family Room With Fireplace Perfect For Central Gathering

| 1,631 total square feet of living area |

Special features

- 9' ceilings throughout this home
- Utility room conveniently located near kitchen
- Roomy kitchen and dining areas boast a breakfast bar and patio access
- Raised ceiling accents master suite
- 3 bedrooms, 2 baths, 2-car drive under garage
- Basement foundation

Price Code B

SINGLE-STORY under 2,000 square feet

Plan #X20-0237
To order blueprints use the form on page 322 or call toll-free 1-800-DREAM HOME (373-2646)

Covered Porch Adds Charm To Entrance

SINGLE-STORY under 2,000 square feet

| 1,655 total square feet of living area |

Special features

- Master bedroom features 9' ceiling, walk-in closet and bath with dressing area
- Oversized family room includes 10' ceiling and masonry see-through fireplace
- Island kitchen with convenient access to laundry room
- Handy covered walkway from garage to dining/kitchen area
- 3 bedrooms, 2 baths, 2-car garage
- Crawl space foundation

Price Code B

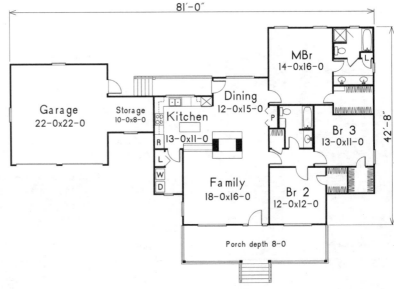

81'-0"

Garage 22-0x22-0

Storage 10-0x8-0

Kitchen 13-0x11-0

Dining 12-0x15-0

MBr 14-0x16-0

Br 3 13-0x11-0

Family 18-0x16-0

Br 2 12-0x12-0

42'-8"

Porch depth 8-0

BAY RANCH

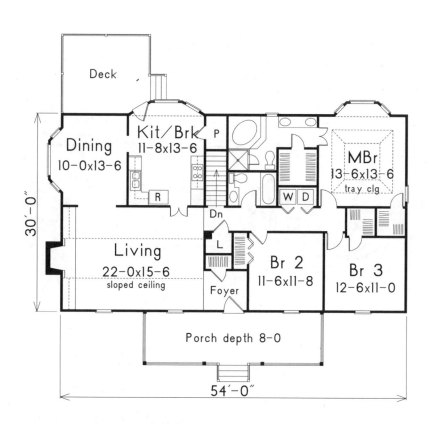

Deck

Dining
10-0x13-6

Kit/Brk
11-8x13-6

P

MBr
13-6x13-6
tray clg

R

W D

Dn

30'-0"

Living
22-0x15-6
sloped ceiling

L

Br 2
11-6x11-8

Br 3
12-6x11-0

Foyer

Porch depth 8-0

54'-0"

Bay Window Graces Luxury Master Bedroom

| 1,668 total square feet of living area |

Special features

- Large bay windows in breakfast area, master bedroom and dining room
- Extensive walk-in closets and storage spaces throughout the home
- Handy entry covered porch
- Large living room has fireplace, built-in bookshelves and sloped ceiling
- 3 bedrooms, 2 baths, 2-car drive under garage
- Basement foundation

Price Code C

SINGLE-STORY under 2,000 square feet

Plan #X20-0112
To order blueprints use the form on page 322 or call toll-free 1-800-DREAM HOME (373-2646)

Circle-Top Windows Grace The Facade Of This Home

| 1,672 total square feet of living area |

Special features

- Vaulted master suite features walk-in closet and adjoining bath with separate tub and shower
- Energy efficient home with 2" x 6" exterior walls
- Covered front and rear porches
- 12' ceilings in living room, kitchen and front secondary bedroom
- Kitchen complete with pantry, angled bar and adjacent eating area
- Sloped ceiling in dining room
- 3 bedrooms, 2 baths, 2-car side entry garage
- Crawl space foundation, drawings also include basement and slab foundations

Price Code C

SINGLE-STORY under 2,000 square feet

Floor plan labels:

Garage 22-0x22-0
Patio
Stor. 16-0x6-0
Deck
Br 3 12-0x12-0
Dining 14-0x13-0
skylt
MBr 16-0x14-0 vaulted
Brk 10-0x 12-0
Kit 12-0x 13-0
Living 18-0x18-0
Br 2 12-0x12-0
Porch Depth 6-0
54'-0"
68'-0"
D W
R
P

Plan #X20-0284
To order blueprints use the form on page 322 or call toll-free 1-800-DREAM HOME (373-2646)

ROCKWOOD

Sculptured Roof Line And Facade Add Charm

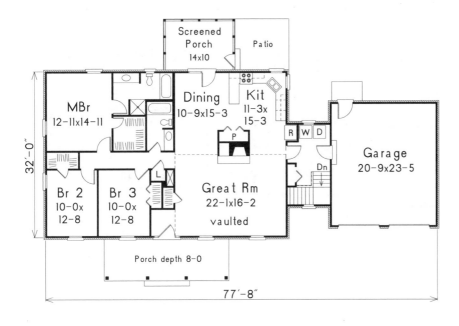

Screened Porch 14x10

Patio

MBr 12-11x14-11

Dining 10-9x15-3

Kit 11-3x 15-3

R W D

Garage 20-9x23-5

32'-0"

Br 2 10-0x 12-8

Br 3 10-0x 12-8

P

Dn

Great Rm 22-1x16-2 vaulted

Porch depth 8-0

77'-8"

1,674 total square feet of living area

Special features

- Great room, dining area and kitchen, surrounded with vaulted ceiling, central fireplace and log bin

- Convenient laundry/mud room located between garage and family area with handy stairs to basement

- Easily expandable screened porch and adjacent patio with access from dining area

- Master bedroom features full bath with tub, separate shower and walk-in closet

- 3 bedrooms, 2 baths, 2-car garage

- Basement foundation, drawings also include crawl space and slab foundations

Price Code B

SINGLE-STORY under 2,000 square feet

Plan #X20-0227

To order blueprints use the form on page 322 or call toll-free 1-800-DREAM HOME (373-2646)

Vaulted Ceilings And Light Add Dimension

1,676 total square feet of living area

Special features

- The living area skylights and large breakfast room with bay window provide plenty of sunlight

- The master bedroom has a walk-in closet; the secondary bedrooms are accented with a circle-top window in one and large closets in both

- Vaulted ceilings, plant shelving and a fireplace provide a quality living area

- 3 bedrooms, 2 baths, 2-car garage

- Basement foundation, drawings also include crawl space and slab foundations

Price Code B

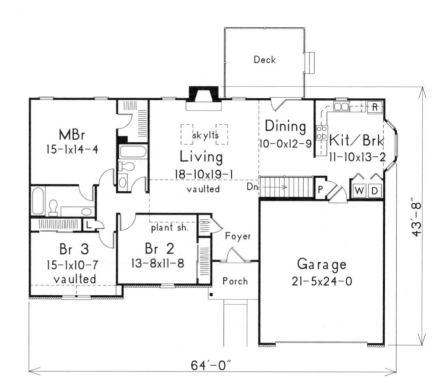

SINGLE-STORY under 2,000 square feet

214

BRADLEY

See-Through Fireplace Joins Gathering Rooms

1,684 total square feet of living area

Special features

- Convenient double-doors in dining area provide access to large deck
- Family room features several large windows for brightness
- Bedrooms separate from living areas for privacy
- Master bedroom suite offers bath with walk-in closet, double-bowl vanity and both shower and whirlpool tub
- 3 bedrooms, 2 1/2 baths, 2-car garage
- Basement foundation

    Price Code B

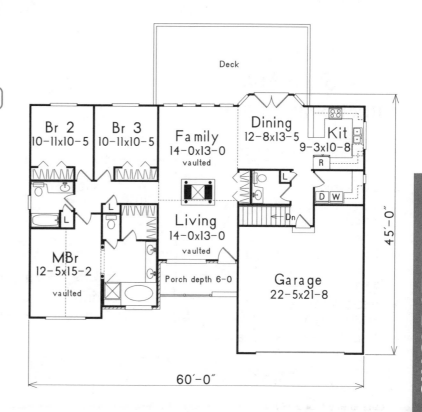

Deck

Br 2
10-11x10-5

Br 3
10-11x10-5

Family
14-0x13-0
vaulted

Dining
12-8x13-5

Kit
9-3x10-8

MBr
12-5x15-2
vaulted

Living
14-0x13-0
vaulted

Porch depth 6-0

Garage
22-5x21-8

45'-0"

60'-0"

SINGLE-STORY
under 2,000 square feet

Plan #X20-0393

To order blueprints use the form on page 322 or call toll-free 1-800-DREAM HOME (373-2646)

215

Balance Of Style And Functional Design

1,698 total square feet of living area

Special features

- Kitchen includes walk-in pantry and corner sink that faces living area
- Breakfast room highlighted by expanse of windows and access to sun deck
- Recessed foyer opens into vaulted living room with fireplace
- Master suite features private bath with large walk-in closet
- 3 bedrooms, 2 baths, 2-car drive under garage
- Basement foundation

Price Code B

SINGLE-STORY under 2,000 square feet

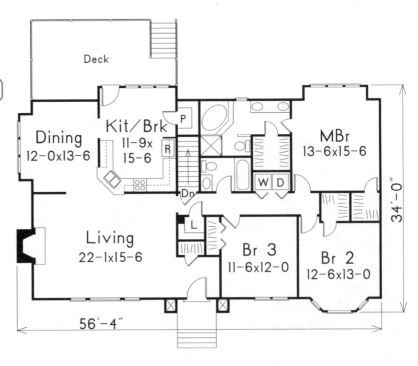

Deck

Dining
12-0x13-6

Kit/Brk
11-9x
15-6

P

R

MBr
13-6x15-6

W D

Dn

Living
22-1x15-6

L

Br 3
11-6x12-0

Br 2
12-6x13-0

34'-0"

56'-4"

High Ceilings Create A Feeling Of Luxury

1,707 total square feet of living area

Special features

- The formal living room off the entry hall has a high sloping ceiling and prominent fireplace

- Kitchen and breakfast areas allow access to garage and rear porch

- Garage with oversized storage/work area provides direct access to the kitchen

- Master bedroom has impressive vaulted ceiling, luxurious master bath, large walk-in closet and separate tub and shower

- Utility room conveniently located near bedrooms

- 3 bedrooms, 2 baths, 2-car garage

- Slab foundation

    Price Code C

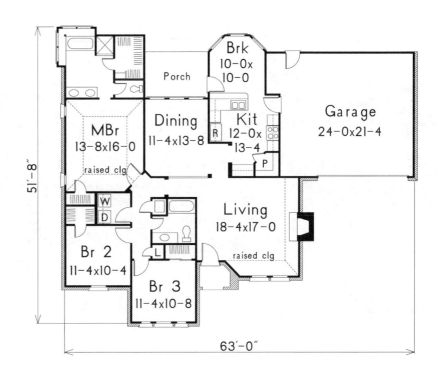

SINGLE-STORY under 2,000 square feet

Plan #X20-0212
To order blueprints use the form on page 322 or call toll-free 1-800-DREAM HOME (373-2646)

Private Breakfast Room Provides Casual Dining

1,708 total square feet of living area

Special features

- Massive family room enhanced with several windows, fireplace and access to porch
- Deluxe master bath accented by step-up corner tub flanked by double vanities
- Closets throughout maintain organized living
- Bedrooms isolated from living areas
- 3 bedrooms, 2 baths, 2-car garage
- Basement foundation, drawings also include crawl space foundation

Price Code B

SINGLE-STORY under 2,000 square feet

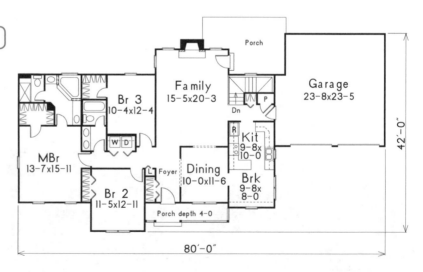

Atrium's Dramatic Ambiance, Compliments Of Windows

1,721 total square feet of living area

Special features

- Roof dormers add great curb appeal
- Vaulted great room and dining room immersed in light from atrium window wall
- Breakfast room opens onto covered porch
- Functionally designed kitchen
- 3 bedrooms, 2 baths, 3-car garage
- Walk-out basement foundation

Price Code C

Rear View

SINGLE-STORY under 2,000 square feet

Plan #X20-0370

To order blueprints use the form on page 322 or call toll-free 1-800-DREAM HOME (373-2646)

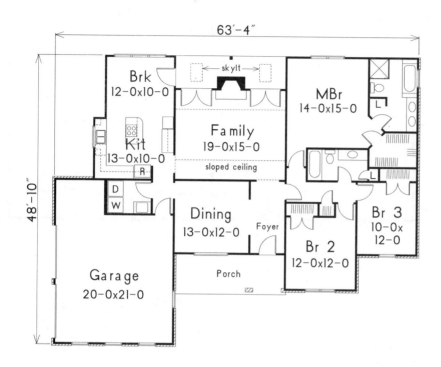

Classic Styling With Framed Entry

1,739 total square feet of living area

Special features

- Utility room has convenient work area, laundry sink and storage space
- Vaulted ceiling lends drama to the family room with fireplace and double french doors
- Island kitchen is enhanced by adjoining breakfast area with access to the patio
- Formal dining room features a 10' ceiling
- Private hallway separates bedrooms from living area
- 3 bedrooms, 2 baths, 2-car side entry garage
- Slab foundation

Price Code B

SINGLE-STORY under 2,000 square feet

Plan #X20-0240

DANVILLE

Distinctive Turret Surrounds The Dining Bay

1,742 total square feet of living area

Special features

- Efficient kitchen combines with breakfast and great room creating spacious living area
- Master bedroom includes private bath with huge walk-in closet, shower and corner tub
- Great room boasts a fireplace and outdoor access
- Laundry room conveniently located near kitchen and garage
- 3 bedrooms, 2 baths, 2-car garage
- Slab foundation, drawings also include crawl space foundation

Price Code B

SINGLE-STORY under 2,000 square feet

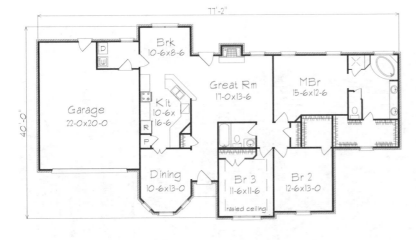

Garage 22-0x20-0

Brk 10-6x8-6

Kit 10-6x 16-6

Great Rm 17-0x13-6

MBr 15-6x12-6

Dining 10-6x13-0

Br 3 11-6x11-6

Br 2 12-6x13-0

raised ceiling

77'-2"

40'-0"

Plan #X20-0410

HAYWOOD

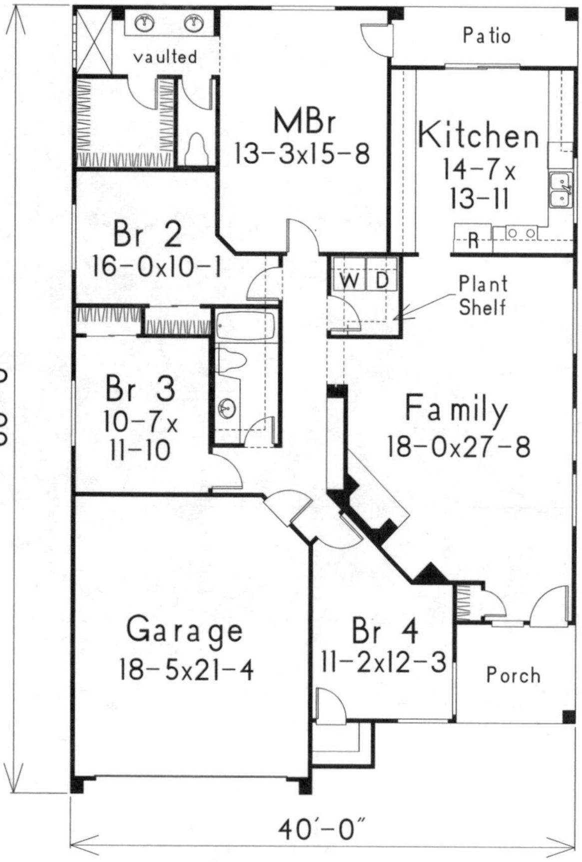

Patio
vaulted
MBr
13-3x15-8
Kitchen
14-7x
13-11
R
Br 2
16-0x10-1
W D
Plant
Shelf
Br 3
10-7x
11-10
Family
18-0x27-8
Garage
18-5x21-4
Br 4
11-2x12-3
Porch
60'-0"
40'-0"

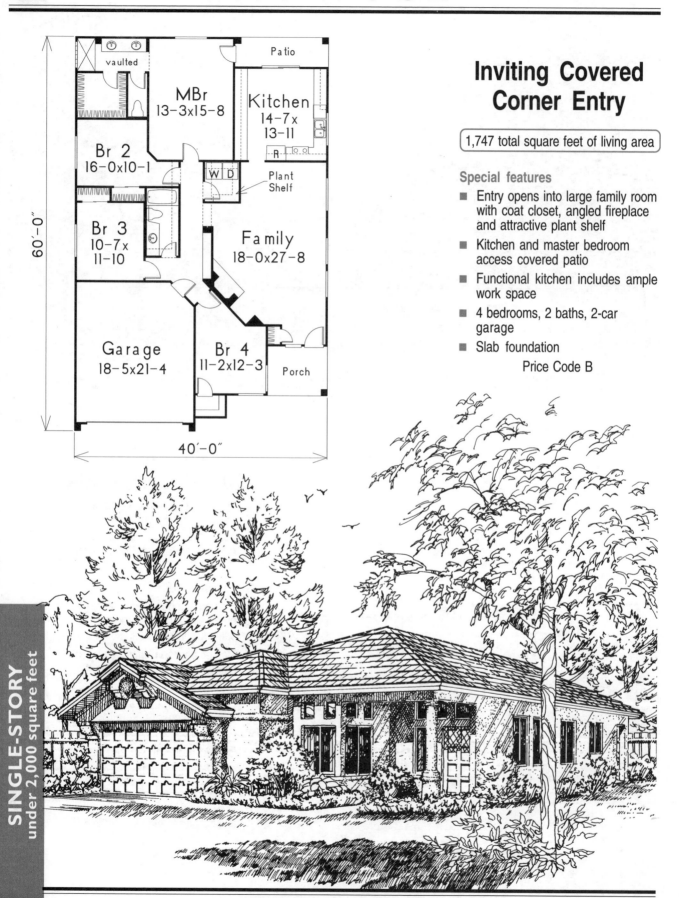

Inviting Covered Corner Entry

1,747 total square feet of living area

Special features

- Entry opens into large family room with coat closet, angled fireplace and attractive plant shelf
- Kitchen and master bedroom access covered patio
- Functional kitchen includes ample work space
- 4 bedrooms, 2 baths, 2-car garage
- Slab foundation

Price Code B

Plan #X20-0441

To order blueprints use the form on page 322 or call toll-free 1-800-DREAM HOME (373-2646)

PAGEHURST

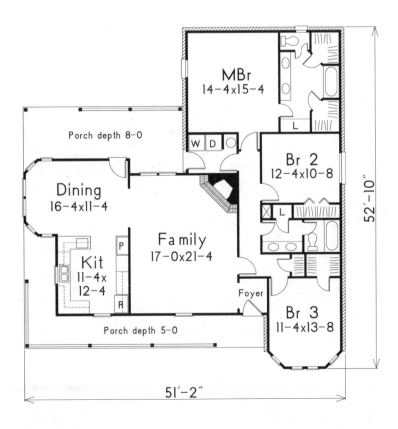

Old-Fashioned Comfort And Privacy

1,772 total square feet of living area

Special features

- Extended porches in front and rear provide a homey touch
- Large bay windows lend distinction to dining room and front bedroom
- Efficient U-shaped kitchen
- Master bedroom suite includes two walk-in closets
- Full corner fireplace in family room
- 3 bedrooms, 2 baths, 2-car detached garage
- Slab foundation, drawings also include crawl space foundation

Price Code C

SINGLE-STORY under 2,000 square feet

Plan #X20-0163

To order blueprints use the form on page 322 or call toll-free 1-800-DREAM HOME (373-2646)

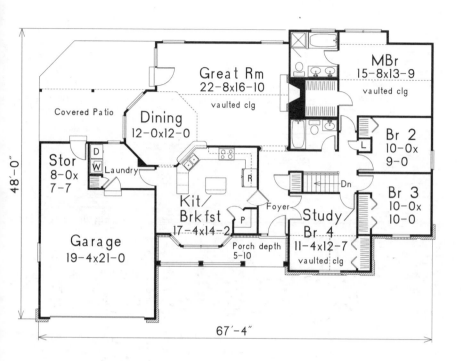

Great Rm
22-8x16-10
vaulted clg

MBr
15-8x13-9
vaulted clg

Covered Patio

Dining
12-0x12-0

Stor
8-0x
7-7

D
W
Laundry

Br 2
10-0x
9-0

48'-0"

**Kit/
Brkfst**
17-4x14-2

R

P

Dn

Foyer

Br 3
10-0x
10-0

Garage
19-4x21-0

Porch depth
5-10

**Study
Br 4**
11-4x12-7
vaulted clg

67'-4"

Classic Exterior Employs Innovative Planning

1,791 total square feet of living area

Special features

- Vaulted great room and octagonal dining enjoy views of covered patio

- Kitchen features a pass-through to dining, center island, large walk-in pantry and breakfast room with large bay window

- Master bedroom is vaulted with sitting area

- 4 bedrooms, 2 baths, 2-car garage with storage

- Basement foundation

    Price Code B

SINGLE-STORY
under 2,000 square feet

Plan #X20-0706

COLLISON

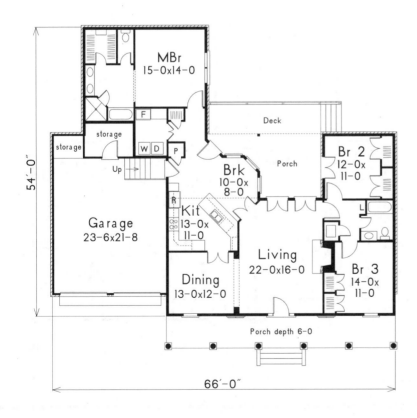

MBr
15-0x14-0

storage

storage

F

W D P

Up

Garage
23-6x21-8

Deck

Porch

Brk
10-0x
8-0

Kit
13-0x
11-0

R

Dining
13-0x12-0

Living
22-0x16-0

Br 2
12-0x
11-0

Br 3
14-0x
11-0

54'-0"

66'-0"

Porch depth 6-0

Full Pillared Porch Makes A Grand Entrance

1,800 total square feet of living area

Special features

- Stylish kitchen and eating areas feature large windows that allow a great outside view
- Covered front and rear porches provide an added dimension to this home's living space
- Generous storage areas and large utility room
- Energy efficient home with 2" x 6" exterior walls
- Large separate master suite and adjoining bath with large tub and corner shower
- 3 bedrooms, 2 baths, 2-car garage
- Crawl space foundation, drawings also include slab foundation

Price Code C

SINGLE-STORY under 2,000 square feet

Plan #X20-0188

To order blueprints use the form on page 322 or call toll-free 1-800-DREAM HOME (373-2646)

Transom Windows Create Impressive Front Entry

1,800 total square feet of living area

Special features

- Energy efficient home with 2" x 6" exterior walls
- Covered front and rear porches add outside living area
- 12' ceilings in kitchen, eating area, dining and living rooms
- Private master suite features expansive bath
- Side entry garage with 2 storage areas
- Pillared styling with brick and stucco exterior finish
- 3 bedrooms, 2 baths, 2-car side entry garage
- Crawl space foundation, drawings also include slab foundation

    Price Code D

SINGLE-STORY under 2,000 square feet

Plan #X20-0283

To order blueprints use the form on page 322 or call toll-free 1-800-DREAM HOME (373-2646)

SAVANNAH

Double Gables
Frame Front Porch

1,832 total square feet of living area

Special features

- Distinctive master suite enhanced by skylights, garden tub, separate shower and walk-in closet

- U-shaped kitchen features convenient pantry, laundry area and full view to breakfast room

- Foyer opens into spacious living room

- Large front porch creates enjoyable outdoor living

- 3 bedrooms, 2 baths, 2-car detached garage

- Crawl space foundation, drawings also include basement and slab foundations

    Price Code C

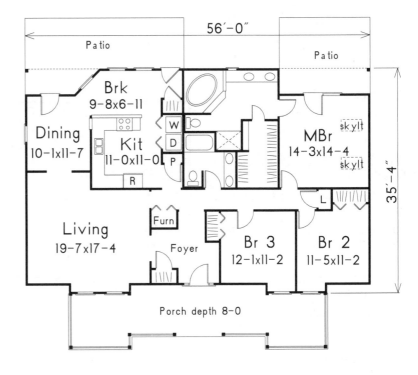

Patio 56'-0" Patio

Brk 9-8x6-11

Dining 10-1x11-7

Kit 11-0x11-0

MBr 14-3x14-4 skylt skylt

W D P R

35'-4"

Living 19-7x17-4

Furn

Foyer

Br 3 12-1x11-2

Br 2 11-5x11-2

Porch depth 8-0

Plan #X20-0542

To order blueprints use the form on page 322 or call toll-free 1-800-DREAM HOME (373-2646)

Divided Bedroom Areas Lend Privacy

1,833 total square feet of living area

Special features

- Master bedroom suite comes with a garden tub, walk-in closet and bay window
- Walk-through kitchen and breakfast room
- Front bay windows offer a deluxe touch
- Foyer with convenient coat closet opens into large vaulted living room with attractive fireplace
- 3 bedrooms, 2 baths, 2-car drive under garage
- Basement foundation

Price Code C

SINGLE-STORY
under 2,000 square feet

Plan #X20-0119

To order blueprints use the form on page 322 or call toll-free 1-800-DREAM HOME (373-2646)

BELFORD

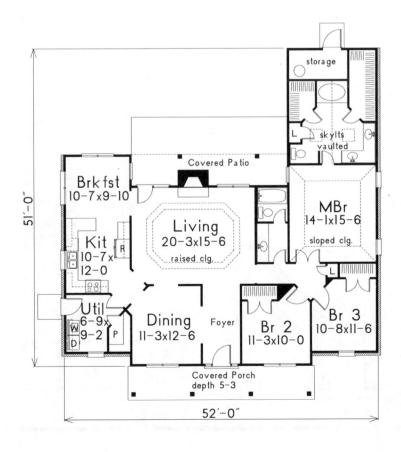

Bright Spacious Living Area Perfect For Entertaining

1,844 total square feet of living area

Special features

- Luxurious master bath is impressive with vaulted ceiling, large walk-in closets, and oversized tub
- Living room has high ceiling and large windows that flank the fireplace
- Front and rear covered porches create homey feel
- Cozy breakfast room adjacent to kitchen for easy access
- Spacious utility room includes pantry and is accessible to both kitchen and outdoors
- 3 bedrooms, 2 baths
- Slab foundation

Price Code C

SINGLE-STORY under 2,000 square feet

Plan #X20-0685

To order blueprints use the form on page 322 or call toll-free 1-800-DREAM HOME (373-2646)

Stylish Features Enhance Open Living

1,846 total square feet of living area

Special features

- Enormous living area combines with dining and breakfast rooms complemented by extensive windows and high ceilings

- Master bedroom has walk-in closet, display niche and deluxe bath

- Secondary bedrooms share a bath and feature large closet space and a corner window

- Oversized 2-car garage has plenty of storage and work space with handy access to the kitchen through the utility area

- Breakfast nook has wrap-around windows adding to eating enjoyment

- 3 bedrooms, 2 baths, 2-car garage

- Slab foundation

    Price Code C

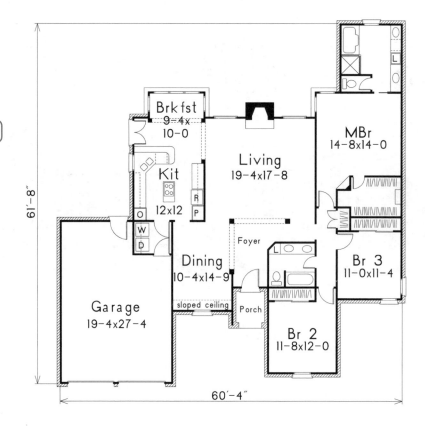

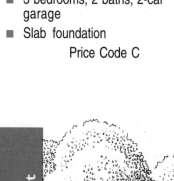

SINGLE-STORY under 2,000 square feet

Plan #X20-0215

To order blueprints use the form on page 322 or call toll-free 1-800-DREAM HOME (373-2646)

Isolated Master Suite Has Grand Master Bath

1,856 total square feet of living area

Special features

- Living room features include fireplace, 12' ceiling and skylights
- Energy efficient home with 2" x 6" exterior walls
- In kitchen and eating areas common vaulted ceiling creates open atmosphere
- Garage with storage areas conveniently accesses home through handy utility room
- Private hall separates secondary bedrooms from living areas
- 3 bedrooms, 2 baths, 2-car side entry garage
- Slab foundation, drawings also include crawl space foundation

Price Code C

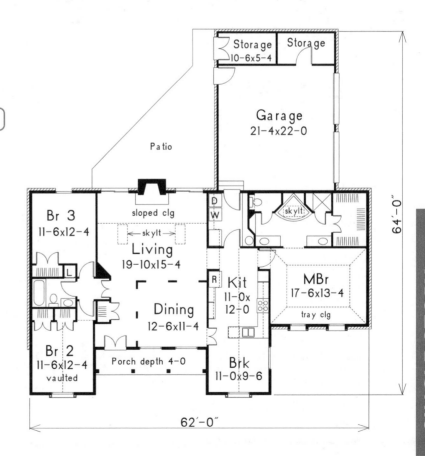

SINGLE-STORY under 2,000 square feet

Large Great Room Perfect For Entertaining

1,862 total square feet of living area

Special features

- Master bedroom includes tray ceiling, bay window, access to patio, and private bath with oversized tub and generous closet space

- Corner sink and bar faces into breakfast area and great room

- Spacious great room features vaulted ceiling, fireplace and access to rear patio

- 3 bedrooms, 2 baths, 2-car garage

- Slab foundation, drawings also include crawl space foundation

Price Code C

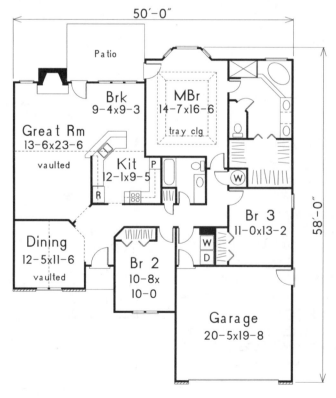

50'-0"

58'-0"

Patio

Brk
9-4x9-3

MBr
14-7x16-6
tray clg

Great Rm
13-6x23-6
vaulted

Kit
12-1x9-5

P

R

W

Br 3
11-0x13-2

Dining
12-5x11-6
vaulted

W
D

Br 2
10-8x
10-0

Garage
20-5x19-8

Plan #X20-0257

To order blueprints use the form on page 322 or call toll-free 1-800-DREAM HOME (373-2646)

WYNDHAM

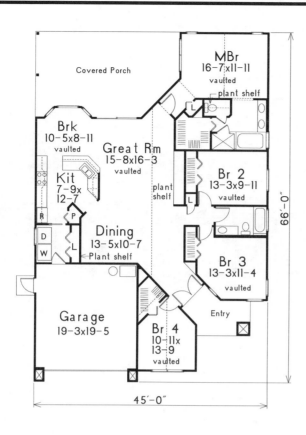

Wonderful Great Room

1,865 total square feet of living area

Special features

- Large foyer opens into expansive dining/great room area
- Home features vaulted ceilings throughout
- Master suite features bath with double-bowl vanity, shower, tub and toilet in separate room for privacy
- 4 bedrooms, 2 baths, 2-car garage
- Slab foundation, drawings also include crawl space foundation

Price Code D

SINGLE-STORY under 2,000 square feet

Plan #X20-0335
To order blueprints use the form on page 322 or call toll-free 1-800-DREAM HOME (373-2646)

Open Living Areas Separate Remote Bedrooms

> 1,868 total square feet of living area

Special features

- Luxurious master bath is impressive with its angled, quarter-circle tub, separate vanities and large walk-in closet
- Energy efficient home with 2" x 6" exterior walls
- Dining room is surrounded by series of arched openings which complement the open feeling of this design
- Living room has a 12' ceiling accented by skylights and a large fireplace flanked by sliding doors
- Large storage areas
- 3 bedrooms, 2 baths, 2-car side entry garage
- Slab foundation, drawings also include crawl space foundation

Price Code D

SINGLE-STORY under 2,000 square feet

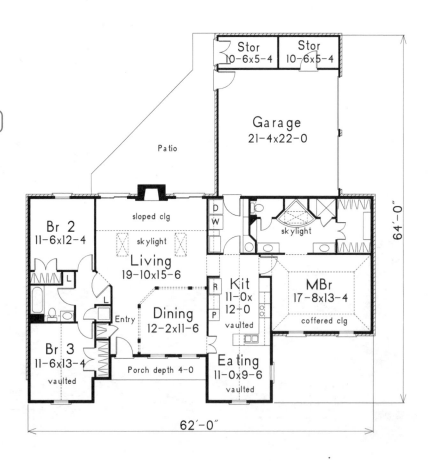

Stor 10-6x5-4 Stor 10-6x5-4

Patio

Garage 21-4x22-0

64'-0"

Br 2 11-6x12-4

sloped clg

skylight

Living 19-10x15-6

skylight

D W

MBr 17-8x13-4

coffered clg

Entry

Kit 11-0x 12-0 vaulted

R P

Dining 12-2x11-6

Br 3 11-6x13-4 vaulted

Porch depth 4-0

Eating 11-0x9-6 vaulted

62'-0"

Plan #X20-0191

MOORELAND

Traditional Exterior, Handsome Accents

> 1,882 total square feet of living area

Special features

- Wide, handsome entrance opens to the vaulted great room with fireplace
- Living and dining areas are conveniently joined but still allow privacy
- Private covered porch extends breakfast area
- Practical passageway runs through laundry and mud room from garage to kitchen
- Vaulted ceiling in master bedroom
- 3 bedrooms, 2 baths, 2-car garage
- Basement foundation

Price Code D

Plan #X20-0162

To order blueprints use the form on page 322 or call toll-free 1-800-DREAM HOME (373-2646)

Secluded Kitchen, Center Of Activity

1,882 total square feet of living area

Special features

- Handsome brick facade
- Spacious great and dining room combination brightened by unique corner windows and patio access
- Well-designed kitchen incorporates breakfast bar peninsula, sweeping casement window above sink and walk-in pantry island
- Master suite features large walk-in closet and private bath with bay window
- 4 bedrooms, 2 baths, 2-car side entry garage
- Basement foundation

Price Code C

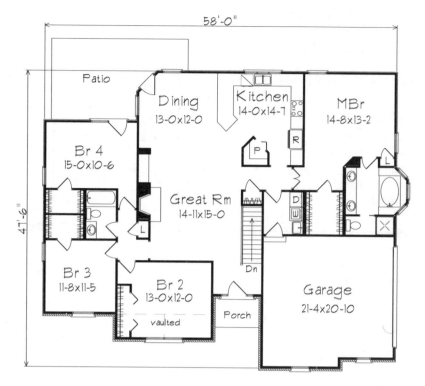

58'-0"

47'-6"

Patio

Dining
13-0x12-0

Kitchen
14-0x14-7

MBr
14-8x13-2

Br 4
15-0x10-6

P

R

Great Rm
14-11x15-0

D
W

L

Br 3
11-8x11-5

Br 2
13-0x12-0
vaulted

Dn

Porch

Garage
21-4x20-10

Plan #X20-0419

To order blueprints use the form on page 322 or call toll-free 1-800-DREAM HOME (373-2646)

HAMILTON

Handsome Facade Welcomes Guests

1,908 total square feet of living area

Special features

- Distinguished front entry features circle-top window and prominent center gable

- Sundeck/patio is nestled between living space for easy access from adjacent room

- Oversized 2-car garage has large work/storage area and convenient laundry room

- Vaulted ceiling and floor-to-ceiling windows in family and breakfast rooms create an open, unrestricted space

- Master suite with deluxe bath, large walk-in closet and recessed ceiling

- 3 bedrooms, 2 baths, 2-car garage

- Crawl space foundation, drawings also include slab foundation

Price Code C

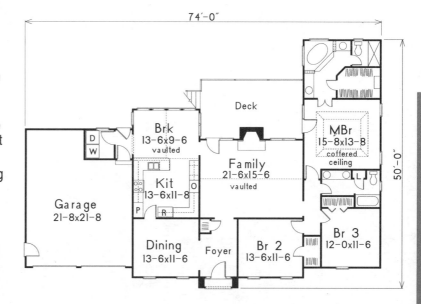

SINGLE-STORY under 2,000 square feet

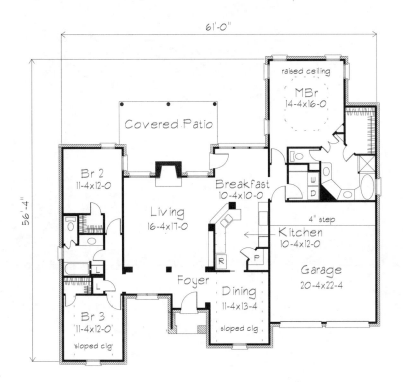

61'-0"

56'-4"

raised ceiling

MBr
14-4x16-0

Covered Patio

Br 2
11-4x12-0

Breakfast
10-4x10-0

Living
16-4x17-0

4" step

Kitchen
10-4x12-0

Garage
20-4x22-4

Foyer

Dining
11-4x13-4

Br 3
11-4x12-0

sloped clg

'sloped clg'

Inviting And Cozy Covered Arched Entry

1,923 total square feet of living area

Special features

- Foyer opens into spacious living room with fireplace and splendid view of covered porch

- Kitchen with walk-in pantry adjacent to laundry and breakfast rooms

- All bedrooms feature walk-in closets

- Secluded master bedroom includes unique angled bath with spacious walk-in closet

- 3 bedrooms, 2 baths, 2-car garage

- Slab foundation

  Price Code C

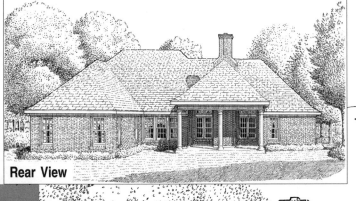

Rear View

SINGLE-STORY
under 2,000 square feet

Plan #X20-0400

To order blueprints use the form on page 322 or call toll-free 1-800-DREAM HOME (373-2646)

LAUREL

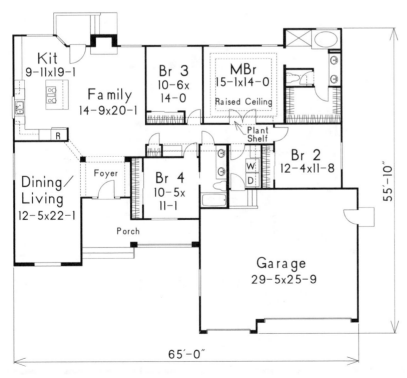

Upscale Ranch Boasts Both Formal And Casual Areas

1,950 total square feet of living area

Special features

- Large corner kitchen with island cooktop opens to family room
- Master suite features double-door entry, raised ceiling, double-bowl vanities and walk-in closet
- Plant shelf accents hall
- 4 bedrooms, 2 baths, 3-car garage
- Crawl space foundation

  Price Code C

SINGLE-STORY
under 2,000 square feet

Plan #X20-0442

To order blueprints use the form on page 322 or call toll-free 1-800-DREAM HOME (373-2646)

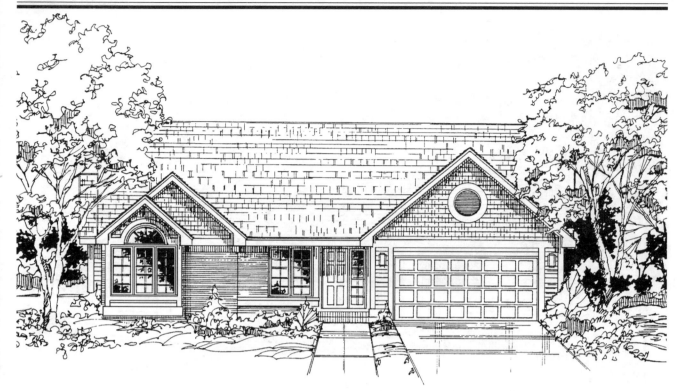

Casual Exterior, Filled With Great Features

1,958 total square feet of living area

Special features

- Large wrap-around kitchen opens to bright cheerful breakfast area with access to large covered deck and open stairway to basement

- Kitchen nestled between the dining room and breakfast room

- Master suite includes large walk-in closet, double-bowl vanity, garden tub and separate shower

- Foyer features attractive plant shelves and opens into living room that includes attractive central fireplace

- 3 bedrooms, 2 baths, 2-car garage

- Basement foundation

  Price Code C

SINGLE-STORY under 2,000 square feet

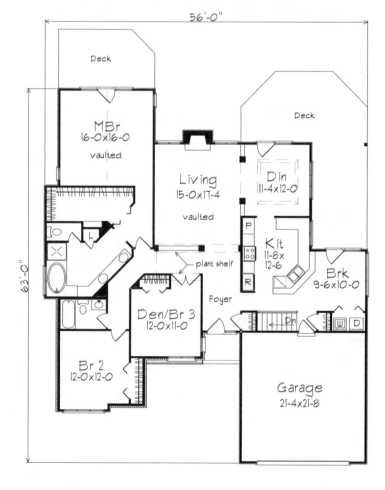

56'-0"

63'-0"

Deck

MBr
16-0x16-0
vaulted

Living
15-0x17-4
vaulted

Din
11-4x12-0

Deck

plant shelf

Kit
11-8x
12-6

Brk
9-6x10-0

Foyer

Den/Br 3
12-0x11-0

Br 2
12-0x12-0

Garage
21-4x21-8

Plan #X20-0387

To order blueprints use the form on page 322 or call toll-free 1-800-DREAM HOME (373-2646)

Provides Family Living At Its Best

> 1,993 total square feet of living area

Special features

- Spacious country kitchen with fireplace and plenty of natural light from windows
- Formal dining room features large bay window and steps down to sunken living room
- Master suite features corner windows, plant shelves and deluxe private bath
- Entry opens into vaulted living room with windows flanking the fireplace
- 3 bedrooms, 2 baths, 2-car garage
- Basement foundation

    Price Code D

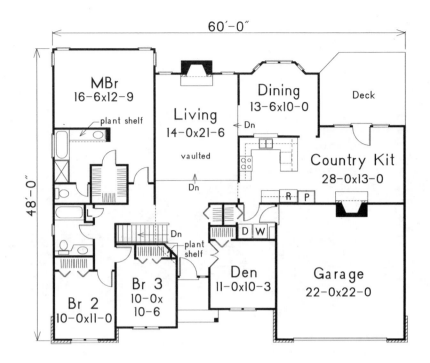

Plan #X20-0279

To order blueprints use the form on page 322 or call toll-free 1-800-DREAM HOME (373-2646)

SINGLE-STORY under 2,000 square feet

LINDENWOOD

Comfortable Family Living In This Ranch

1,994 total square feet of living area

Special features

- Convenient entrance from the garage into the main living space through the utility room
- Standard 9' ceilings, bedroom #2 features a 12' vaulted ceiling and a 10' ceiling in the dining room
- Master bedroom offers a full bath with oversized tub, separate shower and walk-in closet
- Entry leads to formal dining room and attractive living room with double french doors and fireplace
- 3 bedrooms, 2 baths, 2-car garage
- Slab foundation

Price Code D

SINGLE STORY
under 2,000 square feet

64'-8"

56'-0"

MBr
13-4x14-0

Living
17-4x17-4

Brk
12-0x11-0

Kit
12-0x
12-0

Storage

W D

Garage
20-4x21-4

Dining
11-8x13-0

Foyer

Br 3
13-4x11-8

Br 2
11-4x14-8

sloped clg

Plan #X20-0244

Open Living Centers On Windowed Dining Room

2,003 total square feet of living area

Special features

- Octagonal dining room with tray ceiling and deck overlook
- L-shaped island kitchen serves living and dining rooms
- Master bedroom boasts luxury bath and walk-in closet
- Living room features columns, elegant fireplace and a 10' ceiling
- 3 bedrooms, 2 baths, 2-car garage
- Basement foundation

Price Code D

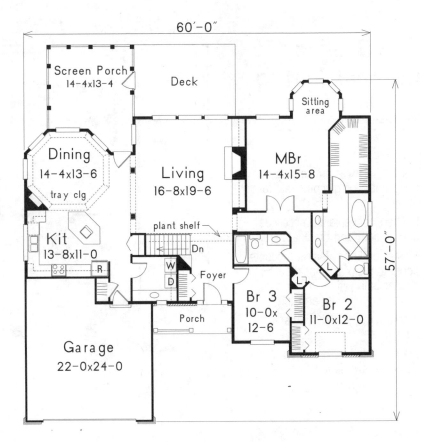

60'-0"

Screen Porch 14-4x13-4

Deck

Sitting area

Dining 14-4x13-6 tray clg

Living 16-8x19-6

MBr 14-4x15-8

Kit 13-8x11-0

plant shelf

Dn

57'-0"

W D

Foyer

Br 3 10-0x 12-6

Br 2 11-0x12-0

Porch

Garage 22-0x24-0

Soaring Covered Portico

2,056 total square feet of living area

Special features

- Columned foyer projects past living and dining rooms into family room

- Kitchen conveniently accesses dining room and breakfast area

- Master bedroom features double-doors to patio and pocket door to master bath with walk-in closet, double-bowl vanity and tub

- 4 bedrooms, 2 baths, 2-car garage

- Slab foundation, drawings also include crawl space foundation

Price Code C

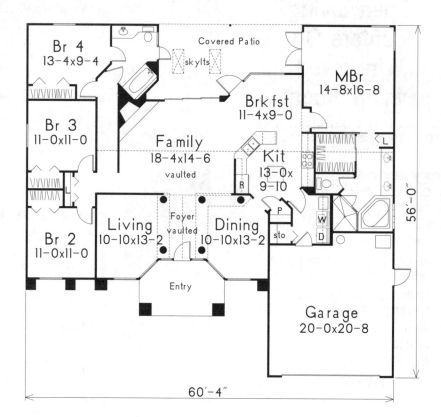

Plan #X20-0343

To order blueprints use the form on page 322 or call toll-free 1-800-DREAM HOME (373-2646)

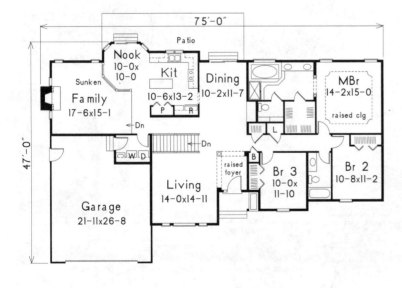

Raised Foyer And Archways Create An Impressive Entry

2,070 total square feet of living area

Special features

- Access to rear deck through kitchen/nook area
- Energy efficient home with 2" x 6" exterior walls
- Master bedroom features arched entrance into bath with separate shower and tub, dressing area and walk-in closet
- Sunken family room with fireplace
- 3 bedrooms, 2 baths, 2-car garage
- Basement foundation, drawings also include slab and crawl space foundations

Price Code C

SINGLE-STORY over 2,000 square feet

Floor plan labels:
- 75'-0"
- 47'-0"
- Patio
- Nook 10-0x 10-0
- Kit 10-6x13-2
- Dining 10-2x11-7
- MBr 14-2x15-0 raised clg
- Sunken Family 17-6x15-1
- Dn
- W D
- Dn
- Living 14-0x14-11
- raised foyer
- Br 3 10-0x 11-10
- Br 2 10-8x11-2
- Garage 21-11x26-8
- P R
- B
- L

Stately Covered Front Entry

2,089 total square feet of living area

Special features

- Family room features fireplace, built-in bookshelves and triple sliders opening to covered patio

- Kitchen overlooks family room and features pantry and desk

- Separated from the three secondary bedrooms, the master bedroom becomes a quiet retreat with patio access

- Master suite features oversized bath with walk-in closet and corner tub

- 4 bedrooms, 3 baths, 2-car garage

- Slab foundation

Price Code C

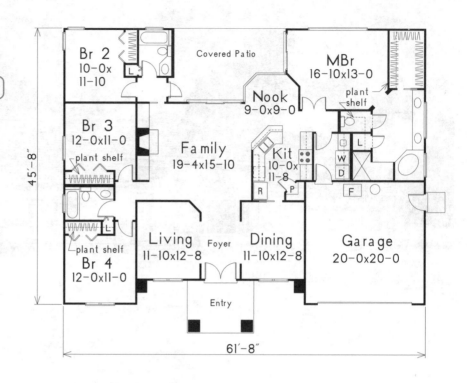

Plan #X20-0342

SANIBEL

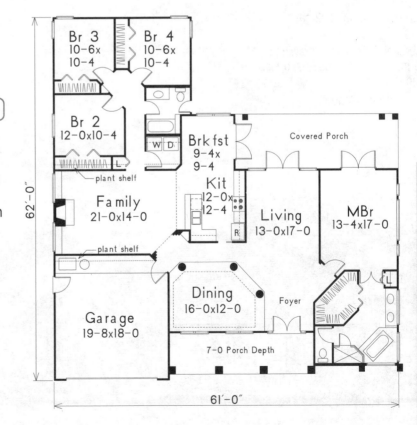

Family Room Features Barrel Vaulted Ceiling

2,153 total square feet of living area

Special features

- Foyer leads directly into formal living room which accesses porch
- Master suite features wall of windows and also accesses porch
- Family room boasts twelve foot barrel vaulted ceiling and built-in bookshelves on each side of dramatic fireplace
- Varied ceiling heights throughout
- Three bedrooms, a bath and the utility room are located off of the family room
- 4 bedrooms, 2 baths, 2-car garage
- Slab foundation

Price Code C

Br 3
10-6x
10-4

Br 4
10-6x
10-4

Br 2
12-0x10-4

plant shelf

Family
21-0x14-0

plant shelf

Garage
19-8x18-0

W D

Brkfst
9-4x
9-4

Kit
12-0x
12-4

Dining
16-0x12-0

Living
13-0x17-0

Covered Porch

MBr
13-4x17-0

Foyer

7-0 Porch Depth

62'-0"

61'-0"

SINGLE-STORY over 2,000 square feet

Plan #X20-0340

To order blueprints use the form on page 322 or call toll-free 1-800-DREAM HOME (373-2646)

247

Facade Combines Siding And Brick With Feature Window

2,159 total square feet of living area

Special features

- Energy efficient home with 2" x 6" exterior walls
- Covered entry opens into large foyer with skylight and coat closet
- Master bedroom includes private bath with angled vanity, separate spa and shower and walk-in closet
- Family and living rooms feature vaulted ceilings and sunken floors for added openness
- Kitchen features an island counter and convenient pantry
- 3 bedrooms, 2 baths, 2-car garage
- Basement foundation, drawings also include crawl space and slab foundations

Price Code C

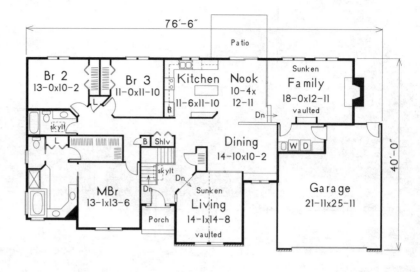

SINGLE-STORY over 2,000 square feet

Plan #X20-0261

To order blueprints use the form on page 322 or call toll-free 1-800-DREAM HOME (373-2646)

DARTMOUTH

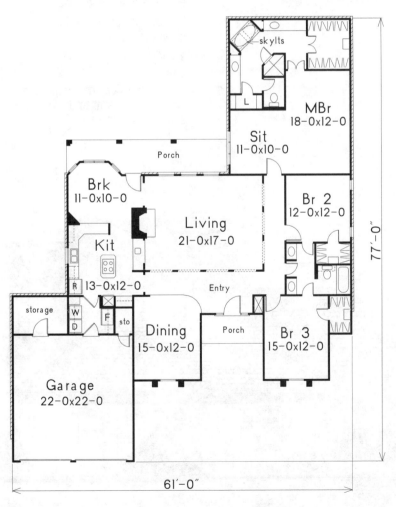

Prominent Central Living Room Adds Luxurious Focus

2,177 total square feet of living area

Special features

- Master suite features sitting area and double-door entry to elegant master bath

- Secondary bedrooms are spacious with walk-in closets and a shared bath

- Breakfast room with full windows open to the rear porch

- Exterior window treatments create a unique style

- Kitchen features an island cooktop, eating bar, and wet bar that is accessible from the living room and breakfast area

- 3 bedrooms, 2 baths, 2-car garage

- Slab foundation, drawings also include basement and crawl space foundations

Price Code C

SINGLE-STORY over 2,000 square feet

Plan #X20-0189

HD

Bold Windows Enhance Front Entry

2,252 total square feet of living area

Special features

- Central living area
- Private master bedroom with large walk-in closet, dressing area and bath
- Energy efficient home with 2" x 6" exterior walls
- Secondary bedrooms are in a suite arrangement with plenty of closet space
- Sunny breakfast room looks out over the porch and patio
- Large entry area highlighted by circle-top transoms
- 4 bedrooms, 2 baths, 2-car garage
- Slab foundation, drawings also include basement and crawl space foundations

Price Code D

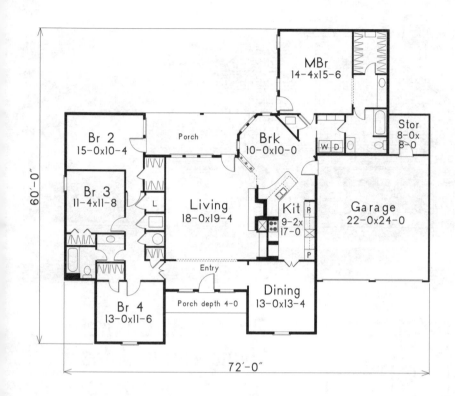

Floor plan labels:
- MBr 14-4x15-6
- Porch
- Brk 10-0x10-0
- Stor 8-0x 8-0
- W D
- Br 2 15-0x10-4
- Br 3 11-4x11-8
- L
- Living 18-0x19-4
- Kit 9-2x 17-0
- R
- P
- Garage 22-0x24-0
- Entry
- Br 4 13-0x11-6
- Porch depth 4-0
- Dining 13-0x13-4
- 60'-0"
- 72'-0"

SINGLE-STORY over 2,000 square feet

Plan #X20-0193

To order blueprints use the form on page 322 or call toll-free 1-800-DREAM HOME (373-2646)

ALEXANDER

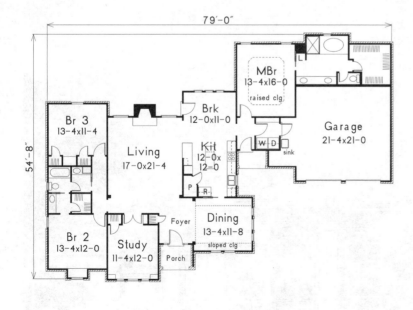

Dramatic Roof Line Accents This Ranch

2,260 total square feet of living area

Special features

- Luxurious master suite includes raised ceiling, bath with oversized tub, separate shower and large walk-in closet

- Convenient kitchen and breakfast area with ample pantry storage

- Formal foyer leads into large living room with warming fireplace

- Convenient secondary entrance for everyday traffic

- 3 bedrooms, 2 baths, 2-car garage

- Slab foundation

   Price Code D

SINGLE-STORY over 2,000 square feet

Plan #X20-0245

Impressive Master Suite

2,287 total square feet of living area

Special features

- Double-doors lead into impressive master suite which accesses covered porch and features deluxe bath with his and her closets and step-up tub
- Kitchen easily serves formal and informal areas of home
- The spacious foyer opens into formal dining and living rooms
- 4 bedrooms, 2 1/2 baths, 2-car side entry garage
- Slab foundation

Price Code E

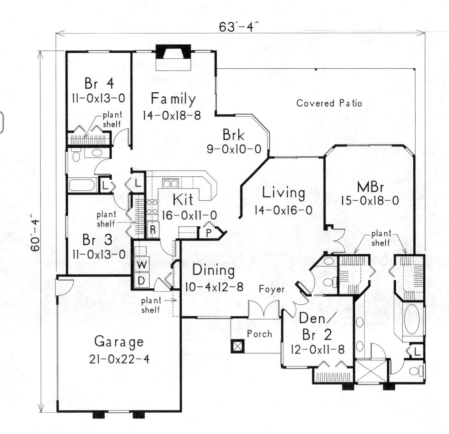

SINGLE-STORY over 2,000 square feet

Plan #X20-0339

To order blueprints use the form on page 322 or call toll-free 1-800-DREAM HOME (373-2646)

SUGARCREEK

Bright, Spacious Plan With Many Features

2,308 total square feet of living area

Special features

- Efficient kitchen designed with many cabinets and large walk-in pantry adjoins family/breakfast area featuring beautiful fireplace

- Dining area has architectural colonnades that separate it from living area while maintaining spaciousness

- Enter master suite through double-doors and find double walk-in closets and beautiful luxurious bath

- Living room includes vaulted ceiling, fireplace and a sunny atrium window wall creating a dramatic atmosphere

- 3 bedrooms, 2 baths, 2-car garage

- Walk-out basement foundation
  Price Code D

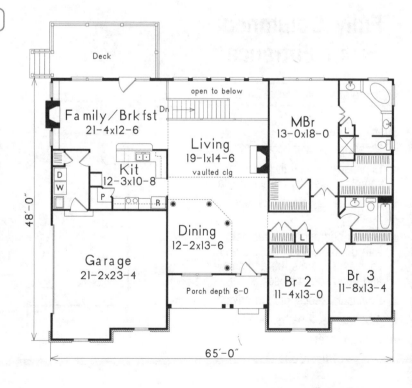

SINGLE-STORY over 2,000 square feet

Plan #X20-0701
To order blueprints use the form on page 322 or call toll-free 1-800-DREAM HOME (373-2646)

253

Fully Columned Front Entrance

2,365 total square feet of living area

Special features

- 9' ceilings on first floor
- Expansive central living room complemented by corner fireplace
- Breakfast bay overlooks rear porch
- Master bedroom features bath with double walk-in closets and vanities, separate tub and shower and handy linen closet
- Peninsula keeps kitchen private
- 4 bedrooms, 2 baths, 2-car carport
- Slab foundation

Price Code D

SINGLE-STORY over 2,000 square feet

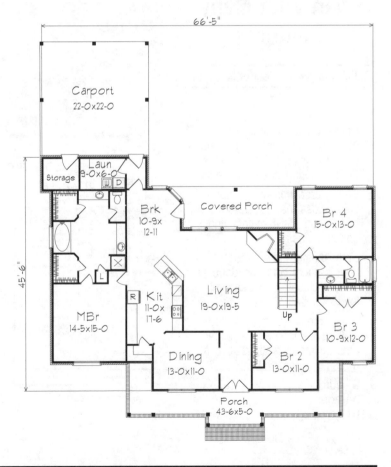

66'-5"

45'-6"

Carport
22-0x22-0

Laun
9-0x6-0

Storage

Brk
10-9x12-11

Covered Porch

Br 4
15-0x13-0

MBr
14-5x15-0

Kit
11-0x17-6

Living
19-0x19-5

Up

Br 3
10-9x12-0

Dining
13-0x11-0

Br 2
13-0x11-0

Porch
43-6x5-0

Plan #X20-0440

To order blueprints use the form on page 322 or call toll-free 1-800-DREAM HOME (373-2646)

Handsome Facade, Spacious Living Arrangement

2,396 total square feet of living area

Special features

- Generous wide entry welcomes guests
- Central living area with a 12' ceiling and large fireplace serves as a convenient traffic hub
- Secluded kitchen, yet easy access to the living, dining and eating areas
- Deluxe master bedroom suite with walk-in closet, oversized tub, shower and other amenities
- Energy efficient home with 2" x 6" exterior walls
- 4 bedrooms, 2 baths, 2-car garage
- Slab foundation, drawings also include basement and crawl space foundations

Price Code D

SINGLE-STORY over 2,000 square feet

Plan #X20-0185

To order blueprints use the form on page 322 or call toll-free 1-800-DREAM HOME (373-2646)

Fountain Graces Entry

2,397 total square feet of living area

Special features

- Covered entrance with fountain leads to double-door entry and foyer

- Kitchen features two pantries and opens into breakfast and family room

- Master bath features huge walk-in closet, electric clothes carousel, double-bowl vanity and corner tub

- 3 bedrooms, 2 1/2 baths, 2-car garage

- Slab foundation

  Price Code E

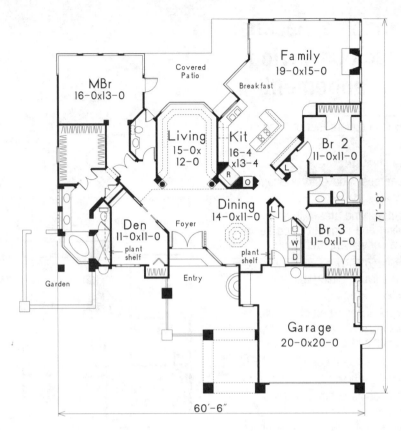

MBr
16-0x13-0

Covered Patio

Family
19-0x15-0

Breakfast

Living
15-0x
12-0

Kit
16-4
x13-4

Br 2
11-0x11-0

71'-8"

Den
11-0x11-0

Foyer

Dining
14-0x11-0

Br 3
11-0x11-0

plant shelf

plant shelf

W
D

Garden

Entry

Garage
20-0x20-0

60'-6"

J.N. HANSEN

SINGLE-STORY over 2,000 square feet

Plan #X20-0338

To order blueprints use the form on page 322 or call toll-free 1-800-DREAM HOME (373-2646)

ASHBURY

Rear View

Cozy Breakfast Bay With Full Outside View

(2,397 total square feet of living area)

Special features

- Varied ceiling heights throughout home
- All bedrooms boast walk-in closets
- Garage includes convenient storage area
- Angled kitchen counter overlooks spacious living room with fireplace
- Master bedroom with coffered ceiling and luxurious bath
- 4 bedrooms, 3 baths, 2-car side entry garage
- Slab foundation

Price Code D

SINGLE-STORY over 2,000 square feet

ROSEWOOD

Appealing Gabled Front Facade

2,412 total square feet of living area

Special features

- Coffered ceiling in dining room adds character and spaciousness
- Great room enhanced by vaulted ceiling and atrium window wall
- Spacious well-planned kitchen includes breakfast bar and overlooks breakfast room and beyond to deck
- Luxurious master suite features enormous walk-in closet, private bath and easy access to laundry area
- 4 bedrooms, 2 baths, 3-car garage
- Walk-out basement foundation

Price Code D

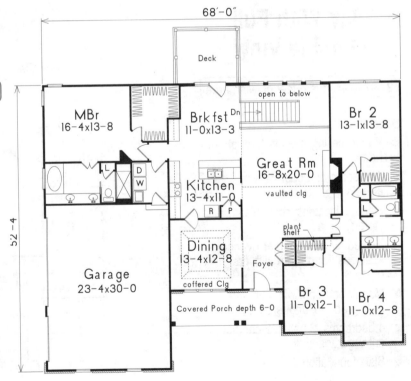

Deck

68'-0"

MBr
16-4x13-8

Brkfst Dn
11-0x13-3

open to below

Br 2
13-1x13-8

Great Rm
16-8x20-0
vaulted clg

Kitchen
13-4x11-0

plant shelf

Dining
13-4x12-8
coffered Clg

Foyer

Garage
23-4x30-0

Br 3
11-0x12-1

Br 4
11-0x12-8

Covered Porch depth 6-0

52-4

Plan #X20-0703

To order blueprints use the form on page 322 or call toll-free 1-800-DREAM HOME (373-2646)

Charming Design Features Home Office

> 2,452 total square feet of living area

Special features

- Cheery and spacious room with private entrance, guest bath, two closets, vaulted ceiling, and transomed window perfect for home office or a 4th bedroom
- Delightful great room with vaulted ceiling, fireplace, extra storage closets, and patio doors to sundeck
- Extra large kitchen features walk-in pantry, cooktop island and bay window
- Vaulted master suite includes transomed windows, walk-in closet and luxurious bath
- 4 bedrooms, 2 1/2 baths, 3-car garage
- Basement foundation

Price Code D

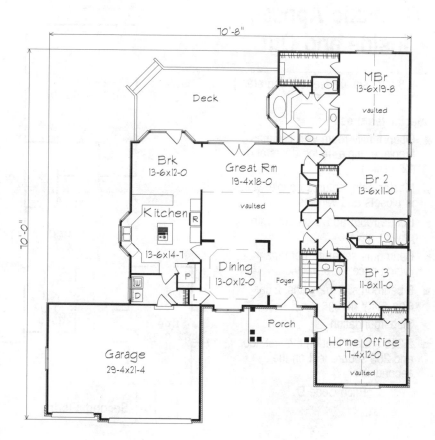

Plan #X20-0368

To order blueprints use the form on page 322 or call toll-free 1-800-DREAM HOME (373-2646)

SINGLE-STORY over 2,000 square feet

Dramatic Appeal, Inside and Out

2,468 total square feet of living area

Special features

- Open family room with columns, fireplace, triple french doors and 12' ceiling

- Master bath features double walk-in closets and vanities

- Bonus room above garage with private stairway

- Bedrooms separate from main living space for privacy

- 3 bedrooms, 2 1/2 baths, 2-car side entry garage

- Slab foundation

- 2,215 square feet on the first floor and 253 square feet on the second floor

Price Code D

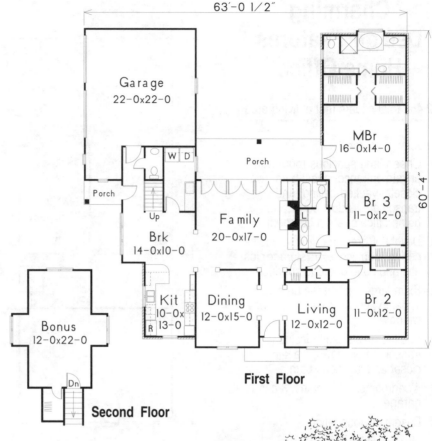

63'-0 1/2"

Garage
22-0x22-0

MBr
16-0x14-0

Porch

Br 3
11-0x12-0

W D

Porch

Family
20-0x17-0

Brk
14-0x10-0

Up

Br 2
11-0x12-0

60'-4"

Kit
10-0x
13-0

Dining
12-0x15-0

Living
12-0x12-0

First Floor

Bonus
12-0x22-0

Dn

Second Floor

SINGLE-STORY over 2,000 square feet

Plan #X20-0238

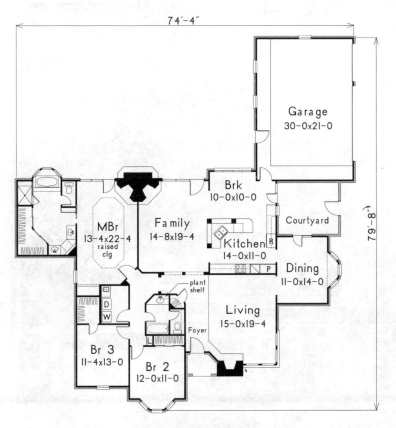

74'-4"

79'-8"

Garage
30-0x21-0

Brk
10-0x10-0

Courtyard

MBr
13-4x22-4
raised
clg

Family
14-8x19-4

Kitchen
14-0x11-0

Dining
11-0x14-0

plant
shelf

D
W

Living
15-0x19-4

Foyer

Br 3
11-4x13-0

Br 2
12-0x11-0

Fireplaces Are Unique Focal Points

2,481 total square feet of living area

Special features

- Varied ceiling heights throughout this home

- Master bedroom features built-in desk and pocket door entrance into large master bath

- Master bath includes corner vanity and garden tub

- Breakfast area accesses court-yard

- 3 bedrooms, 2 baths, 3-car side entry garage

- Slab foundation

Price Code D

SINGLE-STORY over 2,000 square feet

Plan #X20-0315

Terrific Master Suite Provides Escape

2,517 total square feet of living area

Special features

- Central living room with large windows and attractive transoms
- Varied ceiling heights throughout home
- Secluded master suite features double-door entry into luxurious bath with separate stool and shower, step-up whirlpool tub, double vanities and walk-in closets
- Kitchen with walk-in pantry overlooks large family room with fireplace and unique octagonal breakfast room
- Energy efficient home with 2" x 6" exterior walls
- 4 bedrooms, 2 1/2 baths, 2-car garage
- Slab foundation, drawings also include crawl space foundation

Price Code D

SINGLE-STORY over 2,000 square feet

Plan #X20-0407

To order blueprints use the form on page 322 or call toll-free 1-800-DREAM HOME (373-2646)

Rambling Ranch Has Luxurious Master Suite

2,523 total square feet of living area

Special features

- Entry with high ceiling leads to massive vaulted great room with wet bar, plant shelves, pillars and fireplace with harmonious window trio

- Elaborate kitchen with bay and breakfast bar adjoins morning room with fireplace-in-a-bay

- Vaulted master suite features fireplace, book and plant shelves, large walk-in closet and his and her baths

- 3 bedrooms, 2 baths, 3-car garage

- Basement foundation

    Price Code D

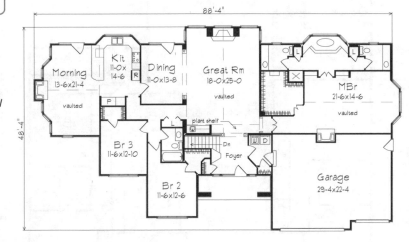

SINGLE-STORY over 2,000 square feet

ASHLEY

63'-6"

64'-0"

Garage
21-4x22-2

Laun
10-0x7-6

Stor.

MBr
17-10x14-0

Covered Porch

Brk
12-4x12-0

Br 3
11-0x12-6

Family
20-0x17-6

coffered ceiling

Kit
12-4x
12-6

Br 2
12-2x13-0

Living
13-4x14-6

Foyer

Dining
13-4x12-0

Br 4
12-1x12-0

Porch

Full Windows Grace Elegant Family Room

2,558 total square feet of living area

Special features

- 9' ceilings throughout home
- Angled counter in kitchen serves breakfast and family rooms
- Entry foyer flanked by formal living and dining rooms
- Garage includes workshop and storage space
- 4 bedrooms, 3 baths, 2-car side entry garage
- Slab foundation, drawings also include crawl space foundation

Price Code D

Plan #X20-0438

To order blueprints use the form on page 322 or call toll-free 1-800-DREAM HOME (373-2646)

AMBSDALE

Elegant Entrance To An Impressive Home

2,563 total square feet of living area

Special features

- Remote master bedroom features bath with double sinks, spa tub and separate room with toilet

- Arched columns separate foyer from great room which includes a fireplace and accesses the nook

- Well-designed kitchen provides plenty of work space and storage plus room for extra cooks

- Energy efficient home with 2" x 6" exterior walls

- 4 bedrooms, 2 baths, 2-car garage

- Basement foundation

    Price Code D

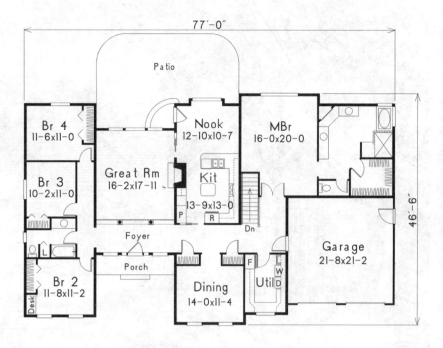

Plan #X20-0308

To order blueprints use the form on page 322 or call toll-free 1-800-DREAM HOME (373-2646)

Columns Accent Great Room And Dining Room

2,598 total square feet of living area

Special features

- Varied ceiling heights throughout home
- Stylish see-through fireplace shared by great room and family room
- Walk-in pantry and laundry room located near kitchen
- Windows in abundance provide natural light
- 4 bedrooms, 2 1/2 baths, 2-car side entry garage
- Slab foundation, drawings also include crawl space foundation

Price Code D

SINGLE-STORY over 2,000 square feet

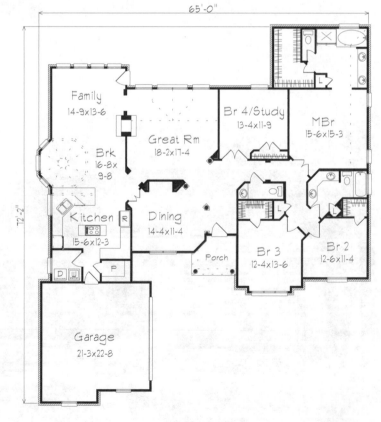

65'-0"

72'-2"

Family
14-9x13-6

Brk
16-8x 9-8

Great Rm
18-2x17-4

Br 4/Study
13-4x11-9

MBr
15-6x15-3

Kitchen
15-6x12-3

Dining
14-4x11-4

Porch

Br 3
12-4x13-6

Br 2
12-6x11-4

P

D   W

Garage
21-3x22-8

LAFAYETTE

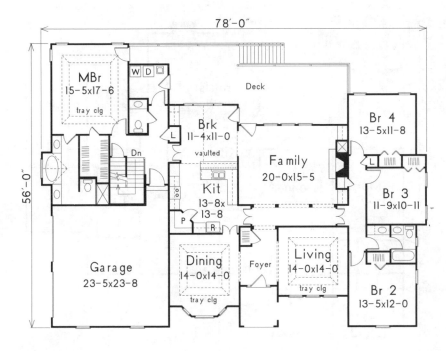

78'-0"

56'-0"

MBr
15-5x17-6
tray clg

W D

Deck

Brk
11-4x11-0
vaulted

Family
20-0x15-5

Br 4
13-5x11-8

L

Dn

Kit
13-8x
13-8

Br 3
11-9x10-11

P
R

Garage
23-5x23-8

Dining
14-0x14-0
tray clg

Foyer

Living
14-0x14-0
tray clg

Br 2
13-5x12-0

Striking Front Facade With Arched Entry

2,718 total square feet of living area

Special features

- Master suite has tray ceiling, access to the rear deck, walk-in closet and impressive private bath

- Dining room and living room flank the foyer and both feature tray ceilings

- Spacious family room features 12' ceiling, fireplace and access to the rear deck

- Kitchen has a 9' ceiling, large pantry and bar overlooking the breakfast room

- 4 bedrooms, 2 1/2 baths, 2-car side entry garage

- Basement foundation

Price Code E

SINGLE-STORY over 2,000 square feet

Plan #X20-0287

To order blueprints use the form on page 322 or call toll-free 1-800-DREAM HOME (373-2646)

Large Family-Sized Kitchen Is Centrally Located

2,731 total square feet of living area

Special features

- Isolated master suite with double walk-in closets, coffered ceiling and elegant bath
- Both dining and living rooms feature coffered ceilings and bay windows
- Breakfast room includes dramatic vaulted ceiling and plenty of windows
- Family room features fireplace flanked by shelves, vaulted ceiling and access to rear deck
- Secondary bedrooms separate from living areas
- 4 bedrooms, 3 1/2 baths, 2-car side entry
- Basement foundation

    Price Code E

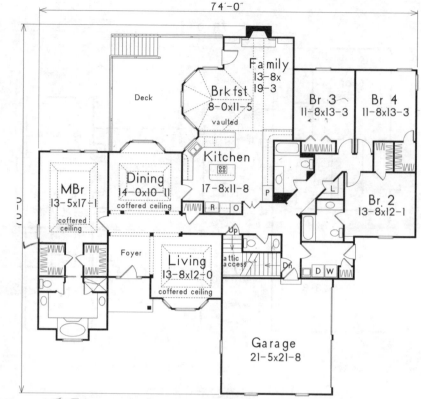

SINGLE-STORY over 2,000 square feet

Plan #X20-0288

Excellent Ranch For Country Setting

2,758 total square feet of living area

Special features

- Vaulted great room excels with fireplace, wet bar, plant shelves and skylight

- Fabulous master suite enjoys a fireplace, large bath, walk-in closet and vaulted ceiling

- Trendsetting kitchen/breakfast room adjoins spacious screened porch

- Convenient office near kitchen is perfect for computer room, hobby enthusiast or fifth bedroom

- 4 bedrooms, 2 1/2 baths, 3-car garage

- Basement foundation
  Price Code E

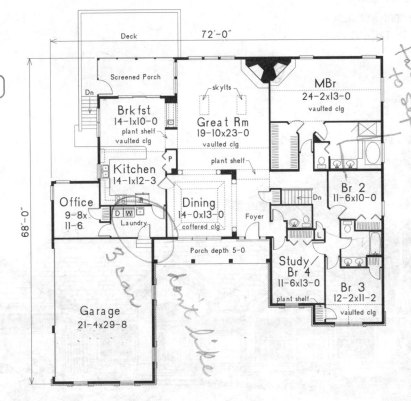

SINGLE-STORY over 2,000 square feet

Plenty Of Bright, Vaulted Spaces

2,847 total square feet of living area

Special features

- Master suite includes skylighted bath, deck access and double closets

- Bedroom #2 converts to guest room with private bath

- Impressive foyer and gallery opens into large living room with fireplace

- Formal dining and living rooms, casual family and breakfast rooms

- Kitchen features desk area, center island, adjacent bayed breakfast area and access to laundry room with half-bath

- 4 bedrooms, 3 1/2 baths, 2-car side entry garage

- Basement foundation

    Price Code E

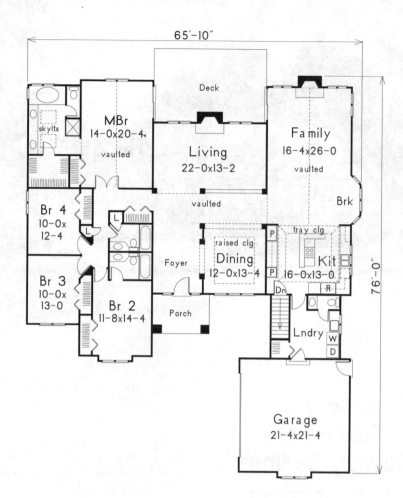

65'-10"

Deck

MBr
14-0x20-4

skylts

vaulted

Living
22-0x13-2

Family
16-4x26-0

vaulted

vaulted

Brk

Br 4
10-0x
12-4

L

L

raised clg

tray clg

P

Dining
12-0x13-4

Foyer

Kit
16-0x13-0

Br 3
10-0x
13-0

P

Dn

Br 2
11-8x14-4

Porch

R

Lndry

W
D

Garage
21-4x21-4

76'-0"

Plan #X20-0278

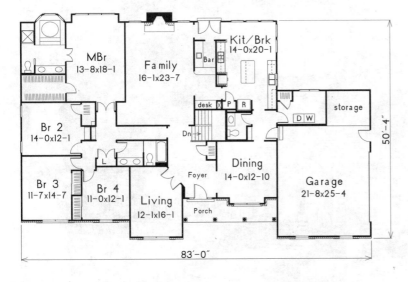

MBr
13-8x18-1

Family
16-1x23-7

Kit/Brk
14-0x20-1

Bar

Br 2
14-0x12-1

desk P R

storage

D W

Dn

Br 3
11-7x14-7

Br 4
11-0x12-1

Living
12-1x16-1

Foyer

Dining
14-0x12-10

Porch

Garage
21-8x25-4

50'-4"

83'-0"

Massive Ranch With Luxurious Features

2,874 total square feet of living area

Special features

- Large family room with sloped ceiling and wood beams adjoins the kitchen and breakfast area with windows on two walls

- Large foyer opens to family room with massive stone fireplace and open stairs to the basement

- Private master bedroom suite with raised tub under the bay window, dramatic dressing area and a huge walk-in closet

- 4 bedrooms, 2 1/2 baths, 2-car side entry garage

- Basement foundation

  Price Code E

SINGLE-STORY
over 2,000 square feet

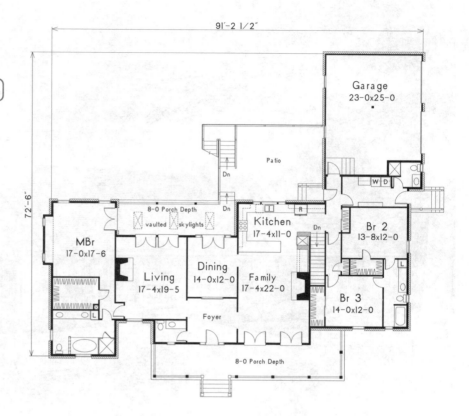

Charming Country Comfort

2,988 total square feet of living area

Special features

- Bedrooms 2 and 3 share a common bath

- Energy efficient home with 2"x 6" exterior walls

- Rear porch has direct access to master bedroom, living room and dining room

- Spacious utility room located off garage entrance features a convenient bath with shower

- Large L-shaped kitchen has plenty of work space

- Oversized master suite complete with walk-in closet and master bath

- 3 bedrooms, 3 1/2 baths, 2-car side entry garage

- Partial basement/crawl space foundation

Price Code E

SINGLE-STORY over 2,000 square feet

Plan #X20-0247

To order blueprints use the form on page 322 or call toll-free 1-800-DREAM HOME (373-2646)

ELLISVILLE

Single Level
Traditional

3,412 total square feet of living area

Special features

- Large formal dining room with vaulted ceiling adjacent to entry foyer

- Expansive great room boasts dramatic fireplace and vaulted ceiling

- Master suite and library are secluded from other living areas

- Family-style kitchen includes pantry, island cooktop and large breakfast area

- Sunken master bedroom has patio access and luxurious private bath

- 3 bedrooms, 2 full baths, 2 half baths, 2-car side entry garage

- Basement foundation

    Price Code F

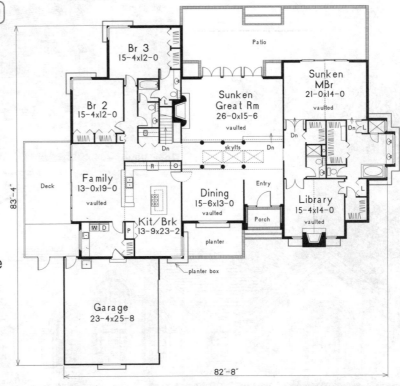

SINGLE-STORY over 2,000 square feet

Plan #X20-0347

To order blueprints use the form on page 322 or call toll-free 1-800-DREAM HOME (373-2646)

Ultimate Atrium
For A Sloping Lot

3,814 total square feet of living area

Special features

- Massive sunken great room with vaulted ceiling includes exciting balcony overlook of towering atrium window wall

- Breakfast bar adjoins open "California" kitchen

- Seven vaulted rooms for drama and four fireplaces for warmth

- Master bath complemented by colonnade and fireplace surrounding sunken tub and deck

- 3 bedrooms, 2 1/2 baths, 3-car side entry garage

- Walk-out basement foundation

- 3,566 square feet on the first floor and 248 square feet on the lower floor atrium

Price Code F

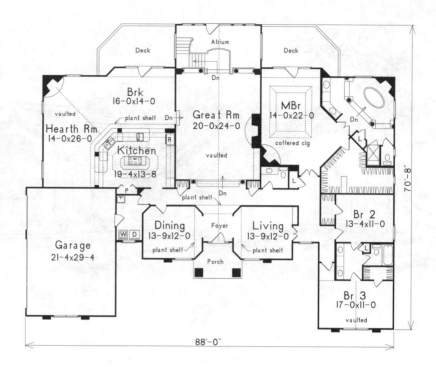

Rear View

Plan #X20-0355

HIGHLANDER

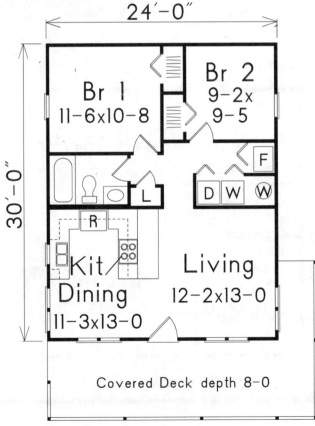

24'-0"

30'-0"

Br 1
11-6x10-8

Br 2
9-2x
9-5

L

F

D W W

R

Kit
Dining
11-3x13-0

Living
12-2x13-0

Covered Deck depth 8-0

Designed For Comfort And Utility

720 total square feet of living area

Special features

- Abundant windows in living and dining rooms provide generous sunlight
- Secluded laundry area with handy storage closet
- U-shaped kitchen with large breakfast bar opens into living area
- Large covered deck offers plenty of outdoor living space
- 2 bedrooms, 1 bath
- Crawl space foundation, drawings also include slab foundation

Price Code AA

VACATION

Plan #X20-0547

To order blueprints use the form on page 322 or call toll-free 1-800-DREAM HOME (373-2646)

Small Home Is Remarkably Spacious

| 796 total square feet of living area |

Special features

- Large porch for leisure evenings
- Dining area with bay window, open stair and pass-through kitchen, creates openness
- Basement includes generous garage space, storage area, finished laundry and mechanical room
- 2 bedrooms, 1 bath, 2-car drive under garage
- Basement foundation
- 118 square feet available on the lower level

Price Code AA

VACATION

28'-0"

28'-0"

Br 2
11-0x9-7

Kit
11-0x8-0

Deck

Dn

L

R

Dining

Dn

MBr
11-0x12-0

Living
12-7x19-4

Dn

Porch depth 5-0

Plan #X20-0657

HAVERHILL

Cottage-Style, Appealing And Cozy

> 828 total square feet of living area

Special features

- Vaulted ceilings in living area enhance space
- Convenient laundry room
- Sloped ceiling creates unique style in upstairs bedroom
- Efficient storage space under the stairs
- Covered entry porch provides cozy sitting area and plenty of shade
- 2 bedrooms, 1 bath
- Crawl space foundation
- 660 square feet on the first floor and 168 square feet on the second floor

Price Code AA

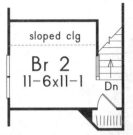

Second Floor

sloped clg

Br 2
11-6x11-1

Dn

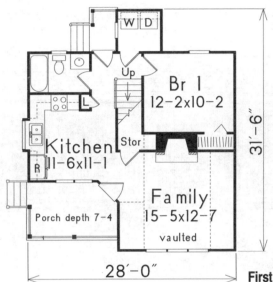

W D

Up

Br 1
12-2x10-2

31'-6"

Stor

Kitchen
11-6x11-1

L

R

Family
15-5x12-7

vaulted

Porch depth 7-4

28'-0"

First Floor

Plan #X20-0461

VACATION

Large Front Porch Adds Welcoming Appeal

829 total square feet of living area

Special features

- U-shaped kitchen opens into living area by a 42" high counter
- Oversized bay window and french door accent dining room
- Gathering space is created by the large living room
- Convenient utility room and linen closet
- 1 bedroom and 1 bath
- Slab foundation

  Price Code AA

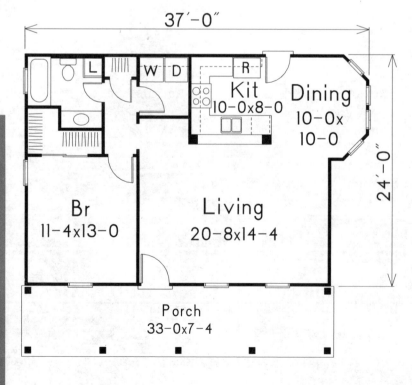

37'-0"

Kit
10-0x8-0

Dining
10-0x
10-0

24'-0"

Br
11-4x13-0

Living
20-8x14-4

Porch
33-0x7-4

VACATION

Plan #X20-0241

To order blueprints use the form on page 322 or call toll-free 1-800-DREAM HOME (373-2646)

SUMMERVIEW

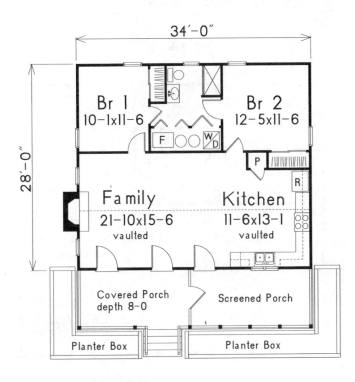

34'-0"

28'-0"

Br 1
10-1x11-6

Br 2
12-5x11-6

F W D

P

R

Family
21-10x15-6
vaulted

Kitchen
11-6x13-1
vaulted

Covered Porch
depth 8-0

Screened Porch

Planter Box

Planter Box

Country Cottage Offers Large Vaulted Living Space

962 total square feet of living area

Special features

- Both the kitchen and family rooms share warmth from the fireplace
- Charming facade features covered porch on one side, screened porch on the other and attractive planter boxes
- L-shaped kitchen boasts convenient pantry
- 2 bedrooms, 1 bath
- Crawl space foundation

Price Code A

VACATION

Plan #X20-0651

To order blueprints use the form on page 322 or call toll-free 1-800-DREAM HOME (373-2646)

Ideal Home or Retirement Retreat

1,013 total square feet of living area

Special features

- Vaulted ceiling in both family room and kitchen with dining area just beyond breakfast bar
- Plant shelf above kitchen is a special feature
- Oversized utility room has space for full-size washer and dryer
- Hall bath is centrally located with easy access from both bedrooms
- 2 bedrooms, 1 bath
- Slab foundation

Price Code A

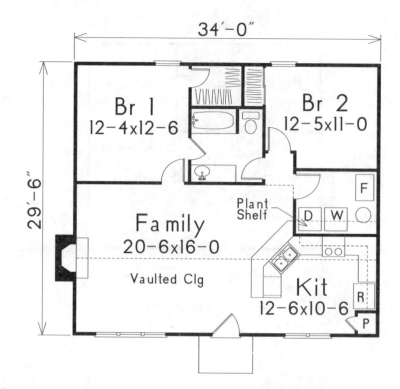

34'-0"

29'-6"

Br 1
12-4x12-6

Br 2
12-5x11-0

Plant Shelf

Family
20-6x16-0

Vaulted Clg

F

D   W

Kit
12-6x10-6

R

P

VACATION

Plan #X20-0693

To order blueprints use the form on page 322 or call toll-free 1-800-DREAM HOME (373-2646)

OAKBERRY

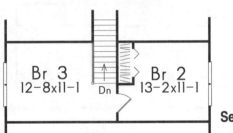

Second Floor

Br 3
12-8x11-1

Dn

Br 2
13-2x11-1

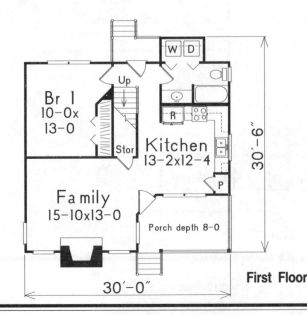

Br 1
10-0x
13-0

Up

Stor

W | D

R

Kitchen
13-2x12-4

P

30'-6"

Family
15-10x13-0

Porch depth 8-0

30'-0"

First Floor

Quaint Country Home Is Ideal

1,028 total square feet of living area

Special features

- Master bedroom conveniently located on first floor
- Well-designed bathroom contains laundry facilities
- L-shaped kitchen with handy pantry
- Tall windows flank family room fireplace
- Cozy covered porch provides unique angled entry into home
- 3 bedrooms, 1 bath
- Crawl space foundation
- 728 square feet on the first floor and 300 square feet on the second floor

Price Code A

VACATION

Plan #X20-0462

To order blueprints use the form on page 322 or call toll-free 1-800-DREAM HOME (373-2646)

CHALET

A Vacation Home For All Seasons

1,039 total square feet of living area

Special features

- Cathedral construction provides the maximum in living area openness
- Expansive glass viewing walls
- Two decks, front and back
- Charming second-story loft arrangement
- Simple, low-maintenance construction
- 2 bedrooms, 1 1/2 baths
- Crawl space foundation
- 764 square feet on the first floor and 275 square feet on the second floor

  Price Code A

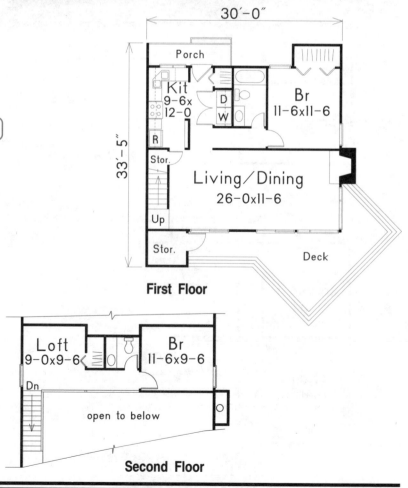

30'-0"

33'-5"

Porch

Kit
9-6x
12-0

R

Stor.

Up

Stor.

D
W

Br
11-6x11-6

Living/Dining
26-0x11-6

Deck

First Floor

Loft
9-0x9-6

Dn

Br
11-6x9-6

open to below

Second Floor

Plan #X20-0101

To order blueprints use the form on page 322 or call toll-free 1-800-DREAM HOME (373-2646)

TIMBERBROOKE

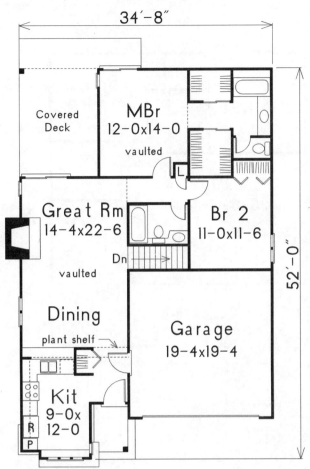

Charming Exterior And Cozy Interior

> 1,127 total square feet of living area

Special features

- Plant shelf joins kitchen and dining room
- Vaulted master suite with double walk-in closets, deck access and private bath
- Great room features vaulted ceiling, fireplace and sliding door to covered deck
- Ideal home for narrow lot
- 2 bedrooms, 2 baths, 2-car garage
- Basement foundation

  Price Code A

VACATION

Plan #X20-0277

To order blueprints use the form on page 322 or call toll-free 1-800-DREAM HOME (373-2646)

Flexible Layout For Various Uses

1,143 total square feet of living area

Special features

- Enormous stone fireplace in family room adds warmth and character
- Spacious kitchen with breakfast bar overlooks family room
- Separate dining area great for entertaining
- Vaulted family and kitchen create open atmosphere
- 2 bedrooms, 1 bath
- Crawl space foundation

Price Code A

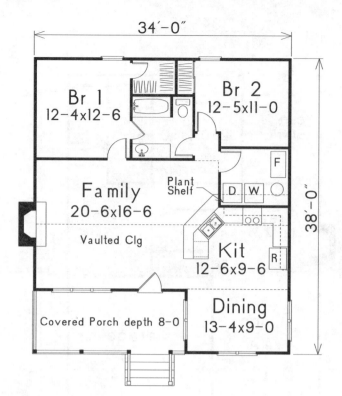

34'-0"

38'-0"

Br 1
12-4x12-6

Br 2
12-5x11-0

F

Plant Shelf

D W

Family
20-6x16-6

Vaulted Clg

Kit
12-6x9-6

R

Covered Porch depth 8-0

Dining
13-4x9-0

VACATION

Plan #X20-0698

To order blueprints use the form on page 322 or call toll-free 1-800-DREAM HOME (373-2646)

WOODBRIDGE

Open Living Area

| 1,154 total square feet of living area |

Special features

- U-shaped kitchen with large breakfast bar and handy laundry area

- Private second floor bedrooms share half bath

- Large living and dining area opens to deck

- 3 bedrooms, 1 1/2 baths

- Crawl space foundation, drawings also include slab foundation

- 720 square feet on the first floor and 434 square feet on the second floor

   Price Code A

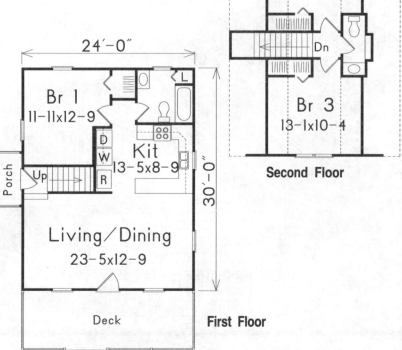

Second Floor

Br 2
13-1x10-4

Dn

Br 3
13-1x10-4

24'-0"

Br 1
11-11x12-9

L

D
W
R

Kit
13-5x8-9

Porch

Up

30'-0"

Living/Dining
23-5x12-9

Deck

First Floor

VACATION

Perfect Vacation Home

1,230 total square feet of living area

Special features

- Spacious living room accesses huge sun deck
- One of the second floor bedrooms features balcony overlooking deck
- Kitchen with dining area accesses outdoors
- Washer and dryer tucked under stairs
- 3 bedrooms, 1 bath
- Crawl space foundation, drawings also include slab foundation
- 780 square feet on the first floor and 450 square feet on the second floor

Price Code A

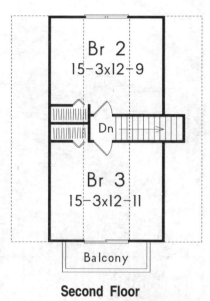

Second Floor

Br 2
15-3x12-9

Br 3
15-3x12-11

Dn

Balcony

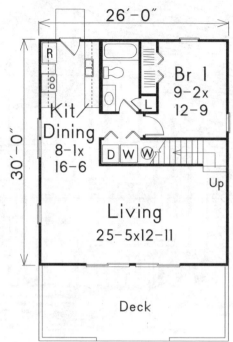

First Floor

26'-0"

30'-0"

R

Kit
Dining
8-1x
16-6

Br 1
9-2x
12-9

L

D W W

Up

Living
25-5x12-11

Deck

Plan #X20-0549

To order blueprints use the form on page 322 or call toll-free 1-800-DREAM HOME (373-2646)

VACATION

286

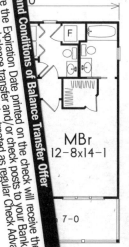

Yea...
W...
Geta...

1,339 total sq...

Special feature...

- Full length c... enhances fron...
- Vaulted ceiling... fireplace add c... room
- Walk-in closets... provide ample s...
- Combined kitche... adjoins family roo... entertaining spac...
- 3 bedrooms, 2 1/2...
- Crawl space found...
- 924 square feet on... and 415 square feet... second floor

Price Code ...

First Floor

F

MBr
12-8x14-1

7-0

Loft/
Br 3
10-7x11-11

Dn

Open To Below

Br 2
12-8x10-0

...Floor

Dramatic Sloping Ceiling In Living Room

1,432 total square feet of living area

Special features

- Enter into the two-story foyer from covered porch or garage

- Living room has square bay and window seat, glazed end wall with floor to ceiling windows and access to the deck

- Kitchen/dining room also opens to the deck for added convenience

- 3 bedrooms, 2 baths, 1-car garage

- Basement foundation, drawings also include slab foundation

- 967 square feet on the first floor and 465 square feet on the second floor

Price Code A

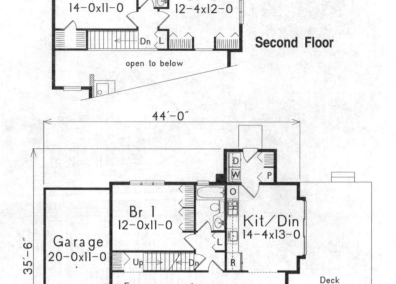

Second Floor

Br 2
14-0x11-0

Br 3
12-4x12-0

Dn

open to below

First Floor

44'-0"

35'-6"

Garage
20-0x11-0

Br 1
12-0x11-0

Kit/Din
14-4x13-0

D W P

Up

Dn

Foyer

wood stove

Deck

Living
23-0x14-4
sloped ceiling

window seat

Covered Porch

VACATION

Plan #X20-0680

To order blueprints use the form on page 322 or call toll-free 1-800-DREAM HOME (373-2646)

IRIS

Dramatic Expanse Of Windows

1,660 total square feet of living area

Special features

- Convenient gear and equipment room
- Spacious living/dining room looks even larger with the openness of the foyer and kitchen
- Large wrap-around deck, a great plus for outdoor living
- Broad balcony overlooks living/dining room
- 3 bedrooms, 3 baths, 1-car drive under garage
- Partial basement/crawl space foundation, drawings also include slab foundation
- 1,292 square feet on the first floor and 368 square feet on the second floor

Price Code B

Second Floor

Br 3
14-10x12-0

skylt

Dn

Balcony

open to below

41'-5"

44'-1"

Br 2
11-0x12-0

MBr
12-0x12-0

Equip.

Dn

Up

L

W D

R

Kitchen
12-7x7-6

Living
12-9x15-7
vaulted

Dining
12-9x14-0
vaulted

Deck

First Floor

VACATION

Spacious A-Frame

1,769 total square feet of living area

Special features

- Living room boasts elegant cathedral ceiling and fireplace
- U-shaped kitchen and dining area combine for easy living
- Secondary bedrooms include double closets
- Secluded master bedroom with sloped ceiling, large walk-in closet and private bath
- 3 bedrooms, 2 baths
- Basement foundation, drawings also include crawl space and slab foundations
- 1,306 square feet on the first floor and 463 square feet on the second floor

Price Code B

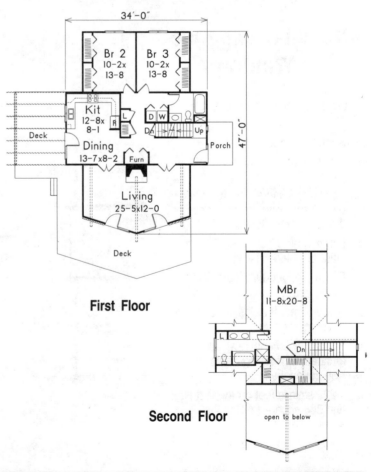

First Floor

Second Floor

Plan #X20-0539

To order blueprints use the form on page 322 or call toll-free 1-800-DREAM HOME (373-2646)

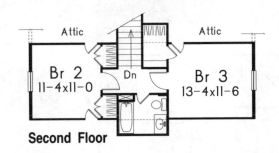

Roomy Two-Story Has Screened-In Rear Porch

1,600 total square feet of living area

Special features

- Energy efficient home with 2" x 6" exterior walls

- Lower level master suite accessible from two points of entry

- Master suite dressing area includes separate vanity and mirrored make-up counter

- Second floor bedrooms with generous storage, share a full bath

- 3 bedrooms, 2 baths, 2-car side entry garage

- Crawl space foundation, drawings also include slab foundation

- 1,136 square feet on the first floor and 464 square feet on the second floor

Price Code B

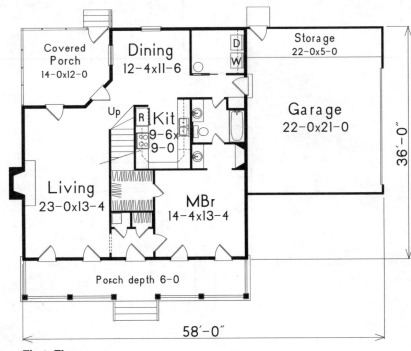

Second Floor

First Floor

1 1/2 STORY

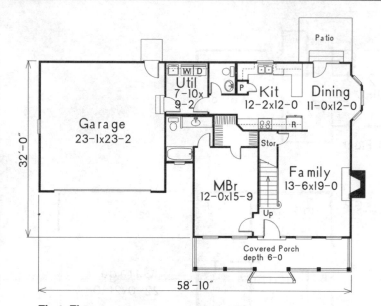

First Floor

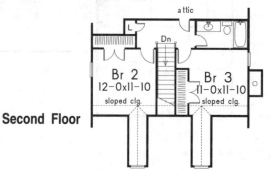

Second Floor

Charming Home Arranged For Open Living

1,609 total square feet of living area

Special features

- Kitchen captures full use of space with pantry, ample cabinets and workspace
- Master bedroom well secluded with walk-in closet and private bath
- Large utility room includes sink and extra storage
- Attractive bay window in dining area provides light
- 3 bedrooms, 2 1/2 baths, 2-car garage
- Slab foundation
- 1,072 square feet on the first floor and 537 square feet on the second floor

Price Code B

I 1/2 STORY

Plan #X20-0686

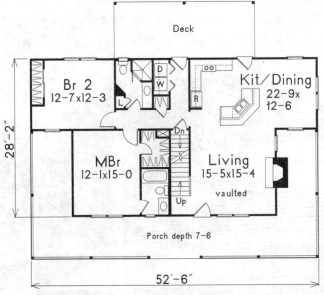

Deck

Br 2
12-7x12-3

Kit/Dining
22-9x
12-6

28'-2"

MBr
12-1x15-0

Living
15-5x15-4

vaulted

Dn

Up

Porch depth 7-6

52'-6"

First Floor

Br 3
12-1x13-7

open to
below

Dn

Second Floor

Wrap-Around Porch Adds Country Charm

1,619 total square feet of living area

Special features

- Private second floor bedroom and bath
- Kitchen features a snack bar and adjacent dining area
- Master bedroom with private bath
- Centrally located washer and dryer
- 3 bedrooms, 3 baths
- Basement foundation, drawings also include crawl space and slab foundations
- 1,259 square feet on the first floor and 360 square feet on the second floor

Price Code B

1 1/2 STORY

Plan #X20-0221

To order blueprints use the form on page 322 or call toll-free 1-800-DREAM HOME (373-2646)

HD

Quaint Exterior, Full Front Porch

| 1,657 total square feet of living area |

Special features

- Stylish pass-through between living and dining areas
- Master bedroom is secluded from living area for privacy
- Large windows in breakfast and dining area
- 3 bedrooms, 2 1/2 baths, 2-car drive under garage
- Basement foundation
- 1,046 square feet on the first floor and 611 square feet on the second floor

Price Code B

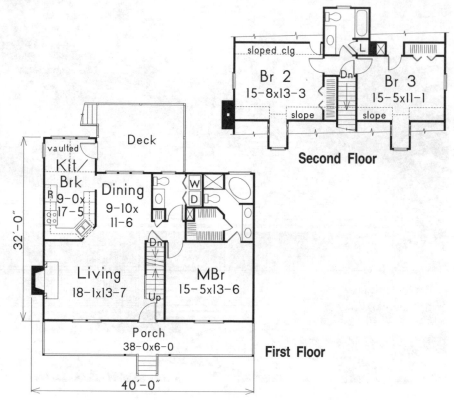

Second Floor

Br 2 15-8x13-3
Br 3 15-5x11-1
sloped clg
slope

Deck
Kit/ vaulted
Brk 9-0x 17-5
Dining 9-10x 11-6
Living 18-1x13-7
MBr 15-5x13-6
Porch 38-0x6-0
W D

32'-0"
40'-0"

First Floor

1 1/2 STORY

Plan #X20-0174
To order blueprints use the form on page 322 or call toll-free 1-800-DREAM HOME (373-2646)

GEORGETOWN

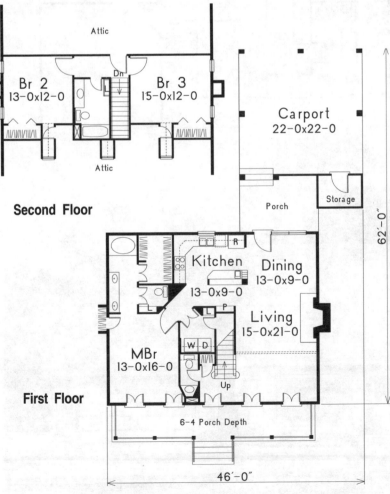

Second Floor

Attic

Br 2
13-0x12-0

Br 3
15-0x12-0

Dn

Attic

Carport
22-0x22-0

Storage

Porch

62'-0"

First Floor

Kitchen
13-0x9-0

Dining
13-0x9-0

Living
15-0x21-0

MBr
13-0x16-0

W D

Up

6-4 Porch Depth

46'-0"

Stucco Finish And Authentic Southern Home Styling

1,700 total square feet of living area

Special features

- Fully appointed kitchen with wet bar
- Energy efficient home with 2" x 6" exterior walls
- Linen drop from upper level bath to utility room
- Master bath includes raised marble tub and sloped ceilings
- 3 bedrooms, 2 1/2 baths and 2-car attached carport
- Crawl space foundation, drawings also include basement and slab foundations
- 1,160 square feet on the first floor and 540 square feet on the second floor

Price Code B

1 1/2 STORY

Plan #X20-0290

Charming Two-Story With Dormers And Porch

1,711 total square feet of living area

Special features

- U-shaped kitchen joins breakfast and family rooms for open living atmosphere
- Master bedroom has secluded covered porch and private bath
- Balcony overlooks family room that features a fireplace and accesses deck
- 3 bedrooms, 2 1/2 baths, 2-car garage
- Basement foundation
- 1,228 square feet on the first floor and 483 square feet on the second floor

Price Code B

open to below

Br 3
11-3x11-0

Dn

Br 2
9-11x10-0

Storage

open to below

Storage

Second Floor

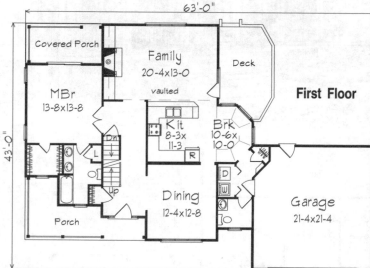

63'-0"

43'-0"

Covered Porch

Family
20-4x13-0

Deck

vaulted

MBr
13-8x13-8

First Floor

Kit
8-3x11-3

Brk
10-6x10-0

Dn

Dining
12-4x12-8

Garage
21-4x21-4

Porch

1 1/2 STORY

Plan #X20-0379

FARMVIEW

Two-Story Foyer Adds Spacious Feeling

1,814 total square feet of living area

Special features

- Large master suite includes a spacious bath with garden tub, separate shower and large walk-in closet

- Spacious kitchen and dining areas brightened by large windows and patio access

- Detached 2-car garage with walkway leading to house adds to the charm of this country home

- Large front porch

- 3 bedrooms, 2 1/2 baths, 2-car detached garage

- Crawl space, drawings also include slab foundation

- 1,288 square feet on the first floor and 526 square feet on the second floor

Price Code D

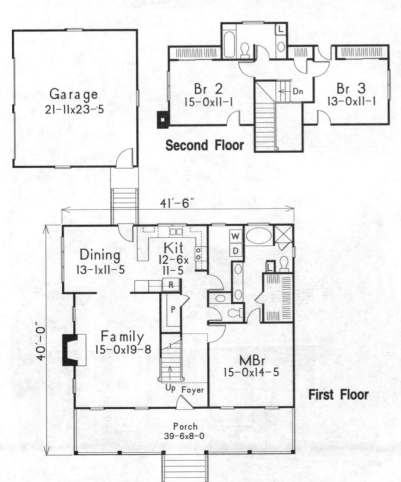

Garage
21-11x23-5

Br 2
15-0x11-1

Br 3
13-0x11-1

Dn

Second Floor

41'-6"

40'-0"

Dining
13-1x11-5

Kit
12-6x
11-5

W
D

R

P

Family
15-0x19-8

MBr
15-0x14-5

Up   Foyer

First Floor

Porch
39-6x8-0

I 1/2 STORY

Plan #X20-0201

To order blueprints use the form on page 322 or call toll-free 1-800-DREAM HOME (373-2646)

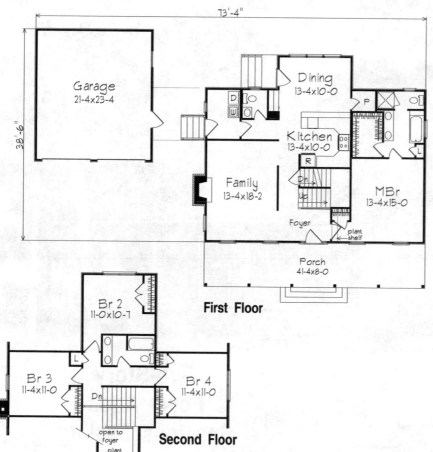

Garage
21-4x23-4

73'-4"

38'-6"

Dining
13-4x10-0

D

W

Kitchen
13-4x10-0

P

R

Dn

Up

Family
13-4x18-2

MBr
13-4x15-0

Foyer

plant shelf

First Floor

Porch
41-4x8-0

Br 2
11-0x10-7

L

Br 3
11-4x11-0

Dn

Br 4
11-4x11-0

open to foyer

plant shelf

Second Floor

Breezeway
Joins Living Space
With Garage

1,874 total square feet of living area

Special features

- 9' ceilings throughout first floor
- Two-story foyer opens into large family room with fireplace
- First floor master suite includes private bath with tub and shower
- 4 bedrooms, 2 1/2 baths, 2-car garage
- Basement foundation, drawings also include slab foundation
- 1,241 square feet on the first floor and 633 square feet on the second floor

Price Code C

I 1/2 STORY

Plan #X20-0362

To order blueprints use the form on page 322 or call toll-free 1-800-DREAM HOME (373-2646)

SPRINGWOOD

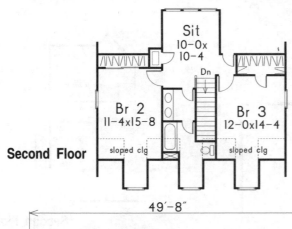

Second Floor

Sit
10-0x
10-4

Dn

Br 2
11-4x15-8

Br 3
12-0x14-4

sloped clg   sloped clg

49'-8"

38'-4"

MBr
13-0x13-4

Brk
10-0x
10-0

W D P

R

Kit
12-0x
10-0

Living
17-4x17-0

Up

Dining
12-4x14-0

First Floor

Veranda depth 7-0

Country Charm Wrapped In A Veranda

2,059 total square feet of living area

Special features

- Octagonal-shaped breakfast room offers plenty of windows and creates a view to the veranda

- First floor master bedroom has large walk-in closet and deluxe bath

- 9' ceilings throughout the home

- Secondary bedrooms and bath feature dormers and are adjacent to cozy sitting area

- 3 bedrooms, 2 1/2 baths, 2-car detached garage

- Slab foundation, drawings also include basement and crawl space foundations

- 1,308 square feet on the first floor and 751 square feet on the second floor

Price Code C

1 1/2 STORY

Plan #X20-0213

Graceful And Functional Front Porch

2,255 total square feet of living area

Special features

- Master suite and adjoining bath with an enormous walk-in closet
- Energy efficient home with 2" x 6" exterior walls
- Deluxe kitchen features a planning desk and a convenient eating area
- Balcony library overlooks living area
- Formal dining area with easy access to the kitchen
- 3 bedrooms, 2 baths, 2-car garage
- Crawl space foundation, drawings also include slab and basement foundations
- 2,159 square feet on the first floor and 96 square feet on the second floor

Price Code D

Second Floor

First Floor

1·1/2 STORY

SALINA

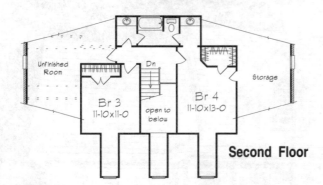

Second Floor

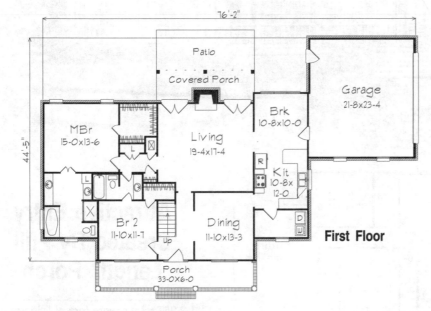

First Floor

Double French Doors Grace Living Room

2,333 total square feet of living area

Special features

- 9' ceilings on first floor
- Master bedroom features large walk-in closet and inviting double-door entry into spacious bath
- Convenient laundry room located near kitchen
- 4 bedrooms, 3 baths, 2-car side entry garage
- Slab foundation, drawings also include crawl space and partial crawl space/basement foundations
- 1,685 square feet on the first floor and 648 square feet on the second floor

Price Code D

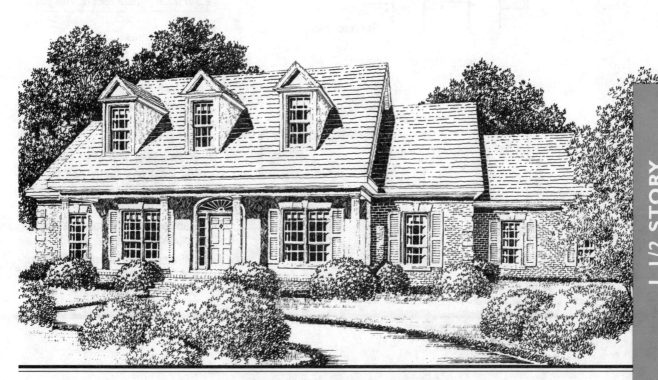

1 1/2 STORY

HARWICK

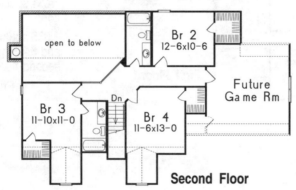

Second Floor

- open to below
- Br 2 12-6x10-6
- Future Game Rm
- Br 3 11-10x11-0
- Dn
- Br 4 11-6x13-0

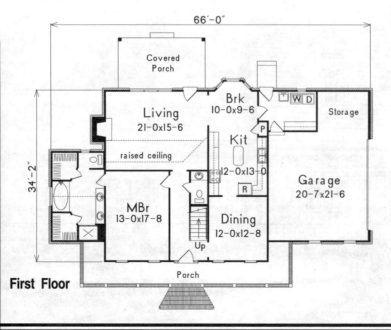

First Floor

66'-0"
34'-2"

- Covered Porch
- Living 21-0x15-6
- raised ceiling
- Brk 10-0x9-6
- W D
- Storage
- Kit 12-0x13-0
- Garage 20-7x21-6
- MBr 13-0x17-8
- Dining 12-0x12-8
- Up
- Porch

I 1/2 STORY

Attractive Entry Created By Full Length Porch

2,357 total square feet of living area

Special features

- 9' ceilings on first floor
- Secluded master bedroom includes private bath with double walk-in closets and vanities
- Balcony overlooks living room with large fireplace
- Second floor with three bedrooms and expansive game room
- 4 bedrooms, 3 1/2 baths, 2-car side entry garage
- Slab foundation, drawings also include crawl space foundation
- 1,492 square feet on the first floor and 865 square feet on the second floor

Price Code D

Plan #X20-0434

To order blueprints use the form on page 322 or call toll-free 1-800-DREAM HOME (373-2646)

LAKEWAY

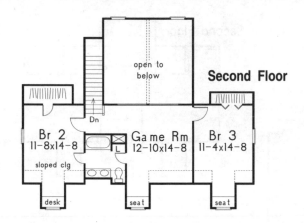

Second Floor

Br 2
11-8x14-8

sloped clg

open to
below

Dn

Game Rm
12-10x14-8
L

Br 3
11-4x14-8

desk

seat

seat

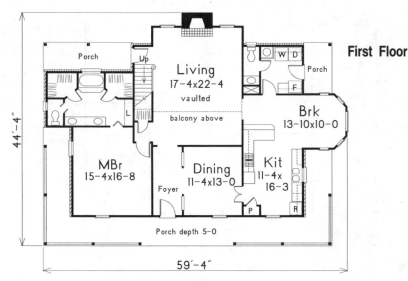

First Floor

Porch

Up

Living
17-4x22-4
vaulted

balcony above

W | D

Porch

F

Brk
13-10x10-0

L

44'-4"

MBr
15-4x16-8

Dining
11-4x13-0

Foyer

Kit
11-4x
16-3

P

R

Porch depth 5-0

59'-4"

Wrap-Around Veranda Softens Country-Style Home

> 2,449 total square feet of living area

Special features

- Striking living area features fireplace flanked with windows, cathedral ceiling and balcony

- First floor master bedroom with twin walk-in closets and large linen storage

- Dormers add space for desks or seats

- 3 bedrooms, 2 1/2 baths, 2-car detached garage

- Slab foundation, drawings also include crawl space foundation

- 1,669 square feet on the first floor and 780 square feet on the second floor

Price Code E

I 1/2 STORY

Plan #X20-0143

To order blueprints use the form on page 322 or call toll-free 1-800-DREAM HOME (373-2646)

Wrap-Around Front Country Porch

2,665 total square feet of living area

Special features

- 9' ceilings on first floor
- Spacious kitchen features many cabinets, center island cooktop and breakfast room with bay, adjacent to laundry room
- Second floor bedrooms boast walk-in closets, dressing areas and share a bath
- Twin patio doors and fireplace grace living room
- 4 bedrooms, 3 baths, 2-car rear entry garage
- Slab foundation, drawings also include crawl space foundation
- 1,916 square feet on the first floor and 749 square feet on the second floor

Price Code E

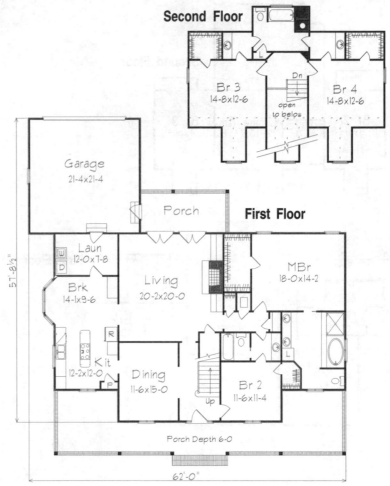

Second Floor

Br 3
14-8x12-6

Br 4
14-8x12-6

open to below

Dn

First Floor

Garage
21-4x21-4

Porch

Laun
12-0x7-8

Brk
14-1x9-6

Living
20-2x20-0

MBr
18-0x14-2

Kit
12-2x12-0

Dining
11-6x15-0

Br 2
11-6x11-4

Up

Porch Depth 6-0

57'-8½"

62'-0"

I 1/2 STORY

Plan #X20-0439

To order blueprints use the form on page 322 or call toll-free 1-800-DREAM HOME (373-2646)

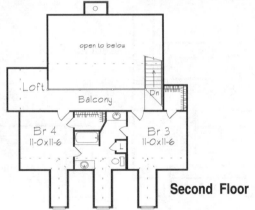

Second Floor

Loft

open to below

Balcony

Dn

Br 4
11-0x11-6

Br 3
11-0x11-6

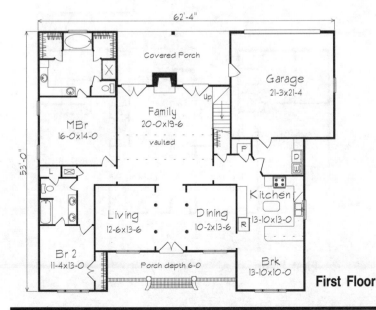

62'-4"

Covered Porch

Garage
21-3x21-4

Up

Family
20-0x19-6
vaulted

MBr
16-0x14-0

53'-0"

P

Kitchen
13-10x13-0

Living
12-6x13-6

Dining
10-2x13-6

R

Br 2
11-4x13-0

Porch depth 6-0

Brk
13-10x10-0

First Floor

Entry Collonade, Circle-Top Windows And Columns

2,869 total square feet of living area

Special features

- Foyer, flanked by columned living and dining rooms, leads to vaulted family room with fireplace and twin sets of french doors

- 10' ceilings on the first floor, 9' ceilings on the second floor

- 4 bedrooms, 3 baths, 2-car rear entry garage

- Slab foundation, drawings also include crawl space foundation

- 2,152 square feet on the first floor and 717 square feet on the second floor

  Price Code E

I 1/2 STORY

Plan #X20-0430

Traditional Classic, Modern Features Abound

> 3,035 total square feet of living area

Special features

- Front facade includes large porch
- Private master bedroom with windowed sitting area, walk-in closet, sloped ceiling and skylight
- Formal living and dining rooms adjoin the family room through attractive french doors
- Energy efficient home with 2" x 6" exterior walls
- 4 bedrooms, 3 1/2 baths, 2-car side entry garage
- Crawl space foundation, drawings also include slab and basement foundations
- 2,008 square feet on the first floor and 1,027 square feet on the second floor

Price Code E

1 1/2 STORY

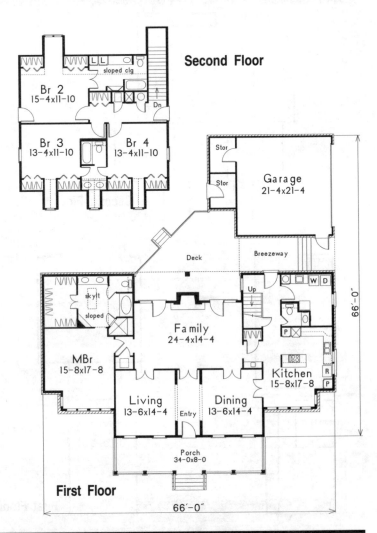

Second Floor

Br 2
15-4x11-10

Br 3
13-4x11-10

Br 4
13-4x11-10

sloped clg

Dn

Garage
21-4x21-4

Stor

Stor

Breezeway

Deck

Up

W D

skylt
sloped

Family
24-4x14-4

MBr
15-8x17-8

Kitchen
15-8x17-8

Living
13-6x14-4

Entry

Dining
13-6x14-4

Porch
34-0x8-0

First Floor

66'-0"

66'-0"

Plan #X20-0187

SALEM II

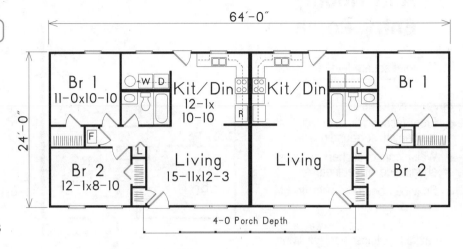

Compact Home With Large Living Area

1,536 total square feet of living area

Special features

- Living room joins the kitchen/dining area for open atmosphere
- L-shaped kitchen with outdoor access and convenient laundry area
- Linen and coat closet
- Welcoming front porch
- Each unit has 2 bedrooms, 1 bath
- Crawl space foundation, drawings also include slab foundation
- Duplex has 768 total square feet of living space per unit

Price Code D

MULTI-FAMILY

Plan #X20-0595

To order blueprints use the form on page 322 or call toll-free 1-800-DREAM HOME (373-2646)

Duplex With Side Garage And Roomy Entry Porch

1,700 total square feet of living area

Special features

- Front facade fits splendidly with residential surroundings
- Well-planned kitchen includes abundance of cabinets
- Spacious bedroom with double closets
- Plant shelf, open stairway and vaulted ceilings highlight living space
- Convenient entrance from garage into main living area
- Dining room accesses deck
- Each unit has 2 bedrooms, 1 bath, 1-car side entry garage
- Basement foundation
- Duplex has 850 square feet of living space per unit

    Price Code D

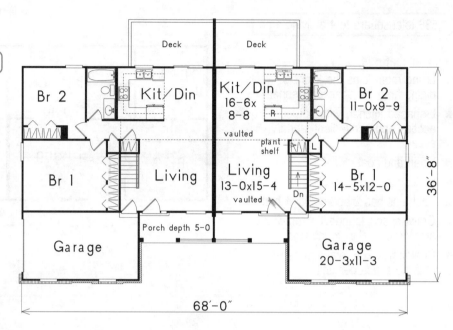

MULTI-FAMILY

PEPPERTREE

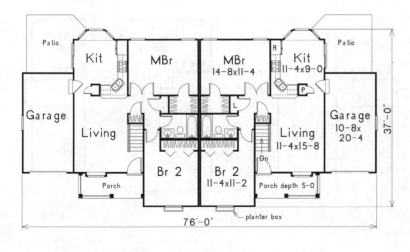

Duplex With Plenty Of Style

> 1,704 total square feet of living area

Special features

- Smartly designed layout with emphasis on efficiency
- Functional kitchen embraces the sun with its bay window, glass sliding doors and pass-through to living room
- Five generously designed closets offer an abundance of storage
- Each unit has 2 bedrooms, 1 bath, 1-car garage
- Basement foundation
- Duplex has 852 square feet of living space per unit

Price Code D

Plan #X20-0465

To order blueprints use the form on page 322 or call toll-free 1-800-DREAM HOME (373-2646)

Duplex With Cozy Front Porch

1,904 total square feet of living area

Special features

- Convenient laundry area and dining adjacent to kitchen
- Bedrooms feature ample closet space
- Garage has plenty of space for work/storage area
- Handy coat closets located near garage and living room
- Dining accesses outdoors
- Each unit has 2 bedrooms, 1 bath, 1-car garage
- Partial basement/crawl space foundation
- Duplex has 952 square feet of living space per unit

Price Code E

MULTI-FAMILY

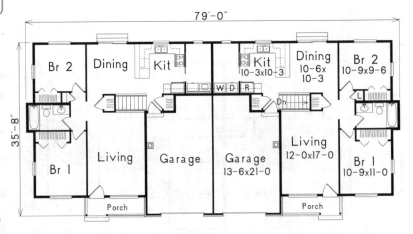

79'-0"

35'-8"

Br 2 | Dining | Kit 10-3x10-3
Br 1 | Living | Garage
Porch

Garage 13-6x21-0 | Living 12-0x17-0
Kit 10-3x10-3 | Dining 10-6x 10-3 | Br 2 10-9x9-6
W D R | Dh | Br 1 10-9x11-0
Porch

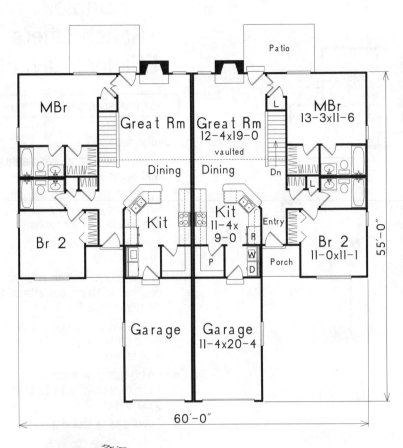

Stylish Living, Open Design

1,992 total square feet of living area

Special features

- Graciously designed ranch home with alluring openness
- Vaulted kitchen with accent on spaciousness features huge pantry, plenty of cabinets and convenient laundry room
- Master bedroom includes its own cozy bath and oversized walk-in closet
- Each unit has 2 bedrooms, 2 baths, 1-car garage
- Basement foundation
- Duplex has 996 square feet of living space per unit

Price Code E

Plan #X20-0464

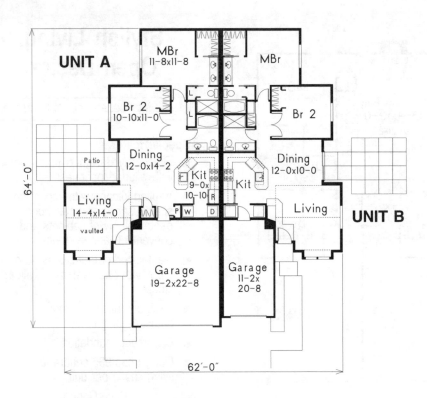

UNIT A

MBr
11-8x11-8

MBr

Br 2
10-10x11-0

Br 2

Patio

Dining
12-0x14-2

Dining
12-0x10-0

Kit
9-0x
10-10

Kit

Living
14-4x14-0

R

P W D

Living

UNIT B

vaulted

Garage
19-2x22-8

Garage
11-2x
20-8

64'-0"

62'-0"

Duplex Ranch Offers Efficient Layout

2,167 total square feet of living area

Special features

- Vaulted ceilings in living areas add spaciousness
- Master bath features separate vanity and dressing area which extends into master suite
- Large patio extends out from dining space
- Wrap-around kitchen counter doubles as snack bar with added counter space
- Unit A has 2 bedrooms, 2 baths, 2-car garage with 1,115 total square feet
- Unit B has 2 bedrooms, 2 baths, 1-car garage with 1,052 total square feet
- Crawl space foundation

Price Code E

MULTI-FAMILY

Plan #X20-0457

SHADYDALE

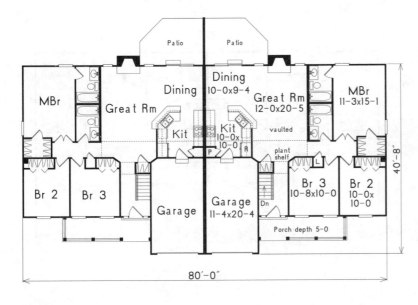

Vaulted Ceilings Add Spaciousness To Living Areas

2,318 total square feet of living area

Special features

- Great room area complemented with fireplace and patio access
- Breakfast bar with corner sink overlooks great room
- Plant shelf graces vaulted entry
- Master suite provides walk-in closet and private bath
- Each unit has 3 bedrooms, 2 baths, 1-car garage
- Basement foundation
- Duplex has 1,159 square feet of living space per unit

Price Code F

MULTI-FAMILY

Plan #X20-0452

Covered Porch Entrance To Duplex

2,830 total square feet of living area

Special features

- Great room, master bedroom and dining accesses covered porch
- Master bedroom features double-door entry, walk-in closet and private bath with shower
- Great room with fireplace and wet bar
- U-shaped kitchen opens to dining room
- Laundry room with plenty of work space conveniently accesses outside, garage and kitchen
- Each unit has 2 bedrooms, 2 baths, 2-car garage
- Basement foundation
- Duplex has 1,415 square feet of living space per unit

Price Code G

MULTI-FAMILY

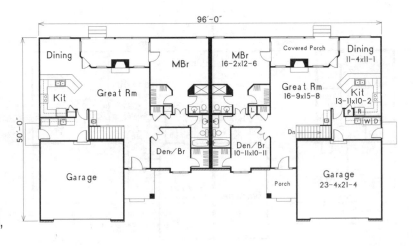

96'-0"

50'-0"

Dining

Kit

Great Rm

Garage

MBr

Den/Br

MBr 16-2x12-6

Den/Br 10-11x10-11

Covered Porch

Great Rm 16-9x15-8

Kit 13-11x10-2

Dining 11-4x11-1

Garage 23-4x21-4

Porch

Dn

Plan #X20-0466

To order blueprints use the form on page 322 or call toll-free 1-800-DREAM HOME (373-2646)

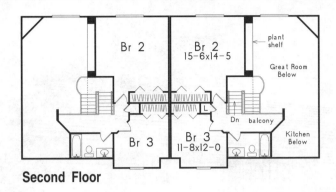

Second Floor

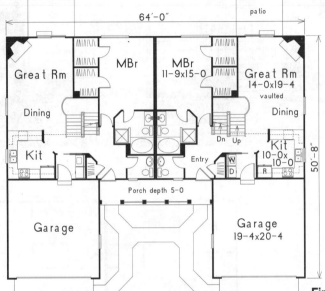

First Floor

Country Charm In A Double Feature

2,986 total square feet of living area

Special features

- Vaulted great room, kitchen and two balconies define architectural drama
- First floor master suite boasts a lavish bath and double walk-in closets
- Impressive second floor features two large bedrooms, spacious closets, hall bath and balcony overlook
- Each unit has 3 bedrooms, 2 1/2 baths, 2-car garage
- Basement foundation
- Duplex has 1,493 square feet of living space per unit with 960 square feet on the first floor and 533 square feet on the second floor

Price Code G

MULTI-FAMILY

Plan #X20-0463

To order blueprints use the form on page 322 or call toll-free 1-800-DREAM HOME (373-2646)

315

Spacious Layout For Comfortable Living

> 3,360 total square feet of living area

Special features

- Bedrooms with ample closet space
- Laundry closet near both bedrooms
- Convenient U-shaped kitchen adjacent to dining room with access to deck on first floor and balcony on second floor
- Adjacent to living room is handy coat and linen closet
- Each unit has 2 bedrooms, 1 bath
- Crawl space foundation, drawings also include slab foundation
- Fourplex has 840 square feet of living space per unit

Price Code H

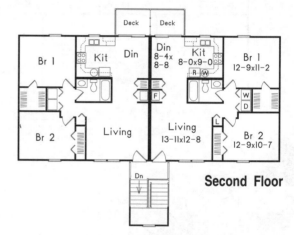

Second Floor

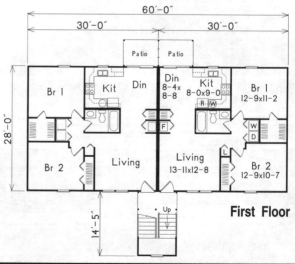

First Floor

PASADENA

Well-Designed Facade, Welcoming And Distinctive

4,240 total square feet of living area

Special features

- Kitchen, brightened by a large bay window, accesses patio on first floor units and deck on second floor units
- Corner fireplace provides warmth and charm
- Bedrooms separated from living areas for privacy
- Laundry located off hall for accessibility
- Each unit has 3 bedrooms, 2 baths, 1-car garage
- Basement foundation
- Fourplex has 1,060 square feet of living space per unit

Price Code H

Second Floor

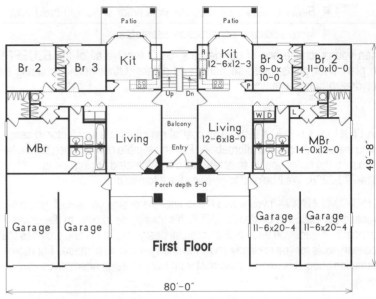

First Floor

Porch depth 5-0

80'-0"

49'-8"

Plan #X20-0454

To order blueprints use the form on page 322 or call toll-free 1-800-DREAM HOME (373-2646)

MULTI-FAMILY

Our Blueprint Packages Offer...

Quality plans for building your future, with extras that provide unsurpassed value, ensure good construction and long-term enjoyment.

A quality home - one that looks good, functions well, and provides years of enjoyment - is a product of many things - design, materials, craftsmanship. But it's also the result of outstanding blueprints - the actual plans and specifications that tell the builder exactly how to build your home.

And with our BLUEPRINT PACKAGES you get the absolute best. A complete set of blueprints is available for every design in this book. These "working drawings," accompanied by our General Building Specifications, are highly detailed, resulting in two key benefits:

- *Better understanding by the contractor of how to build your home, and...*
- *More accurate construction estimates.*

When you purchase one of our designs, you'll receive all of the BLUEPRINT components shown here - elevations, foundation plan, floor plans, cross-sections, and details. Other helpful building aids listed below are also available to help make your dream home a reality.

MATERIAL ESTIMATES - The cost of materials is a key factor in determining the overall cost and affordability. For an estimate of how much the materials will cost for the home you've selected, call our automated pricing line at 1-314-770-2228. We'll be glad to give you the information.

CUSTOMIZING - If you would like to alter the design you select, you can purchase our exclusive Customizer Kit™. It's your guide to custom designing your home. It leads you through the essential design decisions and provides the necessary tools for you to clearly show the changes you want made. For more information about this exclusive product from Home Design Alternatives see page 4.

REPRODUCIBLE MASTERS - If you wish to make minor design changes such as moving a few interior walls, doors, or changing the foundation type, etc., we strongly recommend that you purchase our reproducible masters along with the Customizer Kit. These masters contain the same information as the blueprints, but are printed on erasable, reproducible paper for the purpose of modification.

MATERIAL LISTS - To enhance the quality of our blueprint packages, we offer one of the most precise and thorough material lists in the industry.

Lists are broken down into "packages" such as floor systems, wall framing, roof systems, exterior windows and doors, etc., a real benefit because they are in the order in which these items are needed on the job site.

The lists are very specific. Quantities and exact descriptions are listed for nearly every item needed. The location or point of installation of many materials is also noted to eliminate errors and material waste (e.g. (7) 2x8x8 GRADE MARK 2 OR BETTER, ceiling joist box sill). The lists also include cabinet layouts and truss diagrams where applicable.

OVERNIGHT DELIVERY - Many of our customers need their plans overnight. If you would like yours the next day, please call us by 11 a.m. CST at 1-800-DREAM HOME (373-2646).

TECHNICAL ASSISTANCE - If you have questions, call our technical support lines at 1-314-770-2228. Whether it involves design modifications or field assistance, our designers are extremely familiar with all of our designs and will be happy to help you. We want your home to be everything you expect it to be.

INTERIOR ELEVATIONS

Interior elevations provide views of special interior elements such as fireplaces, kitchen cabinets, built-in units and other special features of the home.

FLOOR PLANS

These plans show the placement of walls, doors, closets, plumbing fixtures, electrical outlets, columns, and beams for each level of the home.

COVER SHEET

This sheet is the artist's rendering of the exterior of the home. It will give you an idea of how your home will look when completed and landscaped.

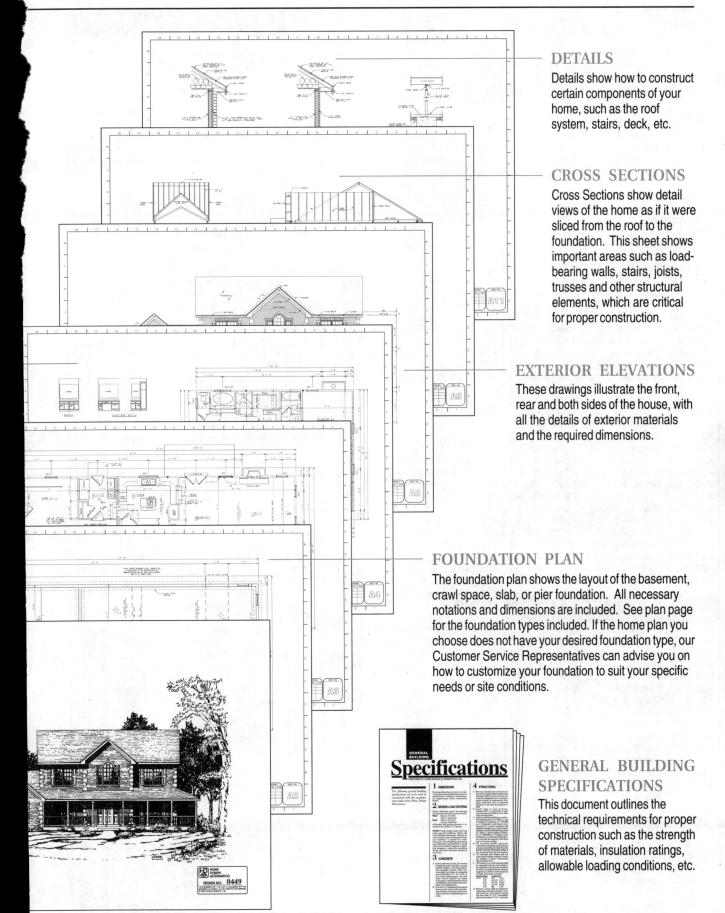

DETAILS

Details show how to construct certain components of your home, such as the roof system, stairs, deck, etc.

CROSS SECTIONS

Cross Sections show detail views of the home as if it were sliced from the roof to the foundation. This sheet shows important areas such as load-bearing walls, stairs, joists, trusses and other structural elements, which are critical for proper construction.

EXTERIOR ELEVATIONS

These drawings illustrate the front, rear and both sides of the house, with all the details of exterior materials and the required dimensions.

FOUNDATION PLAN

The foundation plan shows the layout of the basement, crawl space, slab, or pier foundation. All necessary notations and dimensions are included. See plan page for the foundation types included. If the home plan you choose does not have your desired foundation type, our Customer Service Representatives can advise you on how to customize your foundation to suit your specific needs or site conditions.

GENERAL BUILDING SPECIFICATIONS

This document outlines the technical requirements for proper construction such as the strength of materials, insulation ratings, allowable loading conditions, etc.

HOME PLANS INDEX

Plan Number	Plan Name	Square Feet	Price Code	Page
X20-0502	Provider II	864	AA	148
X20-0503	Grass Roots I	1,000	A	152
X20-0505	Boone	1,104	A	154
X20-0506	Cumberland	1,375	A	179
X20-0507	Manchester	1,197	A	160
X20-0510	Squire I	1,400	A	182
X20-0515	Saxony II	1,344	A	172
X20-0529	Delta Queen I	1,285	B	166
X20-0531	Inverness I	1,504	B	194
X20-0533	Monteray	1,440	A	188
X20-0534	Burlington I	1,288	A	167
X20-0542	Savannah	1,832	C	227
X20-0582	Crosswood	800	AA	147
X20-0585	Ashland	1,344	A	173
X20-0587	Greenridge	1,120	A	155
X20-0670	Strickland	1,170	A	158
X20-0676	Florence	1,367	A	177
X20-0685	Belford	1,844	C	229
X20-0687	Belcourt	1,596	B	204
X20-0689	Wilson	1,539	B	196
X20-0690	Ryland	1,400	A	183
X20-0702	Hollybridge	1,558	B	200
X20-0706	Kinsley	1,791	B	224

SINGLE-STORY HOME PLANS
OVER 2,000 SQUARE FEET

Plan Number	Plan Name	Square Feet	Price Code	Page
X20-0151	Montclaire	2,874	E	271
X20-0185	Jamieson	2,396	D	255
X20-0189	Dartmouth	2,177	C	249
X20-0193	Wrenwood	2,252	D	250
X20-0238	Tavalon	2,468	D	260
X20-0245	Alexander	2,260	D	251
X20-0247	Paterson	2,988	E	272
X20-0261	Seville	2,159	C	248
X20-0262	Darlington	2,070	C	245
X20-0278	Belview	2,847	E	270

Plan Number	Plan Name	Square Feet	Price Code	Page
X20-0287	Lafayette	2,718	E	267
X20-0288	Lewiston	2,731	E	268
X20-0308	Ambsdale	2,563	D	265
X20-0315	Aspen	2,481	D	261
X20-0338	Wynehaven	2,397	E	256
X20-0339	Valrico	2,287	E	252
X20-0340	Sanibel	2,153	C	247
X20-0342	Rosedale	2,089	C	246
X20-0343	Bellerive	2,056	C	244
X20-0347	Ellisville	3,412	F	273
X20-0348	Dennison	2,003	D	243
X20-0355	Clayton	3,814	F	274
X20-0367	Altamont	2,523	D	263
X20-0368	Westport	2,452	D	259
X20-0399	Ashbury	2,397	D	257
X20-0407	Hawthorne	2,517	D	262
X20-0409	Charlotte	2,598	D	266
X20-0438	Ashley	2,558	D	264
X20-0440	Freemont	2,365	D	254
X20-0701	Sugarcreek	2,308	D	253
X20-0703	Rosewood	2,412	D	258
X20-0705	Country Manor	2,758	E	269

VACATION HOME PLANS

Plan Number	Plan Name	Square Feet	Price Code	Page
X20-0101	Chalet	1,039	A	282
X20-0241	Harrison	829	AA	278
X20-0277	Timberbrooke	1,127	A	283
X20-0461	Haverhill	828	AA	277
X20-0462	Oakberry	1,028	A	281
X20-0539	Grandview	1,769	B	290
X20-0547	Highlander	720	AA	275
X20-0548	Woodbridge	1,154	A	285
X20-0549	Lakewood	1,230	A	286
X20-0651	Summerview	962	A	279
X20-0657	Woodsmill	796	AA	276
X20-0680	Lena	1,432	A	288

Plan Number	Plan Name	Square Feet	Price Code	Page
X20-0681	Iris	1,660	B	289
X20-0692	Rosewind	1,339	A	287
X20-0693	Sycamore Hill	1,013	A	280
X20-0698	Walnut Grove	1,143	A	284

1 1/2 STORY HOME PLANS

Plan Number	Plan Name	Square Feet	Price Code	Page
X20-0143	Lakeway	2,449	E	303
X20-0174	Redfield	1,657	B	294
X20-0187	Maxville	3,035	E	306
X20-0201	Farmview	1,814	D	297
X20-0213	Springwood	2,059	C	299
X20-0221	Hickory	1,619	B	293
X20-0290	Georgetown	1,700	B	295
X20-0291	Corsica	1,600	B	291
X20-0304	Lindbergh	2,255	D	300
X20-0362	Auburn	1,874	C	298
X20-0379	Hillview	1,711	B	296
X20-0430	Flagstaff	2,869	E	305
X20-0434	Harwick	2,357	D	302
X20-0437	Salina	2,333	D	301
X20-0439	Mapleridge	2,665	E	304
X20-0686	Springfield	1,609	B	292

MULTI-FAMILY HOME PLANS

Plan Number	Plan Name	Square Feet	Price Code	Page
X20-0451	Brooktree	1,700	D	308
X20-0452	Shadydale	2,318	F	313
X20-0454	Pasadena	4,240	H	317
X20-0457	Oakdale	2,167	E	312
X20-0463	Countryridge	2,986	G	315
X20-0464	Highland	1,992	E	311
X20-0465	Peppertree	1,704	D	309
X20-0466	Roseland	2,830	G	314
X20-0467	Meadowlane	1,904	E	310
X20-0591	Villager I	3,360	H	316
X20-0595	Salem II	1,536	D	307

What Kind Of Plan Package Do You Need?

Now that you've found the home plan you've been looking for, here are some suggestions on how to make your Dream Home a reality. To get started, order the type of plans that fit your particular situation.

Your choices:

The One-set package - This single set of blueprints is offered so you can study or review a home in greater detail. But a single set is never enough for construction and it's a copyright violation to reproduce blueprints.

The Minimum 5-set package - If you're ready to start the construction process, this 5-set package is the minimum number of blueprint sets you will need. It will require keeping close track of each set so they can be used by multiple subcontractors and tradespeople.

The Standard 8-set package - For best results in terms of cost, schedule and quality of construction, we recommend you order eight (or more) sets of blueprints. Besides one set for yourself, additional sets of blueprints will be required by your mortgage lender, local building department, general contractor and all subcontractors working on foundation, electrical, plumbing, heating/air conditioning, carpentry work, etc.

Reproducible Masters - If you wish to make some minor design changes, you'll want to order reproducible masters. These drawings contain the same information as the blueprints but are printed on erasable and reproducible paper. This will allow your builder or a local design professional to make the necessary drawing changes without the major expense of redrawing the plans. This package also allows you to print as many copies of the modified plans as you need.

Customizer Kit™ - Whether you wish to make a lot of changes or just a few to your selected design, out Customizer Kit will simplify the process of modifying that almost perfect home. If your desired changes are minor and do not require a lot of redrawing of the plans, we suggest you order the Customizer Kit along with the reproducible masters. If you plan to make numerous changes including moving exterior walls, we suggest you only order the one-set plan package along with the Customizer Kit. Additional sets can be ordered after your plans are redrawn. See page 4 for details.

Builder's CAD Package™ - This package allows you to make quick drafting and design changes using computer-aided drafting programs that import drawings in a standard DXF format. Specifically, this package includes reproducible vellums of the construction drawings along with 3 1/2" computer disks containing vector drawings of the floor plans and all exterior elevations. The foundation plan, sections and details are only included on the reproducible vellums. This package provides the flexibility a builder needs to create professional work with speed and accuracy.

Mirror Reverse Sets - Plans can be printed in mirror reverse. These plans are useful when the house would fit your site better if all the rooms were on the opposite side than shown. They are simply a mirror image of the original drawings causing the lettering and dimensions to read backwards. Therefore, when ordering mirror reverse drawings, you must purchase at least one set of right reading plans.

ORDER FORM

IMPORTANT INFORMATION TO KNOW
BEFORE YOU ORDER YOUR HOME PLANS

❏ **Building Codes & Requirements -** Our plans conform to most national building codes. However, they may not comply completely with your local building regulations. Some counties and municipalities have their own building codes, regulations and requirements. The assistance of a local builder, architect or other building professional may be necessary to modify the drawings to comply with your area's specific requirements. We recommend you consult with your local building officials prior to beginning construction.

❏ **Exchange Policies -** Since blueprints are printed in response to your order, we cannot honor requests for refunds. However, if for some reason you find that the plan you have purchased does not meet your requirements, you may exchange that plan for another plan in our collection. At the time of the exchange, you will be charged a processing fee of 25% of your original plan package price, plus the difference in price between the plan packages (if applicable) and the cost to ship the new plans to you. *Please note: Reproducible drawings can only be exchanged if the package is unopened, and exchanges are allowed only within 90 days of purchase.*

❏ **Remember To Order Your Material List -** You'll get faster and more accurate bids and you'll save money by paying for only the materials you need.

Prices for plans are subject to change without notice.

BLUEPRINT PRICE SCHEDULE

BEST VALUE

Price Code	One-Set	SAVE $50.00 Five-Sets	SAVE $100.00 Eight-Sets	Material List*	Reproducible Masters	Builder's CAD Package
AA	$195	$265	$305	$40	$405	$505
A	230	300	340	40	440	540
B	265	335	375	40	475	575
C	295	365	405	40	505	605
D	325	395	435	45	535	635
E	350	420	460	45	560	660
F	375	445	485	45	585	685
G	450	520	560	50	660	760
H	525	595	635	50	735	835

OTHER OPTIONS...		
Customizer Kit™*	$ 40.00	**Detail Plan Packages:** *(Buy 2, get 3rd FREE)*
Additional Plan Sets*	$ 30.00	Framing, Electrical & Plumbing $20.00 ea.
Print In Mirror Reverse*	add $ 5.00 per set	**Rush Charges** .... Next Day Air $38.00
Legal Kit	$ 35.00	Second Day Air $25.00

Available only within 90 days after purchase of plan package or reproducible masters of same plan.

ORDER FORM

Please send me Plan Number X20 - _____
Price Code _____
(See Home Plans Index)

❏ Reproducible Masters (see page 321) $ _____
❏ Eight-Set Plan Package $ _____
❏ Five-Set Plan Package $ _____
❏ One-Set Plan Package (no mirror reverse) $ _____
❏ ____ (Qty.) Additional Plan Sets ($30.00 each) $ _____
❏ Print ____ (Qty.) sets in Mirror Reverse (add $5.00/set) $ _____
❏ Builder's CAD Package™ (see page 321) $ _____
❏ Material List (see page 318) $ _____
❏ Customizer Kit (see page 4) $ _____
❏ Legal Kit (see back cover) $ _____
Detail Plan Packages: (see back cover)
  ❏ Framing ❏ Electrical ❏ Plumbing $ _____
  SUBTOTAL $ _____
SALES TAX (MO residents add 7%) $ _____
❏ Rush Charges $ _____
  SHIPPING & HANDLING $ ___12.50___
  TOTAL ENCLOSED (US funds only) $ _____
❏ Enclosed is my check or money order payable to HDA, Inc.
(Sorry, no COD's)

Mail to: **HDA, Inc.**
4390 Green Ash Drive
St. Louis, MO 63045-1219

I hereby authorize HDA, Inc. to charge this purchase to my credit card account (check one):

❏ MasterCard ❏ VISA ❏ DISCOVER NOVUS ❏ AMERICAN EXPRESS Cards

My card number is _____

The expiration date is _____

Signature _____

Name _____
(Please print or type)

Street Address _____
(Please **do not** use P.O. Box)

City, State, Zip _____

My daytime phone number (_____) - _____ - _____

I am a ❏ Builder/Contractor ❏ Homeowner ❏ Renter
I ❏ have ❏ have not selected my general contractor.

Thank you for your order!

322 *Please note that plans are not returnable.*